Gershon Portnoi is currently the deputy editor of *ShortList*, and previously worked on talkSPORT's weekly digital online magazine. Before that he was Sports Editor of *Nuts* and has also worked as a football writer for the Press Association. Gershon has also written for *Observer Sport Monthly* and *F1 Racing* and worked on Sky Sports News. He is the author of *Why Are You So Fat?*, the talkSPORT Book of Cricket's Best Ever Sledges.

The Story of
talkSPORT

Inside the Wacky World of Britain's Wildest Radio Station

GERSHON PORTNOI

SIMON &
SCHUSTER

London · New York · Sydney · Toronto

A CBS COMPANY

First published in trade paperback as *Ten Years of talkSPORT*
by talkSPORT Limited in 2009
This edition published by Simon & Schuster UK Ltd in 2011
A CBS COMPANY

1 3 5 7 9 10 8 6 4 2

Simon & Schuster UK Ltd
1st Floor
222 Gray's Inn Road
London
WC1X 8HB

www.simonandschuster.co.uk

Simon & Schuster Australia
Sydney

A CIP catalogue for this book is available
from the British Library.

ISBN: 978-0-85720-630-5

Typeset by M Rules
Printed in the UK by CPI Cox & Wyman, Reading, Berkshire RG1 8EX

Acknowledgements

A huge thank you to the following people:
Ian Abrahams, Kathryn Anastasi, Keith Arthur, Jack Bannister, Graham Beecroft, Rupert Bell, Antony Bellekom, Tim Bleakley, Bill Borrows, Mike Bovill, Liz Brace, Alan Brazil, Paul Breen-Turner, Bob Bubka, Adam Bullock, Faye Carruthers, Giles Carruthers, Tony Cascarino, Andy Clarke, Charlie Coffey, Ian Collins, Stan Collymore, Chris Cowdrey, George Cummins, Jason Cundy, Kelly Dalglish, Antony D'Angelo, Ian Danter, Moz Dee, Sean Dilley, Kate Dockrell, Jon Driscoll, Adrian Durham, Clint Emmins, Seb Ewen, Stephen Farmer, Liam Fisher, Claire Furlong, Peter Gee, Darren Gough, Asher Gould, Mike Hanson, Steven Hartley, Warren Haughton, Paul Hawksbee, Steve Hodge, Andrew Hughes, Ronnie Irani, Andy Jacobs, Calum Macaulay, John Mahood, Rodney Marsh, Laura Marshall, Dominic McGuinness, Andrew McKenna, Josh Milligan, Steve Morgan, Dennie Morris, Carmel Mullan, Gary Newbon, Jon Norman, Laurie Palacio, Alan Parry, Mike Parry, Nigel Pearson, Victoria Portnoi, Jim Proudfoot, Mick Quinn, Bill Ridley, Rob Sloman, Matt Smith, Scott Taunton, Elizabeth Stevenson, Andy Townsend, Phil von Oppen, Lauren Webster, Josh Williams, Ian Wright and Jonathan Young.

For Victoria and Jake

Contents

1

Chaos Reigns: the Birth of talkSPORT

A week before we were due to go on air, it simply wasn't built. The studios weren't built. I got over there and sat down on the floor because there was no furniture. There was nothing in the room. No studio built, no clocks. It was quite scary really.

ADRIAN DURHAM

It started with a kiss.

Well it didn't actually, but the noise of the engineer's screwdriver furiously rotating and screeching away underneath the studio desk was not unlike a squeaky smacker on the lips. And that was very nearly the first sound transmitted across the airwaves by talkSPORT. Thankfully, it was former ITV football presenter Gary Newbon who uttered the first words to be broadcast on the now-famous 1089 and 1053 on the medium wave – or AM as young, trendy types like to say.

A radio station founded by former *Sun* newspaper editor Kelvin MacKenzie was never going to function traditionally. Even those precious first few seconds after birth were clouded in controversy, as Newbon insisted on changing the name of the programme he was presenting live on air.

With just ten minutes to go until the fledgling station's official launch at 6am on 17 January 2000, Newbon was still trying to confirm the name of the show that he was about to co-present with former sports newsreader Adrian Durham. As radio engineers continued to beaver away under the desk to make sure the station could launch on time, producers told Newbon in no uncertain terms it was to be referred to as 'The Sports Breakfast with Adrian Durham and Gary Newbon'.

The studio clock – which, along with all the furniture, had appeared only in the middle of the night – ticked towards 6am and the sound engineer finally emerged from under the desk with a smile on his face. Job done. What could possibly go wrong now?

'Good morning and welcome to talkSPORT. You're listening to the Sports Breakfast with Gary Newbon and Adrian Durham,' announced Newbon as the clock struck six, deliberately putting his name first in the programme title.

The BBC this was not. In fact, the station's chief executive MacKenzie would go on to invest a great amount of time into taking on the Corporation throughout his shift at talkSPORT's helm. Eighteen months earlier, MacKenzie had fronted a consortium of investors who paid £24.7 million to take control of Talk Radio, a national commercial speech station that had launched in 1995. The largest investor was News Corporation, owned by MacKenzie's former boss at the *Sun*, Rupert Murdoch.

Under Murdoch, MacKenzie had overseen the most successful period in the *Sun*'s history, between 1981 and 1993, and he soon began making dramatic changes at Talk Radio in an attempt to boost ratings and advertising revenue. His reign was littered with a spate of hirings and firings that took the station by storm. MacKenzie's reputation preceded him and Talk Radio's staff trembled under the pressure of knowing each day could be their last.

He drafted in his old *Sun* chums Nick Ferrari and David Banks to present *The Big Boys' Breakfast* and he also began introducing more sports programming by acquiring football commentary rights. Fleet Street columnist Simon Heffer was also brought in to the station as were several other journalistic heavyweights, but ratings barely changed and MacKenzie was unimpressed.

The problem that MacKenzie faced was the same problem Talk Radio had faced since its inception. As the chief executive liked to remind everyone as often as possible, the station didn't know if it was Arthur or Martha.

Advertisers failed to buy in to the station, sensing it lacked a true identity, as they never really knew who was listening. After all, would the same person stay tuned after *The Big Boys' Breakfast* to listen to agony aunt Anna Raeburn talking about the menopause? The lack of consistency was a turn-off to the corporate money men and MacKenzie was not a man who would simply sit around contemplating what changes to make.

Having built a fearsome reputation by ruling the *Sun* with an iron fist, MacKenzie was well known across London's media land. Mike Parry, who went on to become a talkSPORT legend on and off air, was drafted in as MacKenzie's programme director – one of an astonishing number the boss would employ during his stewardship – soon after the Talk Radio takeover. But, following a disagreement between the pair, neither of whom had ever previously worked on radio, Parry was dismissed. He wasn't the first, and was certainly not the last, to receive his marching orders from MacKenzie, but he did return several months later after the two patched up their differences.

Having dabbled with the acquisition of sports broadcasting rights during his first year at Talk Radio (the station already had a deal in place to broadcast Manchester United's Champions League matches), MacKenzie shocked close colleagues in late 1999 by informing them he was going to relaunch Talk Radio as a sports radio station – something that had never been done in the UK.

As is the talkSPORT way, there is even some debate over whose idea the rebranding was, with MacKenzie's colleague Jason Bryant claiming he had come up with the concept, although many insiders begged to differ. Whatever the truth of the matter, the fact remains that talkSPORT was MacKenzie's baby and he went on to drive the whole concept through over the next five years. There were many potential names for the new station including Sports AM, Sports medium wave and Sports Talk, but the boss always favoured talkSPORT.

In true MacKenzie style, he insisted the relaunch had to happen as soon as possible and preferably sooner than that. And, as if completely rebranding the station's content, presenters and name wasn't a tough enough task in barely two months, MacKenzie also decided that the relaunch would coincide with the building of brand new studios in new premises. The whole project was kept completely under wraps from most of the Talk Radio staff, as the majority of the producers and presenters would not be required on the new station. Indeed, some were given their marching orders only as they left for their Christmas holidays – just weeks before the relaunch.

So, while several senior station staff members were frantically working towards the new format, new shows and essentially a new national radio station, others remained at Talk Radio's cramped Oxford Street premises as if it was business as usual, totally in the dark about the creation of talkSPORT. The Oxford Street studios were far too expensive and the change to more spacious, purpose-built facilities made sense – but the location had to be cheaper and instantly available.

Everything was to be leased, MacKenzie told programme director Antony Bellekom, who was actually set to leave for the BBC but had agreed to stay on for the early launch period. As Bellekom recalled, the boss had told him to rent everything: 'Not just the building, but the furniture, the studios – the paint on the walls.'

It was late November and Bellekom, together with a senior engineer, had only until January to view potential locations, draw up floor and studio plans and then employ contractors to begin work. It was inconceivable that this was enough time. Even at a push, a project like this required around a year to plan and then another six months to actualise, according to Bellekom, who took on the task with a mixture of amusement and horror. Eventually, a building close to the South Bank of the River Thames on a road named Hatfields proved to have the best facilities and work began at a furious rate in order to make the impossible possible.

With just a week until the launch of the new project, amazingly the majority of Talk Radio's employees still did not know that their station would soon cease to exist. All staff from Oxford Street were called to a meeting at the new site on Hatfields, where MacKenzie made the dramatic announcement that, as of the following week, talkSPORT would replace Talk Radio. There was a great deal of subsequent upheaval, as many presenters and producers who didn't fit in with his idea of who should work at a sports radio station were sent packing.

That also led to some tough decisions for MacKenzie, as he had to dispense with the services of his friends Banks and Ferrari from *The Big Boys' Breakfast* – although letting Anna Raeburn go was probably not such a heart-wrenching call. She famously burst on to the Talk Radio production floor and screamed: 'I've been fired by Jason fucking Bryant!'

The speed of the transformation from Talk Radio to talkSPORT caught everyone by surprise, but to anybody that knew MacKenzie well enough it was very much business as usual. The synchronisation of moving premises and relaunching led to an unusual situation where presenter Adrian Durham visited the new studios just days before launch to find no furniture in any part of the building. Ostensibly there to test out the facilities and rehearse for the following week's all-singing, all-dancing new launch, he found a makeshift studio that was nowhere near completion and where there was not even a single chair to rest his behind.

Three days before the launch, mayhem reigned at the South Bank site. Contractors were building, painting, stripping and drilling while radio engineers were desperately trying to press on with studio construction. In the middle of this cacophony of industrial noise, producers were transmitting dummy shows using each other as guests, callers and contributors in an attempt to be ready for launch.

MacKenzie scrutinised every aspect of the project. One morning, he was shown around the new building by Bellekom. He explained to him that one particular room was not going to work because the walls were too thin and there would be a problem with sound escaping – therefore extra money was needed to soundproof the walls.

A confused MacKenzie asked what this particular room was that needed extra money spent on it and Bellekom boldly informed his boss: 'It's your office and nobody will be able to work because you're always shouting!' Amazingly, MacKenzie's office ended up partially soundproofed.

At this point, Bellekom informed MacKenzie that it was looking extremely unlikely that either the building or the studios would be ready for the 17 January launch date, but the boss was having none of it. Instead, he demanded that the launch should actually be brought forward instead.

Bellekom ignored that particular request – well, he *was* off to the Beeb anyway – but somehow, in what was to become a talkSPORT trademark, they scraped home literally at the last minute thanks to that engineer under the desk and several people putting in 24-hour shifts. Even then, many of the studio facilities at the station were in no state to be used for a national radio broadcast.

To add to the chaos surrounding the launch, the station was in the middle of broadcasting ball-by-ball commentary from England's Test match in South Africa. The game spanned from the Friday before launch until the Tuesday after and was also heavily rain-affected, meaning the station's output before and after launch was not firmly in place.

With the Oxford Street studios still in use for Talk Radio right up until the point of talkSPORT's launch from its new Hatfields base, there was also confusion about how and when the switch would be made from broadcasting the station's output from one location to another. In the event, the station actually went silent for a period in the small hours of 17 January due to this chaotic state of affairs. It was only when the regional transmitter centre called the station to inform them that they were not broadcasting and were therefore running the risk of burning out their transmitters at a cost of £250,000, that producers realised they were off air. talkSPORT was about to be born, but anybody tuning in would have heard nothing but dead air only hours before.

Despite all the teething problems, talkSPORT was dragged shouting and screaming onto the airwaves just about on time. And the new station's hectic and chaotic feel served only to add to its appeal to a new army of sports-hungry listeners.

Within five minutes of that first breakfast show, reporter Steve Hodge – who would eventually become assistant programme director – had to muck in and think on his feet. He was stationed outside boxer Mike Tyson's Mayfair hotel, as Parry had predicted the fighter's arrival in the UK ahead of his bout with Julius Francis would be the biggest story in town that morning. On a freezing cold night, Hodge wrapped himself up in multiple layers and stood outside the hotel from 4am, finally catching a glimpse of Tyson's arrival an hour later as the boxer entered the hotel with a towel over his head.

Newbon, excited by going live to the hotel just five minutes into the new station's existence, asked Hodge: 'What sort of shape does Tyson look like he's in?'

Cursing the presenter on the inside, Hodge was forced to waffle about the former heavyweight champion from information he had gleaned by speaking to fellow freezing reporters in Mayfair – when all he had to work with was a towelled figure running out of the cold and into a hotel.

But Hodge overcame that particular hurdle and talkSPORT was suddenly up and running with the following launch schedule:

6am	The Sports Breakfast with Adrian Durham & Gary Newbon
10am	Derek Hatton on Sports Break
12pm	Timesmart with Paul Ross
1pm	Sportsday with Tony Lockwood & Alvin Martin
4pm	The Season Ticket with Tom Watt
7pm	The Kickabout with Hawksbee & Jacobs
10pm	James Whale
2am	Ian Collins & The Creatures of the Night
5am	Bloomberg on the Money

The new format struck gold, as both advertisers and listeners understood the rebranded radio station in a heartbeat. For the first time in its history, the station had been given an identity. More blokes tuned in than ever before, with figures for the first quarter of the year showing that 70 per cent of talkSPORT's audience was male.

By June, however, the overall reach of the station had dipped from a phenomenal 2.4 million listeners at launch to 2 million, as many women deserted the 1089 frequency. Sales director Tim 'The Rochdale Cowboy' Bleakley recalled: 'Kelvin was gutted, but I remember being really pleased because of the number of men that were now listening. Suddenly you've got what you were aiming for which was a pure male radio station.'

To complete the advertisers' dream, 53 per cent of listeners fell into the upscale ABC1 demographic – not White Van Man or cab drivers as the stereotype suggested. The advertising industry understood who was listening, meaning talkSPORT had hit the ground running in spectacular fashion.

MacKenzie had ordered as many big-name presenters for the breakfast show as possible. He wanted to wow audiences with high-profile names and this meant that for the first three months, talkSPORT listeners would wake up to a different voice each morning, accompanied by regular anchor Durham.

It could have been Newbon, Sky Sports boxing and football commentator Ian Darke or horse racing expert Brough Scott. Occasionally, former Ipswich, Spurs, Manchester United and Scotland international footballer Alan Brazil would broadcast in the morning. Initially, Brazil was far from keen on doing the breakfast slot as, by his own admission, he was unaware what a prestigious show it was.

It was late-night host James Whale who managed to convince Brazil of how important a role he could play at the station. While having a drink in one of the many South Bank hostelries surrounding talkSPORT's new studios, Whale approached Brazil and convinced him that he was a natural broadcaster and should jump at the chance of presenting the show.

The breakfast roster of top sports names was an impressive line-up, but was also seen to be a confusing policy for the listeners. Brough Scott may have been an intelligent broadcaster, but he worked at a completely different, deliberate pace to somebody like Newbon, who was far more frenetic. It was like listening to two completely different shows and it quickly became obvious Scott did not quite offer the intelligent tabloid debate on which the concept of the station had been based.

MacKenzie had met Scott at the races and thought he would make an excellent radio man, but he never quite suited the station's informal imaging – and he certainly failed to comprehend his boss's burning desire to take on the BBC over sports broadcasting rights. One morning, Durham was giving the nation his thoughts on the previous night's Manchester

United v Arsenal game when Scott admitted on air that he
hadn't actually watched the match because he had been in his
car, although he had tuned in to hear it on BBC Radio 5 Live.
The same 5 Live with whom MacKenzie was about to embark
on a bitter rights battle – and the same 5 Live who had just
received a free plug on talkSPORT.

Whether the story that MacKenzie actually waited outside
the studio that morning holding Scott's coat before ushering
him out of the building is a myth or not, he never broadcast on
the station again.

MacKenzie was never far from the on-air action and he
paid especially close attention in the early days of the launch.
Huge tickings-off, dressings-down or, quite simply, bollock-
ings were meted out on a regular basis to staff who upset him
for whatever reason. And these wouldn't take place in private
either.

On one breakfast show, Durham had made light of a punning *Sun* headline about David Beckham. He belittled the word
play, claiming it was a particularly poor effort. When he finished
the show, MacKenzie, a former *Sun* sub-editor whose speciality
was short, sharp, punning headlines, was waiting outside the
studio door. He pressed his face as close to Durham's as he possibly could without coming into physical contact with him and
said: 'Don't piss on the papers. They will know more than you
will ever fucking know!'

Durham, who had survived the cull at Talk Radio, was also
on the wrong end of a MacKenzie ear-bashing when he per-
sisted with overusing the word 'mate' while on air. This time
it was during an outside broadcast ahead of the Tyson v Francis
fight in Manchester, and the presenter's phone was ringing
almost before he had taken off his headphones at the end of

the show. It was MacKenzie, ranting down the line at him: 'If I ever hear you say that fucking word again, you'll never work for me again!'

Not everyone escaped with verbal maulings. The mid-morning current affairs programme presented by the limousine liberal Derek Hatton – drafted into the station by Bryant – proved to be a disappointment. He was given the elbow after six months and replaced by Mike Dickin, the vastly experienced overnight presenter who had continued to be part of the team after moving over from Talk Radio.

Somebody who lasted far less time than Hatton, and who still holds the talkSPORT record for shortest tenure, was Simon Stainrod, an ex-professional footballer, although the circumstances surrounding his dismissal were not entirely his own fault. Stainrod was drafted in to present the Saturday evening football phone-in at the last minute after MacKenzie had sacked Tom Watt, the regular presenter. At very short notice, senior producer Neil Henderson was given the job of finding a replacement.

Henderson had previously worked with Stainrod in Scotland so asked him to help out. He didn't arrive at the studios until ten minutes to five and was due on air 15 minutes after. In that time, he had to be shown the ropes by producer Maxie Allen, because Henderson was reporting at one of the afternoon's matches and didn't show up at the studios until later – but too late for Stainrod.

With minimum training and not a great deal of broadcasting experience, Stainrod spoke to the nation's football fans at five past five – but instead of introducing the show or encouraging callers to ring in with any topics of discussion, he spent the next ten minutes going straight to the phones, one caller after another, without interjecting with any of his own thoughts.

Within minutes, MacKenzie was on the phone to Allen in the studio: 'What is this **** doing on my radio station?' was his opening gambit. Allen explained the last-minute situation and MacKenzie hung up only to call back two minutes later: 'I've had enough. Get rid of him as soon as possible.'

Allen suggested that would be done after the show. But MacKenzie was having none of that: 'I want him off my radio station as soon as fucking possible. I don't care who it is that replaces him, this **** is going off.'

By some extraordinary luck, the previous show's presenter, Durham, was still in the building and Allen begged him to come back on air and help Stainrod out. Durham obliged and spent the next ten minutes on air with Stainrod, taking calls and talking about the day's games. At the next break, Allen popped his head around the studio door and asked to have a word with Stainrod. Durham never saw the former footballer again and was left to present the rest of the show alone. After 20 minutes, Stainrod's talkSPORT career was over. An hour later, a caller rang in to ask Durham where Stainrod was and the presenter replied: 'He's just had to pop out for a bit.'

It was classic talkSPORT. Unfortunately for Stainrod, he was the victim of the circumstances in which he was recruited but has since gone on to have a successful radio career overseas.

Although the Stainrod experiment failed, talkSPORT did begin a mini-revolution in sports broadcasting by placing ex-professional footballers in front of microphones from a very early stage. Television channel Sky Sports News had started to dabble with the idea and, from the outset, talkSPORT were keen to drag as many former or current players into the studio as possible – whether they were guests or presenters. It was a policy that was far ahead of its time and has been widely imitated since.

MacKenzie's outward no-nonsense persona also had another side, which was shown when talkSPORT was rocked by the news that James Whale had been diagnosed with kidney cancer. Whale had joined Talk Radio in 1995 and was one of only a handful of presenters who made the switch to talkSPORT. His late-night show entertained a loyal audience and he regularly attracted politicians and celebrities as guests. But when a tumour the size of a pizza was discovered on his kidney, Whale was immediately hospitalised and faced a perilous operation to remove it.

He survived, but spent months recovering from the setback, which could have placed him in a tricky position because he was a freelance presenter. However, MacKenzie continued to pay him throughout his illness, showing his loyal and sensitive side. If he valued a member of staff, he would stick by them through thick and thin.

While Whale was convalescing, the presenter-rotation policy on the breakfast show was consigned to the history books – or this book, at any rate. After impressing everyone with his laid-back, natural and informal style, Brazil was offered the show on a permanent basis. He was seen as the prime choice for the slot, although he was still reluctant to get up in the middle of the night for the show.

The Glaswegian never considered himself a 'morning man', as he liked to socialise in the evenings, meaning he would seldom be in bed before the small hours. On top of that, he still lived in Suffolk and arriving in London in time to prepare for the breakfast show meant waking up at around 3am every day.

But after Whale had explained to him the potential of the opportunity that was on offer, he agreed to become the breakfast show's first permanent presenter and he would go it alone from 6am every day (Durham, who sensed impending doom with the presenter rotation policy, had been moved to evenings at his own request). The show relied on reels of pre-recorded audio and live guest slots, which Brazil would link to and then share his thoughts with listeners in between. Nobody realised at the time, but it was the start of one of the most successful breakfast shows in British radio history.

With that problem solved, MacKenzie embarked upon a ferocious campaign to sign up the rights to as many sporting events as possible for talkSPORT to broadcast live. Naturally, he focused on football, but he was met by the formidable obstacle of the BBC who owned the rights to broadcast the Premier League, European Championships and the World Cup. Not a man to shrink from a challenge, MacKenzie rolled up his sleeves and made smashing the BBC's dominance, and what he saw as a monopoly, in the market a major priority throughout his talkSPORT tenure.

From his early days at Talk Radio, MacKenzie had already signed deals to broadcast the Premier League home games of several London clubs, but these were only regional broadcasts and that was nowhere near good enough when Radio 5 Live had the ears of the whole nation.

Unfortunately, talkSPORT and MacKenzie then received bloody noses in their negotiations with the England & Wales Cricket Board to secure the rights to England's home Test series. They lost out to the BBC, despite making a far higher bid, according to the boss who could not hide his disbelief and disgust.

However, one area where MacKenzie enjoyed a great victory over the Beeb was in securing the rights to broadcast the England cricket team's overseas matches. Previously, the BBC had snapped up the rights to England tours for a pittance as no other broadcaster had ever shown an interest in them.

Even before talkSPORT had launched, MacKenzie had left the BBC seething by pinching the rights to England's tour of South Africa from right under their noses. MacKenzie's policy was to make 'take it or leave it' offers of around £50,000 to the heads of each country's cricket board. With the BBC rumoured to be paying paltry sums for the rights, talkSPORT suddenly became the home of ball-by-ball cricket commentary during the winter.

The BBC were furious when they found out and talkSPORT subsequently won the rights to further tours in exactly the same way, leaving the Beeb high and dry before they had even had a chance to bid against them. While not necessarily a resounding commercial success, the cricket rights scored a massive boost in audience terms for talkSPORT and created a buzz of excitement around the station. MacKenzie also convinced former BBC cricket pundit and ex-England captain Geoff Boycott to be the leading analyst for the broadcasts, accompanied by former England international Chris Cowdrey, who had also been work-ing for the Beeb. When he informed his BBC producer, Peter Baxter, that he was considering joining the rival broadcaster, he was told in no uncertain terms: 'You go and work for them and I shall make sure you never work for the BBC again!' There was no love lost between the Corporation and talkSPORT.

Following the cricket coverage, which spanned the period immediately before and after launch, the summer's four-day broad-cast of the Open golf championship from St Andrews in Scotland had featured the voice of Sky Sports football pundit Andy Gray over the airwaves. It was also the first time that respected US golf commentator and analyst Bob Bubka appeared on the station.

Somehow, out of the chaos, confusion and uncertainty of its

launch, talkSPORT had suddenly emerged as a major player in British sports broadcasting, giving the BBC a serious run for their money. But the most bitter battles between the pair would be saved for the football pitch.

2

Live From a Hotel Room
Near Euro 2000

You're listening to live and unofficial commentary of Euro 2000 on talkSPORT. Commentary is from pictures via our studio monitors and all sound effects come from the studio and not from the ground.

ALAN PARRY

It may seem hard to believe, but talkSPORT's football commentators Alan Parry and Jim Proudfoot were forced to interrupt their coverage of Euro 2000 games in order to repeat those words every 15 minutes. And they had to do that in the presence of a lawyer while watching the matches on telly in a hotel room in central Amsterdam. This was no ordinary radio station.

Unsurprisingly, it was MacKenzie's dogged refusal to accept no as an answer that had led to one of the most bizarre situations in British broadcasting history. The boss was in no doubt that the key to talkSPORT's survival and success lay in securing football broadcasting rights. The problem was that not only did the station have almost none, often nobody was even prepared to allow them the privilege of making a bid for any.

The football highlight of 2000, the year of talkSPORT's launch, was the European Championships, staged in the Netherlands and Belgium. Come hell or high water, MacKenzie was insistent that talkSPORT would broadcast live commentary of virtually every game of the tournament, despite not having the rights to do so.

Having come into the broadcasting arena in January 2000, talkSPORT was told it was not allowed to bid for a share of Euro 2000 rights by a group called the European Broadcasting Union. This group was made up of several major European state broadcasters, including the BBC, who, alongside the Capital Radio Group, held the UK radio rights for the tournament. MacKenzie refused to accept this.

As far as he was concerned, talkSPORT were more than willing to pay their way for Euro 2000 rights but had not been allowed to do so by what he believed was a cosy cartel of broadcasters. MacKenzie saw talkSPORT as a passenger on a train who had more than enough money for a ticket but had simply not been given permission to purchase one. The solution was quite simple: jump on board the train anyway.

Originally, the plan had been to cover the tournament from TV screens in the London studios. However, management were worried that commentators and pundits might be recognised in the capital, therefore shattering the illusion that talkSPORT were in the Netherlands and Belgium. So, a week before the opening match, the decision was taken to transfer the whole operation to Amsterdam.

Amid a wave of on-air promotions about its 'live' coverage of the tournament, talkSPORT sent their six-man team, consisting of producer Jim Brown, anchor Adrian Durham and commentators Alan Parry, Jim Proudfoot, Alvin Martin and Frank Stapleton, out to the Netherlands to cover the biggest football event on the continent – all from a room in Amsterdam's Jolly Carlton Hotel.

The plan was to make the commentaries sound like they were coming from inside the stadia – even though nobody from the station was permitted to set foot in any of the grounds as they lacked proper accreditation. To facilitate this, producers Brown and Andrew Hughes had taken charge of an operation that became known as 'The Football Factory'. This was the project that resulted in the creation of a CD of more than 50 sounds that could usually be heard while listening to football on the radio.

In the run-up to Euro 2000, various football matches were recorded to pick up all these noises. Each sound element was then dissected by Hughes and put onto the CD to create 'The Football Factory'. There was a general crowd noise to be played in the background throughout each commentary. Then each layer of sound could be added on top of this for specific incidents like a shot going wide, a referee's whistle or, of course, goals.

There were also many different crowd chanting sounds, but these had all been recorded from English stadia – so when talkSPORT commentated on Germany v Romania, listeners would have been surprised to hear English chanting coming from the stands. And during the crunch group match between England and Germany, anybody comparing the noise of the crowd on talkSPORT's coverage with the BBC's would have noticed the England fans making a great deal more noise on 1089. During the match, while the England fans in the stadium were fairly quiet, on talkSPORT they were banging drums and singing *The Great Escape* theme, mainly because the production team in the studio had simply got carried away.

Similarly, sometimes the sound effect was inappropriate. The recorded noise of a crowd groaning at a missed penalty was used when the Netherlands fluffed a crucial spot-kick, which sealed their exit from the tournament at the hands of Italy. It left commentator Proudfoot wondering why a sound had just been played that was akin to someone narrowly failing to land the top prize on TV game show *Bullseye* when, in the stadium, thousands of Italian fans were roaring with delight at reaching the final.

As Hughes was operating all of the sound effects by pressing buttons back in the London studio, occasionally a slip of the finger could result in chaos. During one match, the referee blew his whistle for a foul, so Hughes attempted to press his whistle button, missed and ended up transmitting a huge groan from the crowd instead. Over in Amsterdam, Proudfoot realised what had happened and began to giggle at the mistake.

But nobody at talkSPORT was laughing after the opening matches of the tournament, when the BBC took out a High Court injunction against talkSPORT describing their commentary as live. Mr Justice Blackburne ordered the station to ensure that they made it clear on air to their listeners that this was not the case.

The BBC were incensed at talkSPORT's chutzpah and Bob Shennan, head of BBC Sport production, said: 'talkSPORT's promotion and coverage over the weekend was duping listeners. talkSPORT aren't in the stadium, they don't have the broadcast rights, they don't have a proper sound feed and they haven't paid for it. Their coverage was simply second hand.'

But MacKenzie was having none of that: 'The BBC belongs to a cartel of state broadcasters who are opposed to the idea of competition from the commercial sector. The idea that we would be responsible for lowering the value of sports rights is preposterous – considering they were instrumental in making sure we were unable to bid against them,' he said.

This verdict led to the extraordinary situation where all talkSPORT's commentaries had to be interrupted every 15 minutes to let listeners know that the commentators were not live at the stadium and that all the crowd noises were sound effects, because the station did not own the rights to broadcast the tournament.

This disclaimer also had to be read out on air within 30 seconds of a goal being scored. By the time the commentator had described the goal and handed over to his summariser, they would have all of a couple of seconds to give the briefest words of wisdom before the commentator would interrupt to read out the legal copy.

Mindful of the heavy fines that could now be imposed if talkSPORT did not comply with the High Court's ruling, the station had been forced to employ a young lawyer to sit in the Jolly Carlton hotel room with the commentators to make sure they didn't forget the legal speak, which was also stuck to the TV screens just for good measure.

For Alan Parry, this was business as usual. The popular TV football commentator was first used by Talk Radio at the 1998 World Cup in France, where chaos had reigned due to a shortage of press passes. That led to several bizarre situations.

Once, co-commentator and Scottish football legend Andy Gray was left at the mercy of thousands of England fans outside the Stade Velodrome in Marseille while two of his colleagues had entered the stadium and were trying to poach another pass to gain access for the Scot. Gray was soon on the phone back to London threatening to leave there and then unless he was in the ground within ten minutes. Another time, Parry had been forced to go it alone inside the stadium, despite having no experience whatsoever on the technical side of radio. Without an engineer or producer, he'd been handed all the equipment and sent in to do his best. Fortunately, another station's techie was able to help Parry and the commentary went ahead.

Although Parry had been expecting to be inside the stadia in the Netherlands and Belgium, he felt strongly that talkSPORT had been treated unfairly and was quite prepared to go along with the project – sound effects, hotel room and all. However, he was slightly more circumspect than he would be on a normal commentary inside the ground, as covering the match from television screens – or off-tube as it's known in the business – meant one was always at the whim of the TV director. If a goal was scored and the director decided to follow the scorer's celebration, oblivious to a linesman's offside flag ruling out the goal, a commentator would have to backtrack.

As if the theatre of covering a tournament in this renegade manner was not enough, in typical talkSPORT fashion, another drama provided a sub-plot to the whole escapade. Heading the outside broadcast in Amsterdam was popular producer Brown, an experienced operator, fundamental to the success of the whole venture.

Brown was an interesting character as he was an openly gay man working in a very macho environment. He was talkSPORT's fixer, the man who made things happen and, believe it or not, his past included working as a producer on the BBC hit show *Jim'll Fix It* – of course the Jim in the title referred to Savile rather than Brown. He once used his fixing skills on that show to take a group of kids from Southampton to New York for a week aboard the *QE2* – all at the expense of licence-fee payers.

Brown's career at talkSPORT, however, very nearly came to an end in Amsterdam when he managed to fall out with MacKenzie. The commentators had complained to Brown about the presence of the lawyer watching over their broadcasts, so Mr 'Jim'll Fix It' then complained to the boss. MacKenzie's response was: 'If you don't like it, you can fuck off!' Much to the boss's surprise, Brown, in his broad Geordie accent, said: 'I'll fuck off then.'

An email was sent around talkSPORT Towers announcing Brown's departure, which was a tremendous shock to staff. Sensing impending doom, Durham decided to put his neck on the chopping block by emailing MacKenzie. He diplomatically explained that everyone in the Netherlands would continue to do their jobs to the best of their abilities, but that they would all perform far better if Brown was reinstated and the issues between him and the chief executive were resolved.

Durham's phone was soon ringing and with baited breath he answered MacKenzie's call, fearing a ferocious broadside at the very least. Amazingly, all the boss asked Durham was whether he thought everybody in the team was in agreement with his feelings, and Durham confirmed that was the case.

Within ten minutes, 'Jim'll Fix It' was back on board and the crisis was averted. A new email was sent around the office straight away announcing that Brown had rejoined the station – he wouldn't have even had time to leave the building.

Just days into the tournament, talkSPORT's coverage had whipped up a media storm, with several newspapers reporting on the cheeky way the station was covering Euro 2000 – at one point, the *Daily Mail* even visited the hotel to write a feature on the unconventional broadcasts. The newspaper compared Alan Parry and Alvin Martin's efforts to John Lennon and Yoko Ono's famous 'bed-in for peace' in 1969. Then, the Beatle and his new wife had stayed in their Amsterdam Hilton hotel room for a full week as part of a peace protest. Parry recalled: 'I am not sure which [of us] was supposed to be which [of them], but it worked because we are both Scousers and kind of suited the angle. But it was odd!'

The team in Amsterdam had felt slightly uneasy about what they'd been asked to do but, at the same time, a strong sense of camaraderie had engulfed them. When the BBC reacted with such outrage, it served only to draw them closer and they became more determined to produce great radio. Any team that plays together is said to stay together and talkSPORT's Euro 2000 troops were no different, making full use of the Amsterdam nightlife, with regular trips to restaurants, bars and clubs, which led to some unusual expenses claim forms.

Spirits were also raised by two beautiful additions to the talkSPORT squad. Brown had overbooked the number of rooms required, meaning that there were two spare bedrooms as well as his own palatial suite (he had a habit of always making sure he stayed in as luxurious surroundings as possible when travelling for work).

Despite the suite, 'Jim'll Fix It' spent a fair amount of time in London during the tournament and while he was back in England, a friend of Durham's had come to visit, accompanied by two stunning ladies. Durham called Brown to check if his friend could stay in one of the spare bedrooms and was told he could use the suite. As it turned out, Durham's mate shared his room and the girls ended up in the suite. As a result, these two stunners, who had never met anybody at the station, had walked straight into the hotel and landed its showpiece room – all on talkSPORT expenses.

Occasionally, broadcasting from a hotel room in front of a television screen created a sense of disillusionment among the team. The sense of being away from the real action in the stadia would sometimes hit home and once, during a rather lifeless group match, Proudfoot and Stapleton decided to spice up proceedings.

The 'commentary' room consisted of the studio and two enormous TV screens. For this particular match, one screen was showing the Euro 2000 Group C fixture between Norway and Yugoslavia while the other was tuned in to the hotel's in-house porn channel. The pair proceeded to play their own game where whoever could insert more double-entendres into their commentary that alluded to the action on the steamier screen would win. Stapleton was particularly fond of his repetition of each team's tactical ploy of playing 'two up front' that night.

Back in London, the unorthodox manner in which talkSPORT covered the tournament registered with the public, many of whom warmed to the station's maverick approach. Ironically, in years to come, when the station *had* purchased sports rights in a legitimate manner, many listeners still assumed the commentators were sitting in front of TV screens and that the crowd noises were sound effects. Not that they were deterred from listening anyway.

Amazingly, talkSPORT had managed to secure sponsorship for their unofficial coverage of the tournament from Nationwide Building Society. Sales director Tim Bleakley reflected: 'That was phenomenal. Broadcasting off the television for the Euros and then getting Nationwide to sponsor it was unheard of. Nobody could believe we were getting away with it. But what a brave and brilliant decision from Nationwide, as the PR they got from it alone was probably worth five times what they paid for it.'

The fallout from the Euro 2000 affair continued for months after the tournament, well into the new domestic football season. Not content with the success of their High Court injunction, the BBC attempted to sue the station for 'passing off' their commentary as live, giving the false impression talkSPORT owned the rights.

Eventually, the case was settled out of court, with both sides claiming victory, as an agreement was reached that talkSPORT could continue to cover events 'off-tube', as long as they reminded listeners at regular intervals that they were not the official rights holders. As far as talkSPORT were concerned, they had won because that was exactly what they had been doing in any case.

By that time, the station had already covered another major sporting event in its own inimitable style by sending a team across the globe for the Sydney Olympics. The plans had been to send a 12-strong crew out to Australia, but the familiar 'lack of accreditation' problem soon arose as talkSPORT wasn't an official Olympic broadcaster – the BBC had taken care of those rights long before.

Without any significant number of press passes and having to rely mainly on more off-tube coverage, talkSPORT sent a team of only three men out to Australia – former British high jumper Steve Smith, reporter Andrew McKenna and producer Gary Burchett. At the last minute, it was also decided to send breakfast host Alan Brazil to broadcast his shows every morning – or afternoon in Sydney.

With the team originally meant to have been 12-strong, the four found themselves based in two lavish apartments in Sydney's Homebush Bay, overlooking the Olympic Stadium. Each apartment had three double-bedrooms as well as a huge living room.

With only two passes available to gain access to the Olympic Stadium, Burchett used one and Smith the other to conduct interviews with British athletes whom he knew from his time with the team. That meant McKenna was left at the flat in front of the television to report on everything that was happening at the different locations across the city. He was kept company by an increasingly bored and restless Brazil, who eventually hired his own car so he could keep himself busy by seeing the sights. He was always due on air between 4pm and 8pm local time and tended to cut it quite fine in terms of making it back to the 'studio' for his shows.

Brazil's trip Down Under hadn't started that well. Because he'd been sent out at the last minute, the only flight he had been found was via Los Angeles. He started off on the wrong foot and spent most of his time complaining that he had nothing to do. At one stage, management in London had to step in and threaten to bring him back home if he didn't calm down and play ball. But eventually the team gelled and, after Brazil's show, they would all go out for dinner together, usually dining at an exclusive top-floor restaurant above a casino in Darling Harbour.

The spirit of the talkSPORT Olympics team was kept high by the British Olympians, and they all gathered at the flat to watch rower Steve Redgrave attempt to make history by winning his fifth consecutive gold medal. They screamed and shouted as Redgrave and Pinsent cruised to victory and, that night, all went out to celebrate. They began drinking on a cruise ship that was permanently moored in Darling Harbour and after knocking back a few lively looseners, a sense of mischief overcame them.

Brazil had spotted a bell on the roof of the ship so he climbed on top of the vessel and, while being recorded for the next day's breakfast show, bellowed at the top of his voice: 'This is for every one of Redgrave's medals!' He then whacked the bell five times, on each occasion yelling a different city's name where Redgrave had claimed gold:

Dong! 'Los Angeles!'

Dong! 'Seoul!'

Dong! 'Barcelona!'

Dong! 'Atlanta!'

Dong! 'Sydney!'

It certainly made for fascinating radio for listeners back in the UK the following morning. The same methods that had served the station well for Euro 2000 and the Olympics actually had their origins in the days just before the new station was founded. Then, Talk Radio had been covering Manchester United's appearance in the inaugural FIFA World Club Championship in Brazil at the turn of the year. Reporter Graham 'Beeky' Beecroft had the onerous task of being despatched to Rio de Janeiro where he stayed in a hotel at the junction of the Copacabana and Ipanema beaches. When he wasn't sightseeing, Beecroft attended United's press conferences and commentated on United's three matches, which were played at the city's majestic Maracana Stadium.

Except Beeky never set foot in the Maracana. With the station having no accreditation for the event, he commentated on the games from his hotel room telly, while Lou Macari provided analysis from the studios in London.

MacKenzie was still doing everything in his power to keep talkSPORT competitive despite its lack of broadcasting rights. He decided to pay the then England manager Kevin Keegan £5,000 a week to appear on the *Alan Brazil Sports Breakfast* every Friday. As part of the deal, Keegan would also do a couple of phone interviews on the 1-4pm show *The Afternoon Sportzone with The Two Macs*, which was presented by Sky Sports pairing Alan McInally and Rob McCaffrey.

In one of these phone interviews, Keegan had just announced his latest England squad and ex-Scotland international and Bayern Munich star McInally innocently said to the England boss: 'Kevin, I have seen your squad and I had high hopes that Rob Lee might be in it this time. He has had a really good season.' The Newcastle midfielder had been playing well but was no shoo-in, yet Keegan was hesitant in his response, saying not everybody could be in the squad. And that was the end of that – an innocuous exchange between Keegan and McInally, for which the England supremo was being paid.

Except the following evening there was a black tie football dinner at Alexandra Palace for the 1966 World Cup winning team. Mike Parry was invited for talkSPORT and was surprised to see Keegan bounding towards him, looking angry: 'I will never do anything for your station again. I have never been so publicly humiliated in my life,' roared the England manager at Parry.

'What are you talking about?' was all the genuinely taken aback Parry could muster.

'Fucking Alan McInally putting me on the spot like that, asking me about Rob Lee. I choose the fucking England team, not him!'

'He was only asking you about it. He only wanted your opinion on it, you know,' offered Parry, but Keegan had already stormed off and never spoke to the station again.

Thankfully, James Whale returned to talkSPORT after making a full recovery, and that freed up Mike Dickin to host the tricky 10am-1pm current affairs slot after Derek Hatton's departure. Dickin was a legendary broadcaster, a veteran of the Talk Radio era, who was opinionated and did not suffer fools gladly. Nevertheless, neither he nor his producers were short of advice from MacKenzie.

One of Dickin's producers was Rob Temple, who was young and enthusiastic and always happy to field calls from MacKenzie about the show. In fact, MacKenzie used to call his programme director and producers regularly at all hours of the day and night, often at weekends. One Sunday morning, MacKenzie called Temple to find out what he had lined up for the following morning's show. The pair chewed the fat for about two or three minutes when Temple suddenly said to MacKenzie: 'Do you mind if I put the phone down for a minute?'

MacKenzie liked to talk for an age and was a little disconcerted so asked Temple what was going on.

'Well, I'm in goal for my Sunday football team,' explained Temple. 'And there's a striker bearing down on goal with the ball and I'd really like to save his shot!'

MacKenzie gave him the go-ahead and heard the phone clunk to the ground, before hearing a yelp followed by a round of applause and then Temple came back on the line.

'So, did you save it?' asked the boss.

'No,' replied Temple.

'Well, in that case, you're fired!' laughed MacKenzie – fortunately for Temple, it was one of those rare occasions where the boss was joking about sacking somebody.

Meanwhile, at talkSPORT Towers, a new era of thriftiness began, meaning the days of flying business class and staying in lavish hotels were over. However, when Durham arrived at his hotel in Barcelona before a Champions League match against Chelsea, he was stunned to find he was staying in a place of supremely magnificent splendour, the likes of which he'd never seen before. His room at the AC Diplomatic boutique hotel was adorned with marble. Huge vases of elaborate flower arrangements were dotted all around and the bathroom featured gold taps and yet more marble. No expense had been spared. Except talkSPORT's.

Within minutes of checking in, his phone rang and it was the office telling him there had been an unfortunate mistake with his booking and he was in the wrong hotel. Despite protesting that he had already checked in, he was forced to check right out and move down the road to vastly inferior accommodation.

Durham was also on the receiving end on his regular trips to Manchester for United's Champions League matches. His hotel for these overnight ventures was inside a walled complex with barbed wire on top just for good measure, but his room was most frightening of all: undecorated, uncomfortable and unable to allow an adult to stand up in it due to the slanted roof of the attic. For future matches, he drove back home on the same night.

Those Manchester United European games were still one of the few examples of live broadcasting rights that talkSPORT owned, although the station continued to cover major football tournaments unofficially.

With the High Court ruling that talkSPORT could broadcast those events, as long as they regularly reminded listeners they weren't official broadcasters and that the crowd sound effects weren't real, the plans for World Cup 2002 in Japan and South Korea were drawn up quickly. They copied what they had done in Amsterdam two years before – except this time the commentary came from the London studios.

As part of the station's World Cup coverage, reporter Dominic 'Our Man in Japan' McGuinness was sent out to Japan to add player interviews, colour and gossip to the station's coverage – a tough gig when talkSPORT still had no accreditation for their man to enter any of the stadia. To his credit, McGuinness managed to wing it in Japan and he had little other choice if he was going to produce the goods. Happy to play the role of a bar fly, 'Our Man in Japan' had no problem with frequenting pubs and clubs in the small hours and he managed to produce some great material from the city of Kobe's nightlife.

The English media were based in the city, but the England fans were not. However, the Brazilian team were staying there and, following their 2-0 second-round win over Belgium, McGuinness chanced upon the only Brazilian bar in Kobe. He was pleasantly surprised to find the tournament's eventual Golden Boot winner Ronaldo, Roberto Carlos and the rest of the Brazil side celebrating inside the bar. He joined them and the hundreds of Brazilian fans who were all dancing together with their heroes and managed to go on air live from the bar at about 1.30am local time, which was still the previous evening in the UK. Standing next to Ronaldo, McGuinness described the colourful, carnival scenes going on around him as the eventual world champions partied the night away.

'Our Man in Japan' gave the station's coverage a more authentic feel – by scuffling his way through the press pack, and with the help of the Football Association, who had always been good to the station, McGuinness managed to secure audio of England player interviews and other football personalities who were in Japan.

He could also accurately report on the atmosphere at all the England games as 'Jim'll Fix It' had struck gold again by sourcing tickets for the group games from the FA, while McGuinness blagged his own for the knockout stages. With

commentary on all the big games provided by Proudfoot and
Alvin Martin back in the London studios – Alan Parry no longer
worked for the station by that stage – talkSPORT made a
decent fist of covering the tournament. Fortunately, by the time
Euro 2004 came around, the eagerly anticipated acquisition of
broadcasting rights changed everything.

McGuinness had also previously reported on his own for the
first few weeks of the 2001 British Lions tour to Australia –
although 'Our Man Down Under' didn't quite have the same
ring to it. With the official rights to broadcast the tour, and with
rugby players being a great deal more accessible than their heavily protected football counterparts, McGuinness spent most of
his time in the team hotel, often interviewing the players pool-
side. In one interview, Austin Healey caused quite a stir when
he claimed he had been on better Lions tours – causing unrest
with coach Graham Henry and ensuring talkSPORT hit the
back pages of newspapers across the UK.

When the talkSPORT commentary team joined McGuinness
for the three Test matches, his main role was to be the station's
pitchside reporter, speaking to replacements before they were
going on to play and interviewing players at full time.

That wasn't an easy task, especially when the Lions managed
to lose the final Test in agonising fashion – and with it the series.
Being so close to the action, McGuinness could smell the disappointment and heartbreak as the red jerseys left the pitch.
With 'Jim'll Fix It' barking instructions in McGuinness's headphones to conduct a post-match interview, the reporter thrust
his microphone into Keith Wood's face. But Wood, who just
weeks earlier had given McGuinness a changing room interview
dressed only in his underpants, barely noticed the talkSPORT
man and trudged off to the dressing rooms.

Captain Martin Johnson was next in McGuinness's sights. He held out the mic as the 6ft 7in, 18-stone Englishman stormed off the pitch. With a look of thunder in his eyes, Johnson almost steamrollered the talkSPORT man, knocking the microphone out of his hand in the process. To his credit, the devastated Johnson held up his hand to apologise and spoke to McGuinness later, but only after he had had time to calm down.

Being so close to the action clearly had its risks, but those were gambles talkSPORT were more than willing to take. Having risen from the squeaky chairs of a tricky launch period, the station was now sitting at the top table of British sports broadcasting.

3

Having Brazil
for Breakfast

*Breakfast show? Forget it. I was always late for training when I was
a player and that started at 10am never mind 6am!*

ALAN BRAZIL

Alan Brazil would never be an obvious choice to present a breakfast show on national radio. His fondness for going out and
having a good time, coupled with his 'we're only here for a visit'
life philosophy, meant he occasionally turned up late, extremely
hungover. And therein lay the genius of the show.

Behaviour that was extremely frustrating for producers suddenly became compulsive listening for millions, as Brazil's life
off-air soon became inextricably linked with his show on-air.

The former professional footballer had been forced to retire
at the age of 27 due to a serious back injury and began work as
a broadcaster on local radio in Suffolk. As an Ipswich legend, he
was popular and went on to spend most of the Nineties
employed by Sky Sports as co-commentator on the satellite TV
giant's live Football League matches.

Talk Radio approached him to present some evening shows in 1999, where he'd field calls and talk about football in a more formatted manner. On his first show, he was joined by ex-Spurs team-mate Paul Miller and, occasionally, Mike Parry would join him in the studio.

Once talkSPORT was up and running, and Brazil had got the nod as the regular breakfast show anchor, he quickly settled into the role – despite his misgivings about the early start. As a natural orator and with an easy, charming manner about him, Brazil was happy broadcasting alone, as he filled the airtime with audio from the previous night's post-match press conferences and the occasional live guest.

Quickly comfortable in the breakfast show hotseat, Brazil rented a London flat around the corner from the studios, opposite the London Eye, and that allowed him the luxury of sampling London's nightlife without worrying about having to trek to and from his family home in Suffolk. Occasionally, after a particularly heavy and long night out, Brazil would have minimal time to return to his flat for a shower before rushing to the studio to make sure he was on air by 6am.

Sometimes, he cut it too fine and producer Claire Furlong would be frantically ringing her presenter while the 6am news and sports headlines were being read. Depending on Brazil's fashionably late arrival, Furlong would instruct the news and sports readers whether to broadcast three- or five-minute bulletins to give the presenter extra time to make it on air.

But, whether it was 6.03am or 6.05am, with adrenalin pumping, the Scot would thrive when he took to the airwaves, and the fact that sometimes he may not have slept at all would give him and the show an edge that won him many fans for its amusing, raw and honest tone.

Towards the end of talkSPORT's first year, Brazil was occasionally joined in the studio by programme director Parry, who would review the morning's newspapers. Parry believed the show was doing well, but thought it could do with being enhanced a little by his presence. He thought Brazil would welcome a little bit of company, instead of just relying on the formula of introducing audio clips.

Within weeks, this slot that Parry had created for himself would go on to provide the spark talkSPORT needed. The station needed a flagship show and breakfast was meant to fill that role. Even though Brazil had been doing well anchoring the slot on his own, the programme still lacked that 'gee wiz' tabloid newspaper factor that Parry had been striving to translate from print to the airwaves.

Like his boss MacKenzie, Parry's background had also been in newspapers – he had been news editor at the *Daily Express* and then moved across the Atlantic to be the newspaper's USA correspondent before joining the *Sun* to work for MacKenzie as an executive editor.

When Parry joined Brazil in the studio, there was an immediate chemistry between the pair. They bounced off each other well and began exchanging exactly the sort of friendly banter that would drive listeners to the station and also to the phones to have their tuppence worth.

Parry decided to act upon his gut feeling and became Brazil's permanent co-host in January 2001. Every morning listeners would be woken up by a passionate, opinionated Scotsman trying to get to grips with an equally passionate and opinionated Englishman, both of whom loved football, had a similar sense of humour and were partial to what they might describe as a sociable drink or two. Good-natured mickey-taking was part of

Brazil's make-up and Parry's short, rotund stature immediately earned him the nickname 'Porky', which stuck faster than glue.

Throughout his time on the station, Brazil was able to create characters for his show. Aside from 'Porky' Parry, later on Graham Beecroft became 'Beeky', while Ronnie Irani is 'Chicken Biryani' and sports newsreader Ian Abrahams is universally known as 'The Moose'. With these characters and the language of his Glaswegian roots, Brazil went some way to creating his own mini talkSPORT sub-culture.

Suddenly, use of the words 'numptie' and 'tube' were becoming commonplace, even popping up on *EastEnders*. talkSPORT had truly arrived and it was all thanks to an anarchic breakfast show – one where listeners felt like they were part of a gang. It was edgy, it was cool and it certainly wasn't conventional. In years to come, the rest of the station would adopt those themes, and the sound and imaging of talkSPORT also reflected that. The station had desperately needed a successful breakfast show to set the tone for the rest of the day.

The natural patter between the pair flowed for four hours every morning. It was good-natured but quick-witted banter and, pretty soon, the booze was also flowing as Brazil and Parry became firm drinking buddies off air, frequenting their favourite wine bars, pubs and restaurants until all hours of the night.

Brazil loved to make fun of Porky, taking advantage of his own razor-sharp memory to pull up his co-presenter if he thought he was contradicting himself. He would remember everything Parry had said and, quite often, he would enlist the help of office juniors to find a clip of Parry from the previous week just so he could prove his friend wrong. Porky was opinionated, loud and wacky but, for the success of the show, was quite happy to have the mickey taken out of him by the former footballer. It was a winning formula.

A typical exchange between the pair went as follows, on the morning after a comfortable England football victory:

Parry: Al, I was proud of the boys and proud to be English.

Brazil: English? But you're Welsh!

Parry: Al, when they gave out the geographical brains you must have been hiding behind the door. I think you'll find that Chester is indeed in England.

Brazil: Maybe. But look at you. All the signs say Celt. Short. Fat. Ginger.

Parry: Al, I'll have you know that I am as English as fish and chips, as Yorkshire pudding, as the Royal Family ...

Brazil: The Royal Family? But she's German and he's Greek!

Parry: Your lack of education fails you, Alan. The Queen is as English as I am. We share many similarities.

Brazil: Aye, I'm sure she'll be thrilled about that!

Exchanging rapid verbal fire for four hours every morning might have come naturally to them but it was not easy, and by the time the show had ended both men would be quite fired up, buzzing with adrenalin and that would lead to a glass of wine once the pubs were open. From that glass, the day could go anywhere, particularly if they were away from the studios, covering an event. Parry was in the difficult position of being the station's programme director as well, so he couldn't abandon his post for the day once the show was over. If anything, he would still put in a full day's work despite having risen at 3.30am to prepare for the breakfast show. Parry recalled: 'It was incredibly intense, but then I had a lot of adrenalin running through me in those days, so I really enjoyed it. It wasn't a problem.'

Brazil, however, saw his co-presenter's workload slightly differently: 'He tried to do everything and I told him "You are mad. You will hurt yourself." And he said "No I won't. I like to work. You shouldn't waste a day not working." He is one of them nutcases!'

Occasionally, Porky and Brazil's on-air banter would turn a little too heated, with Parry mocking Brazil's ex-footballer, carefree attitude to life. The Scot would counter with jibes about Porky's journalist past, insinuating he was part of the gutter press, prepared to stitch people up at all costs. Sometimes, these spats would transfer off air and the pair might go a few days without exchanging a word away from the studio, before a few bottles of wine would solve the problem.

The breakfast show's cast of characters was enhanced by daily slots from Brazil's friend Henk Potts, a financial public relations consultant, and Derek 'Thommo' Thompson who would preview the day's racing – both subjects close to Brazil's heart. On several occasions, Thommo was forced to broadcast his 6.50am piece live from a toilet on a train from Cambridge to Kings Cross as he needed to be in London early. With trains into the capital packed at that time of the morning, the reporter had no choice but to lock himself in the loo before going on air.

That led to the bizarre situation one morning when Thommo was mid-broadcast on the toilet and was interrupted by a furious hammering on the door and a voice screaming: 'Oi! Are you coming out of this toilet or what?' – all live on national radio.

With such a successful formula, talkSPORT quickly discovered the tactic of taking the breakfast show on the road to mark major occasions. The pair broadcasted from events including the Open golf, the Derby, the Grand National and England away matches, including the team's famous 5-1 win in Munich. With

Parry forgetting the pressures and distractions of being in the office as programme director on trips like these, the pair were truly able to let their hair down – often with amusing and potentially disastrous consequences.

On one such trip, England were playing Netherlands in Amsterdam in a midweek friendly. In the hotel bar the night before the game (and the following morning's broadcast), Parry and Brazil were enjoying a quiet glass of wine after a meal and were heading for an early night – at least that was the plan. Suddenly, the bar filled with British journalists who were there for the match but were also enjoying celebratory drinks to mark the retirement of legendary *Sun* hack John Sadler.

With most of them knowing Porky from his Fleet Street days and Brazil from his playing days, before long a full-scale party had broken out from the tedium and tranquillity of the hotel bar. Brazil was in his element and, once the hacks had departed for their next destination, he and Parry headed for a casino, although Porky departed early as he was worried about waking up in time for the following morning's show. Brazil drank champagne and played cards with some friends of his old Ipswich team-mate Frans Thijssen until the early hours and then returned to his hotel to grab some shut-eye before going on air.

While undressing, he was surprised to hear a knock at the door – it was Porky waking him up for the show, although he stunned his friend by opening the door immediately. Parry was shocked Brazil was awake, but the Scot told him he was just having a shower and then he would be along to the studio, which was in a hotel room down the corridor. But in reality, Brazil had other ideas.

Sensing the opportunity to grab a few minutes' sleep, he collapsed on his bed and dozed off, only to be woken by a fierce

thumping on the door. It was one of the assistant producers
trying to shake him out of his slumber. For some reason, during
that short sleep, Brazil had managed to convince himself it was
Sunday and, as he never worked on Sundays, he told the door-
knocker exactly where he could go for disturbing him like that.

Moments later, it was Porky attempting to bash the door
down. Brazil checked his watch. Seven minutes to six. Ouch!
Scrambling out of bed and feeling the effects of the back injury
that ended his playing career, Brazil finally managed to crawl
down the corridor into the studio. The show had started and
Parry was flying solo, so Brazil lay down on a sofa while listening to his friend. He noticed a dish full of M&Ms chocolates on
an adjacent coffee table and his mischievous mind lit up as he
started pinging them at Parry's head during his broadcast. Before
throwing each chocolate at Porky, Brazil popped one into his
mouth and repeatedly muttered: 'One for me, one for him . . .'

At the next commercial break, Porky erupted with anger,
slung Brazil out of the studio and called a meeting at noon to
discuss the Scot's behaviour. After a few hours of sleep, a more
sober Brazil joined a fuming Parry in the hotel lobby. But each
time Porky was about to lay into his colleague, an FA represen-
tative walked past and exchanged greetings with the pair, so
Parry had to slip from bollocking mode straight into the polite-
ness of corporate niceties. Using his old trick, Brazil suggested
it was pure folly to try to achieve anything in a busy hotel lobby
and that they would be better off continuing their discussion at
an Italian restaurant across the road. Game, set and match.

A staggering nine bottles of pinot grigio later, the pair were
best of friends and on their way to the stadium for the evening's
match, with Porky leaning out of the open cab window, belting
out 'Three Lions' at the top of his voice. When the taxi arrived

near the stadium, pandemonium reigned, with England fans everywhere and police looking for troublemakers. Porky immediately joined the throng, but Brazil had other ideas. Being a proud Scot, Brazil was never keen on attending England matches so he jumped back into the taxi and returned to the hotel to watch the game.

The following morning was Porky's turn to struggle as he couldn't remember what had happened in the previous night's match. This time, it was Brazil who came to his rescue by handing him a crib sheet with all the information on the 1-1 draw so that Parry could continue broadcasting and sound authoritative.

MacKenzie was furious with the pair's behaviour and impressed this upon Parry, whose task it was to relay it to the Scot. As Brazil was fond of saying, Parry was MacKenzie's gopher, a 'wee puppy dog' who would be sent to tell Brazil off completely ineffectively or to praise him for a good show:

'It was always at arm's length with Kelvin,' recalled Brazil. 'He used to correspond with me through the gopher, Parry! Mike used to come and tell me off or tell me "Well done, the boss is happy" or "You have got to stop going out at night" and it always came through Mike. We [MacKenzie and I] would pass, you know, have a little chat, sounds good and all that. I never really had a bollocking off him.'

By this stage, Brazil and Parry's breakfast show was such a hit with the punters that the pair had started to do roadshows organised by programme sponsor John Smith's. These would usually take place in the evening, with the breakfast show then going out live from whichever British city they were in the following morning.

But, sometimes the reality of meeting the listeners wasn't all it was cracked up to be, especially when they tended not to forget Parry's uncompromising views on football. In a Newcastle working men's club on one occasion, promotional golf balls with the presenters' heads on them had been distributed to the audience before the roadshow began. When Porky trotted out his long-held belief that Newcastle United's lack of success on the pitch was because the Geordie fans were too comfortable with losing, he started to come under attack as golf balls rained on to the stage from all corners of the room. Then, disaster almost struck, as one crazed fan tried to attack Porky with a chair before Brazil intervened to defuse the situation.

There were similar problems in Glasgow at another roadshow where several locals – and some of Brazil's old pals – had a pop at Parry for the anti-Scottish views they accused him of broadcasting on talkSPORT. This time, Porky escaped unscathed.

With the roadshows in full swing and regular outside broadcasts taking the breakfast team all over Europe, these were heady days for Brazil and Parry. Ratings were up, with the show heard by around one million listeners every day. The listeners tuned in because they loved the banter between the pair – it was like listening to a couple of their mates arguing in the pub, as demonstrated by this conversation between the pair one morning:

Parry: Yes, but Al, your only objective in being rich was to live a life of sloth. Young players now have different ambitions.
Brazil: Such as what?
Parry: Unlike your generation of players, they don't want to own pubs and play snooker all day. They want to make films and go to Hollywood. They want to rear animals and livestock.
Brazil: Animals and livestock? What are you on about now?
Parry: These are ambitious young people who want to use their wealth to fulfil proper ambitions.

Brazil: OK, so what are your ambitions then? Why do you work so hard to earn money?

Parry: In the hope, Al, that I'll get enough so I don't have to sit here every morning looking at your ugly mug!

The other appeal of the breakfast show was that listeners never knew what was going to happen next. A few months after comedian and television presenter Bob Monkhouse passed away, TV critic Garry Bushell appeared on the breakfast show and talked about a BAFTA tribute show for Monkhouse that he'd attended the previous evening. Brazil, Parry and Bushell exchanged anecdotes about Monkhouse together before Brazil asked the critic: 'Garry, what about Bob's health now?'

An awkward silence followed before Brazil was informed that Monkhouse had died at Christmas. The Scot could only counter with: 'Oh, I heard two different versions of it.' Similarly, on another show, the pair were discussing the death of actor John Thaw who had passed away the previous day. The exchange went as follows:

Brazil: I was sad to hear yesterday about the death of Inspector Morse, TV's John Shaw.

Parry: John Thaw, Alan.

Brazil: Do you know, I've been doing that all morning. John, if you're listening, sorry mate!

But, when he wasn't trying to raise the dead, Brazil remained in top form, with a heavy night on the town seemingly helping him to perform at his best – and giving him plenty of material for his shows. The lengthy drinking sessions served only to strengthen the bond between Porky and Brazil as presenters – in fact, many ideas for the following day's show would be born out of a third, fourth or even fifth bottle of wine. And the very next day, listeners would hear all about the previous night's antics, adding to the show's cult status. One such idea from a night out led to an unforgettable trip to Washington DC for a special broadcast of the breakfast show.

In early 2004, a terrorist scare had repeatedly grounded BA Flight 223 from London to Washington. Television news channels were showing the plane sitting on the Heathrow Airport tarmac around the clock and it was while Brazil was counting his losses in a Mayfair casino that he saw the pictures of the jumbo jet and had a brainwave: he needed to board that flight with Porky whenever it finally left to send a message to the terrorists that they could not win. Once in Washington, they would broadcast the breakfast show before returning home to a heroes' welcome.

British Airways were delighted with the idea, as it would give them plenty of positive free publicity, and they footed the bill for the breakfast team's first-class seats. The flight was almost empty after being cancelled for two consecutive days, but that didn't stop Brazil and Parry from taking full advantage of the first-class hospitality. It was third time lucky for the flight, although not before a three-and-a-half-hour delay left Brazil and Porky sitting on the plane with nothing to do other than quaff as much free champagne as possible. In fact, they downed so much bubbly while the plane was on the runway that BA staff had to send out for more before take-off.

Once airborne, talkSPORT's finest continued their two-man assault on BA's champagne stock, finally arriving in Washington in the evening, where temperatures had plummeted down to -22 degrees Celsius. Undeterred by the conditions, Brazil and

Parry continued the party with the help of their own chauffeur-driven limousine – supplied by a talkSPORT fan who ran a worldwide limo firm.

Having worked in the US capital while at the *Express*, Parry still had contacts and knew the places where Brazil would feel most comfortable. The limo took them straight to a Celtic Supporters' Club based in a pub where Brazil was treated like royalty. From there they went to a Georgetown piano bar for a sing-song, pausing only when they realised the time was coming up to 2am in Washington and 7am in the UK, meaning their weekend breakfast show was beginning in an hour.

They dashed to the hotel in time for the broadcast, but technical problems meant there was no line open to the London studios and the show could not go to air. After coming all that way and drinking all that champagne, Brazil and Parry's efforts looked to be in vain.

But, as is the talkSPORT way, with just 20 seconds to go, an engineer managed to correct the problem and the broadcast began on schedule. The American hosts of the studio were amazed at the energy of Porky and Brazil, especially when they heard that the pair were yet to sleep since arriving the previous night. They asked talkSPORT's finest if they used pills to maintain their performance and were stunned to learn that this breakfast show team functioned purely on bubbly.

By the time the show was over, it was 7am local time and a new dawn had broken. Parry and Brazil decided to finally call it a night – or a day – and retired to their rooms only to both find themselves in the hotel bar less than three hours later as neither had been able to sleep due to the adrenalin and the natural high of what they had just done. With their flight back to the UK not leaving until 4am the following morning, there was nothing left to do other than continue the party. They did just that, arriving back at the airport in the early hours, just in the nick of time to make the flight.

Soon after that trip, the breakfast boys took to the skies again, this time to broadcast their show from Monaco, where Chelsea were playing in the Champions League semi-final. With talkSPORT in thrifty mode, the pair flew easyJet to the principality and made sure they were stocked up with red wine for the short journey from London. On this occasion, Brazil and Parry were still in the skies when the mayhem began.

After enjoying a few glasses, Parry was being tutted at and ticked off by a gentleman sitting to his right. The flight was full of football fans going to the game, including Chelsea midfielder Frank Lampard's family, but this passenger was clearly nothing to do with the match, as he openly disapproved of the raucous and boisterous atmosphere that the talkSPORT pair were creating. At one point, he even shoved past Parry to retrieve his home-made sandwiches from a bag in the overhead locker.

As the plane began its descent into the South of France, there was a spell of turbulence which caused poor old Porky to throw his wine up in the air – unfortunately it landed all over this unsuspecting passenger. The wine was still dripping from the man's glasses onto his nose as Parry started to mop him up using some old tissues he had found. He was apologising profusely as the passenger berated him, pleading: 'Get away from me, you disgusting man. Get off me!'

Meanwhile, Brazil and most of the plane were crying with laughter watching Porky having to deal with his irate new friend. At this point, Parry started thrusting £20 notes into the man's hand, saying: 'Get your shirt cleaned! No, get a new shirt! No, get a new outfit!'

Having arrived in hysterics, Brazil also left Monaco chuckling after stopping off at one of his favourite hotels, La Reserve de Beaulieu. It was an exclusive, expensive hotel frequented only by the rich and famous, so Brazil suggested they enjoy a glass of his favourite red wine there while admiring the rugged coastline and listening to the waves crashing against the rocks.

As he perused the wine list, Brazil checked Porky had the talkSPORT credit card before ordering a bottle of red. It was a beautiful wine and Parry was keen on ordering another bottle although, unusually, Brazil asked if he was certain he wanted one more as it was an expensive wine. Parry insisted, much to Brazil's delight, and they knocked back the second bottle before asking for the bill, which came in at a cool £500!

Parry exploded in disbelief, while Brazil started laughing again uncontrollably. For some reason, nobody had told Porky about the Euro, because he was still calculating the price in French francs, believing he had to divide by ten to reach the figure in pounds. Unfortunately, he should have divided by around one and a half. As Brazil giggled, Parry was already trying to work out how he would wangle his way out of trouble back in London, concocting stories about entertaining Ken Bates and Chelsea officials at the game. Needless to say, a bollocking was waiting for Porky on arrival at talkSPORT Towers.

It was becoming unofficial station policy to ensure at least one show – usually breakfast – was broadcast live from the city of any major sporting event. The programme did not necessarily need to come from the venue itself, but as long as talkSPORT were in town to capture the colour and atmosphere, it was job done.

Being a lifelong Celtic fan, it was unsurprising that Brazil got the nod to head to Seville for the UEFA Cup final between his club and FC Porto. After landing at an airport several hours from Seville, the brekkie boys endured a nightmare car journey across the south of the country as several wrong turns left them utterly lost. At one point, they even drove into Portugal.

Driver and sound engineer Phil von Oppen was the unfortunate recipient of plenty of abuse from Brazil and Parry, who complained of their need for a drink from the minute the car journey had begun. It turned out that their flight had experienced severe turbulence so there had been no trolley and, therefore, no booze for the pair as von Oppen distinctly recollected: 'Every time we saw a pub or taverna, Brazil wanted to stop. We made quite a few stops, as Brazil was a very thirsty man. But he made up for it!'

After von Oppen took a wrong turn one too many times for his liking, Brazil hailed down a taxi once they were in Seville and ordered the driver to lead them to their hotel. They didn't get lost again.

After finally arriving at their hotel in the early evening, Brazil wasted no time in catching up with his long-lost Glaswegian brothers – it's fair to say that a glass or two were raised ahead of the following night's match. Porky preferred to take things a little easier that night, especially after the disastrous journey. He left Brazil and friends in the hotel bar and went up to his room, only to discover two Celtic fans asleep on his bed. Knowing only one person could possibly be to blame, poor Porky confronted Brazil back in the bar and found out that the Scottish strangers in his room were old friends of his co-host's who didn't have beds for the night. Now, courtesy of talkSPORT, they did. Brazil knew he had a spare bed in his room, so invited Porky to spend the night with him, although the programme director was far from happy with that arrangement. But that was only the half of it.

After the following morning's show, Porky discovered that Brazil had also given the pair's match tickets away to two more old friends of his who had arrived in Seville without cash or any hope of seeing the game. But Brazil was confident that Porky would be able to pull a few strings and reel in a couple of press passes for them, which he duly did, although, once again, he wasn't best pleased.

After Brazil watched his beloved Celtic lose in the final to Jose Mourinho's Porto, the trip to Spain concluded with a couple of breakfast shows that were broadcast live from the beach in Marbella. Large speakers on the sand ensured that holiday-makers could also hear the show, as Brazil took a call from a rather concerned woman back in Glasgow that morning. She came on air to say that her husband had gone to Seville for the final and still hadn't returned home five days later. While she was on the radio, a man on the beach made his way to the mobile studio to inform producers that he was this woman's husband, so von Oppen put him on air to be reunited with his wife: 'I gave him a set of headphones and a microphone and she started screaming at him down the phone!' After receiving an ear-bashing in front of the nation, the man made his way to the airport with his tail firmly between his legs.

Later that year, the breakfast show team found themselves overseas again. Brazil and Parry had flown over to Istanbul to broadcast a couple of shows either side of England's crucial European Championship qualifier against Turkey. Brazil was not particularly enamoured with being in Istanbul as it wasn't his sort of city – it had no central area offering restaurants and bars where he could kick back and relax while not on air.

On top of that, the atmosphere in the city was a little tense as it was the first time an English team had returned to Turkey since two Leeds fans were stabbed and killed there before a Champions League game in 2001. As a result, Brazil spent most of the trip camped out in the five-star hotel that was the talkSPORT team's base.

The show was broadcast from just outside the hotel, which was the only place where a signal for the satellite could be picked up. While Parry was broadcasting, he noticed Jim'll Fix It, his producer, sprinting away from the makeshift studio in the direction of some local kids. He looked around and realised the youngsters had made off with some of the crew's satellite equipment and his own mobile phone. Parry continued broadcasting while Jim'll gave chase and eventually the thieves dropped the heavy equipment but made off with Porky's phone.

About five minutes later, they returned with the phone and forced Parry to hand over £30 to secure its safe return – apparently, this was common practice in Istanbul. The daylight robbery and bribery was definitely a first for the breakfast show team. But it all ended happily that night, as England secured the draw they needed to qualify for the following year's finals in Portugal. Porky was in far better spirits as he and the crew attempted to drink the hotel bar dry while singing patriotic England football songs through the night.

Naturally, Brazil would have enjoyed a drink too, but the celebrations and the singing were not for him as he remained loyal to Scotland. His dislike of Istanbul was typical of the single-minded way he approached his job and his life. He did exactly what he wanted whenever he wanted, although never in a malicious or selfish way. He simply had a happy-go-lucky attitude to everything he did.

It was this attitude that meant there would be occasions when he would cut his arrival into the studio much too fine and miss the start of shows. In the station's early years Brazil often flew by the seat of his pants and never had to pay the penalty. But, further down the line, the breakfast show presenter's approach would land him in hot water at talkSPORT.

4

Sir Geoffrey, Cricket and a Ratings Ricket

It's bloody hot up here!

CHRIS COWDREY

The decision to broadcast England's overseas cricket tours had proved to be a stroke of genius on the part of Kelvin Mackenzie. After the success of the South Africa tour of 1999-2000, talkSPORT managed to secure the rights to the Pakistan tour the following winter. Signing up Geoff Boycott had been a masterstroke. Not only was he a respected authority on the game across the globe, but he was revered on the sub-continent as some sort of cricketing god.

Everywhere Boycott went in Pakistan he was called Sir Geoffrey, despite the fact he had never been knighted. He had spent a great deal of time coaching cricket in India and Pakistan, as well as playing for England there back in his heyday, and the locals always wanted to show their appreciation. Boycott's presence in the commentary box helped talkSPORT immensely. It smoothed any problems they may have otherwise faced in sometimes difficult conditions abroad and his voice lent more gravitas to the station's broadcast back home.

The main difficulty of touring Pakistan was the lack of available alcohol for winding down purposes during the long, hot evenings. Luckily, talkSPORT commentator Jack Bannister had a contact at the British Embassy who made sure that a new crate of wine followed the station's commentary team around each Test venue. It wasn't that simple, however, as it was still illegal to drink wine in restaurants so the talkSPORT team would smuggle the booze in to their dining venues then ask the waiter for a bottle of water. As soon as it arrived, the water would be poured away and, in a feat of which Jesus Christ himself would have been proud, was immediately replaced by the wine.

After the controversy over Euro 2000, here was talkSPORT playing by the rules – apart from the illegal wine consumption – and doing a tremendous job, even if the BBC were still smarting from being usurped from what they saw as their rightful place as the voice of English cricket.

It also gave MacKenzie great pleasure to see talkSPORT put one over on the Beeb so soon after the High Court action that followed Euro 2000. The only problem for MacKenzie – and talkSPORT – was that many listeners failed to realise they were listening to his new station.

Since 1992, radio audiences had been measured by RAJAR (Radio Joint Audience Research Limited), who used a diary system to record listening figures. This system relied on about 130,000 people filling in a diary by hand to document what they had listened to on the radio each day. MacKenzie was convinced this system was flawed and he may have had a point, as independent research indicated that large numbers of people who had heard talkSPORT's cricket coverage wrote in their diaries that they had heard it on the BBC. In other words, they assumed it was on the Beeb, as that's where they had always heard the cricket.

Battling RAJAR and the BBC would become the two bees in MacKenzie's bonnet throughout his talkSPORT tenure and, through the cricket, he could do both.

In order to impress upon listeners that talkSPORT was broadcasting the 2000-01 tour to Sri Lanka, which followed the Pakistan tour, MacKenzie instructed producers that the coverage should feel unique and as different as possible from the way the Beeb would have done it. With that mission, the *talkSPORT At The Test* team set off for Sri Lanka with Boycott again at the helm, joined by former cricketers Mark Nicholas, Chris Cowdrey, Chris Broad, Jack Bannister and reporter Andrew McKenna – or 'Macca' to the listeners. Organising everything behind the scenes was none other than Jim 'Jim'll Fix It' Brown.

And on day one of the first Test match in the seaside resort of Galle, talkSPORT inflicted a bloody nose on the BBC, although it was not necessarily of their own doing. MacKenzie had paid a fair amount for the rights to cover the series and some bright spark had pointed out to the Sri Lanka Cricket Board chief that the BBC's small reporting team, who were there only to transmit updates, had not paid a penny. So when the Beeb's team of Peter Baxter, Jonathan Agnew and Pat Murphy arrived outside the ground, they were refused entry and a furious row broke out as no news organisation had ever paid to broadcast what is known as 'news access'.

This was all taking place about 15 feet below the talkSPORT commentary box and Cowdrey saw the funny side by throwing down pieces of paper which had slogans such as 'Free The

Murphy One!' scrawled on them. Naturally, that only enflamed the situation and, in the end, the Beeb team had no choice but to set up their satellite equipment on top of an old fort over-looking the ground and report from there while sitting on the grass. It was a sign of the times and showed the shifting balance of power. talkSPORT was now the major British player in cov-ering overseas cricket.

It was in Kandy for the second Test that the talkSPORT crew pulled off a stunt that the Beeb would never have dreamed of. In fact, the BBC would never have even slept next to somebody who would have dreamed of it. Kandy was an area of Sri Lanka where herds of elephants roamed and the local dignitaries had organised an elephant procession around the ground before the start of play one day.

Jim'll Fix It himself decided it would be a great idea if one of the talkSPORT team could ride on one of the elephants while introducing that day's coverage. A live broadcast from on top of an elephant – could any other radio station have even consid-ered this?

Using the 'fix it' knowledge garnered from working with Mr Savile, Brown convinced the locals this would be good fun and they agreed that one of the talkSPORT team could join the ele-phant parade. Former England opening batsman Broad was the chosen man for the job, but when he found out whoever was to sit on top of the elephant would also have to be kitted out in Sri Lankan traditional national dress, he pulled out. Brown turned to Cowdrey who, feeling there was no choice because Boycott was hardly going to do it, told Brown 'You must be mad!' before he accepted the challenge of performing this piece of broad-casting history.

Before the next morning's play, a troop of elephants paraded around the outskirts of the ground as the teams were going through their warm-up and stretching exercises. Sitting on top of one particularly big-eared beast was Cowdrey, dressed in full Sri Lankan traditional costume and armed with a radio mic so that he could introduce the day's cricket to the talkSPORT listeners huddled around their radios in the early hours of the morning in the UK. As he broadcast from the back of the world's largest land mammal, England captain Nasser Hussain and his team-mates stopped their stretches and stood open-mouthed. No RAJAR diary on that day could possibly have contained an entry mistakenly thinking that the Test cricket had been broadcast by the BBC.

Cowdrey was told that he would be up on the elephant for no more than 20 minutes, but he was royally stitched up as Brown abandoned him on top of the enormous creature for a grand total of an hour and 40 minutes. During the morning session commentary on a baking hot day, the talkSPORT team often handed over to Cowdrey for the latest from the elephant and he simply replied: 'It's bloody hot up here!'

Broad's refusal to dress up did not last long, as he and several other members of the talkSPORT crew were soon taking part in a fashion show in Colombo to help out the Sri Lankan press officers who were organising it. Unsurprisingly, Boycott was not involved. He was also revered in Sri Lanka, although perhaps not as much as in India and Pakistan, and he travelled in luxury on the country's dusty and bumpy roads. With potholes everywhere, journeys in more basic cars took an age and were extremely uncomfortable. With his bad back, talkSPORT made sure they had hired Boycott a Mercedes in which to travel. Everyone on the island knew when Boycott was driving past, as he had the only Merc in the country.

Boycott was also given honorary treatment when it came to mealtime during the Test matches. With lunch always a curry derivative and the unrepentant Yorkshireman having no stomach for that kind of dish, he was always given Western cuisine, while everybody else ate the local offerings. During one lunch interval during the third Test in Colombo, the talkSPORT team managed to persuade Boycott to taste one of their curries. The dish was certainly not on the mild side and his eyes started rolling like fruit machine reels, while sweat poured from his forehead. Thankfully, Boycott was able to continue broadcasting for the afternoon session despite his ordeal.

The former England captain was a wily character who could dish out the stick just as easily. Before one morning's commentary had begun, he took Cowdrey to one side and explained to him that he was unhappy with the way he introduced the programme: 'Chris, do you know that every morning, when you come to me in the middle, you've covered everything. You do too big an intro. Off you go and tell everyone what the weather's like, the score from yesterday, the pitch conditions. You do the whole bloody thing then you come down to me and I've got nothing left to say,' complained Boycott.

'This is what you're going to do,' he continued. 'Keep it short, just say that you thought that the pitch played well yesterday.'

Cowdrey was slightly taken aback but was keen to keep Boycott happy, so later that morning, before handing over to the Yorkshireman for his preview of the day's play, he did exactly what he had been asked: 'I thought the pitch played really well yesterday. Let's go over to Geoffrey. . .'

Boycott replied: 'I don't agree! I don't think the pitch did play well. It was a bit up and down actually!' Boycott continued to rubbish Cowdrey's brief analysis, as the talkSPORT presenter realised he had been led a merry dance by the former England opener.

Away from the pranks, what Boycott wanted, Boycott generally got. During that Colombo Test, talkSPORT were broadcasting from a sealed, heavily air-conditioned commentary box, but the former England star complained. He wanted to hear what was going on 'out in the middle', as cricket types like to refer to the centre of the pitch where all the action takes place. Following a conversation between Jim'll Fix It and the Sri Lankan press officials, the next day the window in the box had vanished completely, making it hotter but more authentic as Boycott had requested.

Ratings were up in 2001, no doubt helped by the overseas Test coverage and the fact that the England team were showing signs of improvement. Their winning run came to an end in India in 2001-02, where the Test series was again broadcast in its entirety on talkSPORT with rising audience figures again.

Disaster struck the following year, though, as Boycott was diagnosed with throat cancer, forcing him out of the equation as far as the Ashes tour to Australia was concerned and, more importantly, facing a long battle for survival. Plans were still in place to cover the Test series, but with Boycott ill, the whole operation was canned at the last minute and the rights were sold back to the BBC.

talkSPORT still had a presence Down Under in the shape of young reporter Mike Bovill, who had temporarily left the station to go freelance but had agreed to work for them again during the Test matches. Jim'll Fix It was on the scene in a flash to make sure Bovill, who had been backpacking in South America before arriving in Australia, had all the necessary equipment. He handed the broadcasting gear over to Bovill, who was staying in a six-man dorm in a backpackers' hostel, before speeding back to his four-star luxury hotel in his rented Saab convertible. Jim could fix it for himself too.

The most unforgettable and surreal moment of the tour for Bovill was recording a live interview with Tony Greig in the former England captain's Hobart hotel room. Bovill had been trailing Greig during the Ashes tour, speaking to him for talkSPORT in every Test location at the end of each day's play. On this particular evening, Bovill knocked on Greig's door and the former cricketing god, wearing nothing other than his Y-fronts, let him in. The pair then recorded the interview with no further clothes added to the Greig body. Listeners back home would never have known. That was the beauty of radio, although it's not clear how beautiful Bovill would have found that moment.

Despite these colourful moments on the other side of the globe, the overseas cricketing monopoly was temporarily over for talkSPORT, but they would be back the following year in the West Indies with more controversy than ever before.

Meanwhile, MacKenzie had ploughed thousands of pounds into new technology for measuring radio audience figures, as he still believed the system then employed by RAJAR was flawed and was giving talkSPORT far fewer listeners than it was broadcasting to in reality. Many people still stated in their diaries that they were listening to cricket coverage on the BBC, when in fact it was on talkSPORT.

The answer, according to MacKenzie, lay in Swiss digital watches that were specially designed to record and compress ambient sound. This meant that anybody wearing one of these watches while listening to the radio would have the sound pattern automatically recorded by the watch. To find out exactly what people were listening to on the radio, the watches simply needed to be checked by a control centre to compare the recorded sound patterns with the sound broadcast by each radio station. Any direct matches would incontrovertibly prove that the person wearing the watch was listening to that particular station.

Using trials of this Swiss watch technology, talkSPORT were able to prove how flawed the RAJAR ratings were. With the watches, talkSPORT's weekly reach was quadrupled – going from around the two million mark under RAJAR to an astonishing nine million potential listeners.

As far as MacKenzie was concerned, the system employed by RAJAR was costing his station millions of pounds in lost advertising revenue. If talkSPORT really was being heard by up to three or four times as many listeners as RAJAR's figures suggested, then advertisers should have been paying a great deal more for their on-air commercials.

After much to-ing and fro-ing between talkSPORT and RAJAR, MacKenzie took legal action against the radio audience researchers, suing them for delaying the introduction of an electronic audience measurement tool, rather than relying on the diary system. At great cost to the station, the High Court struck out talkSPORT's action, which was a tremendous blow to MacKenzie and the station.

Following the verdict, RAJAR announced it was committed to sticking to a timetable of research into electronic measurement that would see it implement its chosen preferred method by 2007 to which MacKenzie responded: 'There is as much chance of RAJAR sticking to their timetable as there is of Bin Laden being found in Deptford.'

Sadly, MacKenzie was proved right as RAJAR's diary system is still in use today. Incidentally, Osama bin Laden has yet to be found in Deptford.

5

Buggies, Bogeys
and Booze

*At the Ryder Cup, we ended up literally with my arse sticking out
the window of the caravan because there was so little room.*

MIKE PARRY

The Open Golf Championship, one of the quintessentially
British events of the summer. The Royal & Ancient. The Claret
Jug. Champagne flutes. Hushed crowds of stiff-upper-lip types.
And talkSPORT's camper van.

Somehow, the idea of Britain's rough and ready, tabloid-style
sports radio station broadcasting the Open sounds like the
mother of all culture clashes. But in the early days of talkSPORT,
MacKenzie's bold decision to send a large crew up to St Andrews
to broadcast all four days of a tournament in which Tiger Woods
won his first major championship in the UK was inspired.

There was no major issue in terms of covering the tournament,
despite the large BBC presence in Scotland. The talkSPORT
team, which consisted of commentators Richard Boxall and
Robert Lee, alongside Andy Gray – the ex-footballer and then

Sky Sports co-commentator – American reporter Bob Bubka, Rupert Bell and Sarah Sanderson, were free to roam around the course, following each playing group from hole to hole. Gray's appointment was a MacKenzie decision that was an attempt to persuade the station's many football fans that golf was worth a try and proved to be another tactical triumph. With his voice arguably better known than his face from his Sky football commentaries, Gray was a hit with listeners.

In fact, talkSPORT's golf broadcasts were so popular that the team won a Sony radio silver award for their coverage – a fantastic accolade for a station that was barely six months old during the broadcast.

All this for a team that included horse racing correspondent Bell, who was drafted into the line-up because in one of his reports from Chester races, he had mentioned on air that he had played golf on Michael Owen's nearby course. Parry had heard this, thought it obvious that Bell must be knowledgeable about all things golf and sent him up to Scotland to join the team. The fact that he had a plummy, posh English voice certainly helped too, and Bell was more than happy to be involved although would be the first to admit his golf knowledge did not match his racing expertise. Despite this, he hasn't missed an Open for talkSPORT since.

Apart from the star names and terrific coverage, the highlight of the tournament had to be the spectacular golf buggy driving of reporter Andy Clarke. Having only been working for the station for a couple of months, Clarke was essentially sent up to Scotland to look after Brazil, who was also broadcasting his breakfast show from St Andrews.

These duties included ferrying the Scot around in a buggy, as there was a large amount of ground to cover between the talkSPORT team's living quarters and their temporary studio. There was one small problem. Nobody had realised that Clarke did not hold a driving licence and had no idea how to control the buggy.

On the first morning of the tournament, Clarke had Brazil on board as he raced along the paths next to the course, but he didn't slow down for a turn at a mini-roundabout and nearly managed to kill the station's star presenter in the process. Clearly shaken up by the incident, Brazil refused to travel in the buggy with Clarke again.

The following day, as Clarke was leaving the compound where the TV and radio studios were housed, he wasn't paying full attention to where he was going. Coupled with his atrocious driving skills, this was a recipe for disaster. With another buggy just in front of him, Clarke could only swerve dramatically to avoid shunting into it. Having lost control of the vehicle, he managed to drive straight into the side of a catering stall, destroying a table that held all the condiments and cutlery.

As a result, the Royal & Ancient banned Clarke from operating a buggy anywhere near St Andrews for the rest of the tournament, although he managed to flout that ban on several occasions.

The following year, talkSPORT returned to the Open. Encouraged by the award-winning coverage at St Andrews, MacKenzie sent an even bigger team to Royal Lytham & St Annes for the 2001 championship. As well as additional reporters such as Adrian Durham, the station sent along pretty much all of their top talent for this assault on the British sporting summer. Just because there was no football didn't mean talkSPORT needed to go quiet for three months. So the team was beefed up by Geoff Boycott as well as the breakfast show pairing of Brazil and Parry, who broadcast their programme from the course every morning throughout the tournament.

By the summer of 2001, the breakfast boys had firmly established themselves as a regular fixture on the airwaves, with their reputations going well before them for enjoying a tipple or two after the show. And there were plenty of distractions for them to wet their gullets after their broadcasts, with the Bollinger champagne tent the central attraction. The drinks would flow through the day, and often long into the night, which always made the following morning's very early start the rudest of awakenings.

And when Brazil wasn't in the Bollinger tent, he could usually be found on the driving range, where all the golf equipment manufacturers would greet him and shower him with complimentary accessories like sweaters, rain jackets and golf balls. (The breakfast presenter loved a freebie and was once found outside talkSPORT Towers loading up his car with crates of Fosters lager. The reception area was rammed full with dozens of boxes of the beer from floor to ceiling and Brazil could barely believe his luck. Unfortunately, he was forced to unload his booty when a sponsorship and promotions executive informed him the beer was strictly for competition winners.)

At Lytham, the talkSPORT team had rented a house alongside the course, meaning they were on site for the duration of the tournament. It was only a golf buggy ride away from the temporary studio facility overlooking the 18th green. To be more accurate, this facility was a motorhome. Or to be even more accurate, it was actually a caravan. And, to be brutally honest, it was a caravan in the car park situated behind the 18th with an excellent view of thousands of cars, but not much golf. Well, this was talkSPORT.

Those early-morning golf buggy rides were always treacherous affairs. Dawn had often only just broken and an assistant producer had to navigate the course, knowing that any wrong turn could lead to the embarrassment of driving across a green and being berated by any number of stuffy officials who patrolled the course. Run-ins with the stewards were a regular occurrence for the talkSPORT team.

One morning following the breakfast show, Brazil was sent out with a radio microphone and a backpack with an aerial sticking out of it, as he was due to follow Colin Montgomerie around the course. The breakfast host had risen early that cold and wet morning and was kitted out in waterproofs along with an armband that gave him access to go pretty much wherever he liked as a broadcaster. He quickly warmed to the task, whispering in hushed tones over the airwaves: 'And it's Monty with a five-iron, second shot, 200 yards to the pin...' as he was caught up in the atmosphere of the occasion.

By now, the sun had come out and, still in his heavy waterproofs, Brazil was beginning to tire, having walked a good five or six holes. It was lunchtime and he had been up since around 5am – the heavy burden of doing the breakfast show and walking the course with the backpack was taking its toll. On top of that, he was convinced that the producers were not coming to him regularly enough for updates.

In the heat of the day, Brazil had had enough and, by chance, as he was walking along the fairway on the next hole, he noticed the back of the talkSPORT house on the other side of a fence. Remembering that he had heard the producers tell him that some areas of the course were black spots where his radio mic wouldn't be picked up, he realised he had the perfect alibi and headed for home. Weighed down by the equipment and feeling like an Action Man by now, he enlisted some spectators to help him mount the fence, hop over a railway track, clear another fence and suddenly he was back in his bedroom.

As he was taking off the radio gear, Brazil could hear producer Claire Furlong on the radio mic, screaming: 'Fucking hell, get the engineers out there! Brazil is going to go mad, he's out on the course – I knew these things wouldn't work!' Soaked in sweat, Brazil jumped straight into the shower to cool off and, as he was drying himself, singing away happily, he was surprised to bump into reporter Clarke, who was just on his way out of the house to begin his shift. Brazil handed him the radio equipment and asked him to return it to the caravan before collapsing on to the bed for a well-earned kip.

Back in the car park caravan, Furlong had been ranting at her engineers for what seemed to them like ages. Unable to track down Brazil, with whom she'd been trying to link up several times for updates on Montgomerie's progress, she became more and more agitated, and all the technical people around her were bearing the brunt of her wrath.

Convinced that she was dealing with a faulty radio mic problem or one of the black spot issues that had arisen earlier, Furlong ranted at the engineers, telling them: 'I can't believe you're expecting to be paid for this!' In mid-rant, Clarke came in and, hearing what she had been saying, chuckled quietly to himself as he calmly handed over Brazil's kit and explained that the Scot was fast asleep in bed. Furlong was eating humble pie for breakfast, lunch and supper for the rest of the Open, as the engineers demanded apologies all round.

As usual, Brazil managed to charm his way out of trouble. When he eventually surfaced, he was spotted with Parry in the Bollinger tent by Furlong who demanded an explanation and accused him of being thoroughly unprofessional. Brazil was no liar and honestly held his hands up to explain how he had seen the house, thought of his bedroom and gave in to temptation. Pretty soon, as her colleagues dissolved into laughter with the brekkie boys, she had to see the funny side of it too – even if she did want to throttle Brazil. On the remaining days, Brazil was never asked to return to the course after the breakfast show – he was left to spend his time in the one place where he would always show up punctually, performed consistently and never shirked responsibility – the Bollinger tent.

Meanwhile, Boycott was making his presence felt around the course too. The former England cricketer was justifiably a voice of authority when it came to his old sport of willow on leather and was never afraid to opine to anyone and everyone whenever he had something he felt had to be said. And that remains the case to the present day. A stereotypically proud and forthright Yorkshireman, Boycott 'says what he likes and likes what he bloody well says.'

Now that he was at Lytham to add some colour to four days at the Open golf, Boycott also took it upon himself to assume expertise on what was, after all, another bat and ball sport. On the day before the championship began, Boycott accompanied Ernie Els on his practice round. In fact, Boycott was supposed to be part of a group of reporters who were following Els around the course, but he took it upon himself to stay much closer to the South African so he could offer the two-time US Open champion advice and assistance.

Each time an Els drive went wayward, Boycott could be heard muttering in the background how he would never have used that particular club or taken that line of approach. If comedian Harry Enfield's annoying 'You don't want to do it like that!'

character had been marching around Lytham behind Els, he couldn't have been any more irritating.

Boycott had arrived at Lytham carrying an extremely painful injury, as he had accidentally gashed his wrist after falling and putting his hand through a window. His hand still felt quite fragile, so he was taking extra care of himself and that included being chauffeured around the course in a buggy – fortunately not one driven by Clarke.

When crossing a particular fairway in a bid to make it to the next hole for a broadcast, Boycott's buggy was held up by a large group of a few hundred spectators. A particularly jobsworth steward was insisting the Yorkshireman would not get through the crowds and he started to become agitated, pleading to the official: 'We need to get across there, son!' With his distinctive voice bellowing out to the marshals, the spectators soon realised it was Boycott and spontaneously began parting to allow his buggy through, while giving him a round of applause at the same time.

As the buggy drove between the crowds, Boycott showed his appreciation to the fans by delicately waving his injured hand to acknowledge their assistance and good wishes. With his hand raised in the air, fixed in a very slow and deliberate waving motion, one spectator assumed Boycott was issuing a high-five invitation. He took it upon himself to slam his palm straight into the former cricketer's very sensitive and badly damaged hand, causing him to wince in pain and wring his hand while screaming: 'Fucking hell, I didn't expect that one!'

Boycott survived, although he kept his hands firmly to himself for the rest of the tournament, and he wasn't the only member of the talkSPORT team to narrowly avoid serious injury.

Bell was sent out to follow David Duval on the American's

final round, which would lead to him lifting the Claret Jug by its conclusion. But disaster struck for the reporter when a contact lens cracked, meaning he was rendered virtually blind for most of the day. Luckily, armed with his radio mic and earpiece, he took information from the producers who were advising him exactly how Duval was doing, more or less commentating in his ear from the television pictures back in the caravan.

At one hole, Bell was on the edge of the fairway and, in his ear, he heard that Duval had struck his tee-shot and it was in the air but drifting left. Bell looked up to the skies but, without his lenses, he would barely have known whether they were blue or grey, let alone find Duval's ball. His earpiece was telling him the ball was still in the air but on its way down when suddenly Bell heard a fizzing sound in his other ear and the ball whizzed past him, clunking the spectator next to him fully on the knee. Thanking his lucky stars for his good fortune, Bell inquired about the spectator's health, who told him he didn't mind being hit as, after all, he had been whacked by the Open champion. It was the only time all day that Bell knew what was happening without the aid of his earpiece.

The golf and racing reporter endured his fair share of scrapes working for talkSPORT, none more so than at Ascot in 2009 when he managed to trip and fall in the weighing room. He ended up with eight stitches in his face and a magnificent black eye of which a heavyweight boxer would have been proud. As Bell's brother trained some of the Queen's horses, the dishevelled state of talkSPORT's correspondent did not go unnoticed by Her Majesty. She enquired of one of her racing managers: 'What is the brother of my trainer doing? Has he been drinking?' To ask a question like that, even Elizabeth Windsor must have been a talkSPORT fan.

Bell was also famously lost for words on one occasion at Aintree when he was covering Ladies' Day at the Liverpool course. In a live broadcast on the Hawksbee & Jacobs afternoon show, Bell was interviewing a young lady who wasn't wearing very much, so he innocently asked: 'How are you keeping warm?'

'I have got two thongs on!' she replied.

Back at Lytham, that particular tournament proved to be an eventful one for many at talkSPORT. Parry kept his head down, as he was expecting a torrid time from British star Lee Westwood, whom he had publicly rebuked on the breakfast show for missing the US Masters. A couple of months earlier, the Nottingham-based pro had decided to remain alongside his wife, who was expecting their first child, rather than fly out to Augusta to play in the year's first major. Parry, who has never married, called Westwood a wimp on air, saying that his first priority should have been his golf, while Brazil attempted to explain why Westwood's action was correct.

Westwood was rumoured to be on the lookout for Parry – for some strange reason he never tried the Bollinger tent – and eventually took out his frustration on Durham, who interviewed him after a poor performance in the first round. He was monosyllabic throughout the interview, refusing to play ball and trying to make life as difficult as possible for the talkSPORT man. Durham countered by asking Westwood what he thought the cut score (the traditional point after two rounds of a tournament where those who are too far behind the leaders leave the competition) would be. After only one round, it's considered quite insulting to ask a pro a question like that and Westwood stormed off, leaving his agent to reprimand Durham: 'Don't you ever interview one of my boys like that again!' All this while the real villain Parry was quaffing champers just down the road.

Somehow, through the mayhem, madness and madcap nature of everything that went on around their coverage, talkSPORT managed to bring the Open to life on air, sharing many of these experiences with the listeners and transporting the colour of the event into the homes of millions. The station continued its Open coverage for the next few years, providing a genuine alternative to the BBC and showing that there was a slightly different way to approach golf – the talkSPORT way.

When the BBC turned up at the Open they did so with a crew hundreds strong and with about 20 trucks. When talkSPORT turned up, usually running late, they would have around a dozen people and something resembling a motorhome. The following year at Muirfield proved particularly trying, as the wet weather ensured the mobile studio leaked for the duration of the tournament, while the Open at Sandwich in 2003 was memorable for the accommodation booked by Bell.

The reporter had been assigned this task with a severely restricted budget and the team stayed in what became affectionately known as The Toblerones. This was a row of small chalets, usually frequented by holidaymakers, with roofs shaped like pointed triangles. The problem with the chalets was that all the electricity was run by individual coin-slot meters. So golf commentators like Richard Boxall and Rob Lee, who were accustomed to Sky's no-expense-spared hospitality, were having to post pound coins into their meters so they could have the lights on at night.

The financial clampdown was also felt at the Belfry in 2002 where coverage of the eagerly anticipated Ryder Cup, postponed from the previous year because of the 9/11 terrorist attacks, came from an even smaller than usual caravan. This vehicle had so little space that there was barely room in it for Brazil, Parry, producer Jim Brown plus all the equipment that was required to go live from the Midlands. There was so little space that Porky was forced to broadcast the breakfast show while sitting on a ledge with his portly behind sticking out of the window.

Back at Sandwich a year later, once they had managed to accumulate as many pound coins as possible, the talkSPORT crew were up and running, with Brazil and Parry once again presenting the station's flagship show from the course every morning. This time, the station had sourced a far more glamorous location for their broadcasts: a tower overlooking the 18th green – in the right direction.

Immediately after their show on the first morning, the breakfast boys hit the Guinness tent – already aided and abetted by a few cheeky glasses of champagne they had managed to down during the final hour of the programme. That was the last anybody saw of them until the following morning's show, when Porky was up bright and early as usual, preparing for the broadcast alongside Jim'll Fix It. It was the responsibility of sports newsreader and reporter Mike Bovill to make sure that Brazil was brought to the studio on time – Clarke's buggy nightmares of previous years continued to haunt him.

Bovill, a bright, enthusiastic member of the talkSPORT team, had joined the station close to its inception in circumstances that were typical of the nature of the talkSPORT launch. He was still doing a journalism course at college when he wrote to talkSPORT in search of a two-week work experience placement. It was very much a case of amazing timing for Bovill, as his CV landed on Parry's desk the same day that someone else at talkSPORT had been given their marching orders – though that would have been the case on most days in the station's early stages. One Friday morning, Bovill was called in for an interview with Parry, who took him into a small room that was full of boxes and said: 'Sorry son, you can't sit down. We haven't got any chairs. Now, have you ever read a news bulletin before?'

Bovill, who had experience of one shift at Slough local radio station Star FM, replied: 'Yeah, I worked for Star FM.'

'Do you live locally?'

'Yeah, just the other side of the river – a twenty-minute walk from here.'

'So you wouldn't have to get cabs in or anything?'

'No.'

'Right, can you start on Monday?'

'Start what on Monday, Mike?'

'Sports newsreader on the breakfast show.'

And, just like that, Bovill had a job at a national radio station while still at college. But he had to survive a baptism of fire in his first few days. His first broadcasting experience at talkSPORT was to read the sports headlines alongside Alan Brazil, who was joined by special guest Kevin Keegan. The England manager was there as part of the five-show deal before it turned sour. If Bovill hadn't been nervous enough at making his national radio debut just days after applying to the station for work experience, reading the sports news in front of Keegan sent him over the edge.

He lasted just two days on breakfast before producer Furlong had him transferred to afternoons, as she was far from impressed with his nervous and hesitant style. In his defence, the first three months of his talkSPORT career were combined with completing his college broadcast journalism course, which was hardly an ideal start.

That meant the legend of one shift at Slough's Star FM was now working on *The Two Macs* instead. The old football dressing-room mentality kicked in straight away, as McInally pounced on Bovill for being the new boy, ribbing him whenever he could.

One afternoon, Bovill was reading the sports news when he looked up to see the whole production team in the gallery laughing hysterically. He couldn't really understand why – he hadn't made any more mistakes than usual and nobody had messed around with the audio he was using in his bulletin, a regular occurrence at the time. He pressed on with his headlines until he had finished, whereupon he removed his headphones and turned around to see McInally standing behind him. The former footballer was not wearing a stitch of clothing and was waving his 'old fella' in the direction of Bovill's ear. That had been going on throughout the bulletin, much to everyone's amusement and Bovill's utter horror.

The sports reporter recalled: 'I was so new and so young, I found it very difficult to see the funny side. Luckily everyone else did; they found the funny side for me. That was my introduction to working live.'

Young Bovill was also caught on the hop when he was filling in as a producer for Tom Watt, one Saturday lunchtime back in 2001. The 'God Line' – a studio number to which only MacKenzie had access – rang in the control room just ten minutes into the show, which filled Bovill with panic before he had even answered it. He knew that meant not only was the boss calling in, but he was clearly unhappy about something. Bovill answered and MacKenzie's opening gambit was: 'Why the fucking hell has Tom not mentioned the massive fucking traffic jam on the M25?'

'We didn't know there was a traffic jam on the M25,' replied Bovill.

This provoked his boss to scream: 'I am stuck in a fucking

traffic jam on the fucking M25 and I want to hear about it on my fucking radio station!'

With that, MacKenzie slammed the phone down.

Now, with three years of experience at the station, it was 5.30am on a warm Friday morning at Sandwich when Bovill approached Brazil's door and tentatively knocked to wake him up for the breakfast show. He was met by silence. The young reporter knocked again with the same response and, finally, started hammering on the door until he heard a loud groan from inside the room. Jim'll Fix It had given Bovill strict instructions not to allow Brazil to drive – he was to drive the Scot to the 18th to do the show.

The door opened and Bovill was forced to take a step back. The sight of Brazil wearing nothing but a pair of bright green briefs was an image that has been burned on his retina ever since – most probably alongside Tony Greig's underpants in his Hobart hotel room. Calmly, Brazil told him he needed another ten minutes in bed and that he would make his own way to the 18th to do the show. Bovill immediately informed Jim'll Fix It of the situation, who told him to leave Brazil to his own devices.

Back in the studio, it was approaching 6am and Parry seemed to have resigned himself to starting the show without Brazil. Suddenly, there was a commotion down below as the screeching of brakes was followed by angry voices. Parry, Bovill and Jim'll Fix It looked down to see Brazil's BMW come to a halt at the back of the 18th green in a spot that would have been a wonderful vantage point to watch the day's final hole action, but probably wasn't overly suitable as a parking space.

Brazil emerged from the car and started to climb the steps up to the studio as several security guards and stewards gave chase on foot, yelling at him not to leave his car there. With the car park a few miles away, Brazil had simply decided to drive directly to the studio, ignoring road blocks and driving straight on to the course, causing fury among the officials. Undeterred, he made it to air on time and began the show as if it was just another morning – which to him it was.

Bovill was utterly astounded by Brazil's antics: 'Even for him it was something special and it was the first time I had seen it at close hand. I had heard all the stories, but it was the first time I had really witnessed it.'

Unfortunately, the security guards were persistent types, insisting that Brazil move his car off the back of the 18th and they probably had a point. Amazingly, 20 minutes into the show, Brazil relented. He took off his headphones, climbed down the stairs and drove off in search of the car park, leaving Parry on his own for the next hour.

Parry held the fort admirably and, once Brazil had returned, it was business as usual for the rest of the day – and that meant long stints in the Guinness and Bollinger tents, where Porky would no doubt have been accosted by Adrian, the Hare Krishna Scottish monk. Adrian used to visit the Open every year to raise funds for his monastery by targeting wealthy punters in the champagne tents. And every year without fail, he would find Parry waiting for him – or was it the other way around? He would engage Parry in deep conversation about spiritualism and the after-life while the breakfast show host knocked back the champagne. At the end of every discussion, Porky would hand Adrian £50 for his cause. And this would happen every day of every tournament. Occasionally, after one or two glasses too many, Parry would tell Brazil he was seriously considering becoming a monk. The Scot reckoned his friend must have handed the monk more than £1,000 over the years, although that was typical of Parry's warm-hearted generosity.

Porky was not so generous towards Bovill on another morning at Sandwich, although this was purely accidental. Golf equipment manufacturers Callaway had organised a promotional 'longest drive' competition between talkSPORT's breakfast presenters. Each presenter had to strike the golf ball into netting and then computerised equipment would measure how far they had driven it. Standing about ten feet away and at a safe 90 degree angle from each presenter was Bovill, who was providing commentary for the listeners.

Brazil stepped up to take his shot, thumped it firmly into the netting, then returned to the studio to continue broadcasting while Parry made his way outside to take his turn. A crowd had gathered and Bovill was doing his best to ramp up the drama by whispering about how the tension was building. The pressure no doubt affected Parry, who swung and missed twice, leading to gasps – not to mention a few laughs – from the spectators. With the spotlight firmly on him and the pressure at boiling point, Porky swung his club for a third time and managed to make contact. Unfortunately, he only caught the ball with the toe end of his club, walloping it straight into Bovill's shin, despite the reporter standing at right angles to the presenter. Bovill was laid out on the ground, enjoying some banter with Porky and the crowd, before clambering back to his feet to describe Parry finally making good contact with the ball. Bruised, but not necessarily battered, Bovill returned to reporting on the Open.

Two days later, the reporter received a phone call from his mother demanding to know why he hadn't told her he was in hospital. Somewhat puzzled, Bovill explained the reason he hadn't told her was because he wasn't actually in hospital. His mother told him she had read in the *Daily Mail* that he was in hospital with a broken leg, much to the reporter's befuddlement. It turned out that Porky had told the paper's sports diarist Charles Sale that he had whacked Bovill so hard with the golf ball that he had ended up in A&E with a suspected broken leg – and Parry's version of events had made it into print, much to the reporter's amusement.

Another talkSPORT golfing regular was larger-than-life American Bob Bubka, a respected golf writer and broadcaster with more than two decades' experience of covering the PGA Tour. He had started out covering football and basketball, but switched his attention to golf from 1981. His distinctive and smooth voice was part of the reporting team from the outset of talkSPORT's coverage when the PGA Tour received a request from the station for a US-based correspondent. And he quickly became a cult figure with listeners and fellow broadcasters. Bubka always told it like it was on air and he was no different when the microphone was switched off.

Accompanied everywhere by his loyal PA and editor Janis Self, another bubbly character, Bubka was always great company on nights out, with a penchant for pints of beer and vodka chasers. On one evening out in Liverpool, Bubka was asked to quieten down by a diner on a nearby table, as he had been making so much noise. His retort to the startled woman was: 'I'll turn my microphone off when you take your top off!'

In the early stages of talkSPORT's golf coverage, Bubka was sent out to Germany to report on a tournament in which Tiger Woods was making a rare appearance in a European event. When he arrived, he was told that he would be joined for the broadcast by none other than 'the great Geoffrey Boycott', although, being an American, Bubka had absolutely no idea who this great man was. He was briefed to expect an English cricketing legend with a bit of an ego, which Bubka totally understood knowing that many of the world's great sportsmen needed large reserves of self-belief to give them that extra edge.

Boycott arrived in Germany and the pair chatted for a while before the ex-cricketer enquired if there was any chance that he might be able to see Woods in action. So Bubka led him down to the driving range where the young American was in full flow, effortlessly driving balls almost 300 yards.

Boycott and Bubka had been at the driving range for all of a minute, in which time Woods had taken no more than three swings, when the former cricketer announced: 'That's enough, let's go!' Amazed, Bubka led Boycott away but had to ask his colleague what he had thought of the world's greatest golfer.

'Absolutely incredible,' enthused Boycott. 'Unbelievable. What an amazing athlete that guy is, reminds me so much of myself!'

It wasn't often that Bubka was rendered speechless, but Boycott was after all a special talent. The American broadcaster remembered: 'I said to him "Well Geoffrey, they told me you had a little bit of an ego, I didn't think it was that big!" But we got along pretty well. He worked with us covering some golf and I enjoyed his company.'

Bubka's highly individual and natural broadcasting voice was working wonders for talkSPORT across the UK. Once, the American was on his way to cover a tournament in Scotland when he decided to stop in Aberdeen to buy some batteries for his radio. He found an electronics shop in the city centre, approached the clerk and asked for some DD batteries. On hearing his voice, the shop assistant took a step back, pointed at him and said: 'You're Bob Bubka! You're on talkSPORT!'

Bubka was astonished: 'It totally flabbergasted me and just

about anywhere I go over here people associate me with talkSPORT. It is just amazing the amount of penetration talkSPORT has developed and they have the most loyal listeners in the world.'

The golf worked well for talkSPORT, bringing in good numbers thanks to the talented team working on all the Opens that the station covered. But, breakfast show aside, talkSPORT was still struggling to come up with a winning formula for other programmes and staff were still being hired and fired with alarming regularity.

The 1-4pm show, *The Two Macs*, presented by McCaffrey and McInally, was one of the more high-profile shows, as listeners knew the pair from their Sky Sports commitments. But MacKenzie wasn't a fan – and that was the end of *The Two Macs*.

Then Tom Watt was sacked from his drivetime show soon after. The former *EastEnders* star was an Arsenal fan who was extremely knowledgeable about football, but management wanted a change, and that led to the first talkSPORT afternoon appearance of Paul Hawksbee and Andy Jacobs. Ironically, Jacobs was good friends with Watt, yet he was now replacing him on drive.

'It was extremely awkward,' said Jacobs. 'Two days before Christmas, at five past four, I get a phone call from Tom saying "Do you know anything about this?" Ten minutes after that I got a phone call from Kelvin saying "We want you to do four to seven every day." It was embarrassing.'

Throughout its first year, the Hawksbee & Jacobs show regularly received emails asking 'Where's Tom?' Watt had moved to present a Saturday football preview show while H&J, as they quickly became known, stayed on drive for 18 months before it was decided that the timeslot needed to have a more sports news-based agenda. They were moved to the early afternoon shift where they have stayed ever since.

One of their many regular items that has gained iconic status among both talkSPORT staff and listeners is their 'Clips of the Week' round-up, which features audio of the best on-air cock-ups on the station from the past seven days. It all started when Jacobs would hear the odd funny moment on the airwaves and then play it on the show to everybody's great amusement. Usually, Brazil would be a target, with some of his slightly wilder moments being captured. That led to a phone call from Parry, in his programme director guise, saying: 'Boys, I must ask you to refrain from taking the piss out of Mr Alan Brazil, a former Scotland international and a renowned football star. I think some of the banter is going a bit too far.'

No sooner had that reprimand been taken on board than MacKenzie was on the phone to H&J, enthusing about how much he loved the Brazil clips and how they should continue with them because they were great. With that change of mood, the 'Clips of the Week' feature was born. Some of the presenters who were featured were not overly keen at first, but they soon realised that this wasn't malicious. If anything, that segment of the show opened up the station's other programming to listeners, so it may well have been doing a favour to anybody that was featured. At least, that's how Hawksbee and Jacobs justified it. Occasionally, certain clips reduced H&J to giggling schoolkids, particularly when Brazil was commentating on golf and mentioned the fact that it was 9.32am at least five times in the space of 30 seconds.

Now and again, H&J could almost have ended up in the clips package themselves, although they would usually make instant light of their mistakes to avoid the ignominy of starring in their own feature. Once, during a commercial break, Jacobs was watching his beloved Chelsea on their way out of the UEFA Cup at the hands of minnows St Gallen when Jimmy Floyd Hasselbaink fluffed a golden opportunity to score. With the break about to end and the studio on the verge of going live, the presenter screamed out his frustration by yelling: 'Oh Hasselbaink, you absolute ****!' Just at that moment, the studio's red light lit up and listeners were welcomed back from the ad break to hear the last consonant emerge from Jacobs' mouth as he held his head in his hands, realising his faux-pas.

That sort of language would frequently emerge from MacKenzie's mouth but he also had a different side which not many people knew about. One Friday afternoon, he ventured down to the talkSPORT Towers basement, where the engineering department was located. He was horrified to see the entire floor in complete disarray – there was mess and clutter everywhere. He gathered all the engineers together and warned them in no uncertain terms: 'You've got a week to sort this out and if I can't eat my fucking dinner off the fucking floor, you'll all be fucking sacked!'

A monumental tidy-up operation began and new shelves were quickly assembled and erected. By the following Friday evening, the basement looked far more respectable and the engineers were speculating whether MacKenzie would even bother to check if they had taken his threat seriously. Suddenly, the door opened and the boss's personal assistant walked in carrying a crate of beer, which she placed on the floor. She was followed by MacKenzie who was carrying several large boxes of pizza. He sat down on the floor surrounded by beer and pizza, told everyone what a 'fucking good job' they had done, then invited all the engineers to join him for dinner. For the next 45 minutes, MacKenzie and the talkSPORT engineers sat on the basement floor happily eating and drinking together. It was one of the more surreal moments at talkSPORT Towers, even by the station's bizarre standards.

6

Off the Wall and
On Another Planet

The belly dancing music – where did you get it? It's very, very good!

ABU HAMZA

Some of modern media's greatest creations have been born in the pub. From the booze-fuelled ideas meetings held by tabloid newspapers around Fleet Street to the lads' mag generation originated by *Loaded*, there have been plenty of gems discovered at the bottom of many pint glasses. Unfortunately, there have also been some absolute stinkers.

Despite its obvious macho branding, talkSPORT wasn't just about sport. With a strong current affairs line-up in the mid-morning and late-night slots, MacKenzie was in touch with the sports fans' extra-curricular needs. However, in its early years the station also experimented with other programming that ticked neither the sport nor 'general chat that may interest the listener' boxes. One such show was *Champagne and Roses*, presented by actor Gerald Harper and dreamed up in the boozer one night.

The programme was a surprising departure for the speech radio station, mainly because it was a music show. And not just any music – this was a show dedicated to the genres of lounge or swing. Actor-turned-broadcaster Harper had previously presented the show on Capital Radio and then BBC Radio 2 decades earlier, always beginning with the immortal line: 'Hello, I'm Gerald Harper. Welcome to my Saturday selection.' The title came from Harper's tradition of sending champagne and flowers to every listener who wrote in with requests that he played – and he fully intended on doing the same at talkSPORT.

The speech station had to apply for a change of licence so talkSPORT could also feature a music programme in its line-up on Saturday nights. From December 2002, Harper took to the sporting airwaves. It wasn't just the fact that listeners may not have been overly fond of Peggy Lee, Bing Crosby or Ella Fitzgerald, but it was more the juxtapositioning of the show straight off the back of the Saturday evening football phone-in that made it stick out like a sore thumb. It was one of the most surreal gear changes in British radio history, as talkSPORT went from Dave on Merseyside ranting about the incompetent referee who had cost his side three points to Ella Fitzgerald singing 'When My Sugar Walks Down The Street' in the blink of an eye.

The full *Champagne and Roses* playlist from his first show illustrates the point perfectly:

'Chicago'	Tony Bennett
'Nancy (With The Laughing Face)'	Frank Sinatra
'Fever'	Peggy Lee
'Moonlight Becomes You'	Bing Crosby
'Is You Is Or Is You Ain't My Baby'	Louis Jordan

'T'ain't What You Do, It's The Way You Do It'	Ella Fitzgerald
'Back Bay Shuffle'	Artie Shaw
'Walkin' My Baby Back Home'	Dean Martin
'Georgia On My Mind'	Billie Holiday
'Jumpin' Jive'	Cab Calloway
'Moon River'	Judy Garland
'Unforgettable'	Nat 'King' Cole
'One O'Clock Jump'	Count Basie
'Beyond The Blue Horizon'	Jeanette Macdonald
'Whispering Grass'	The Ink Spots
'I Wanna Be Loved By You'	Marilyn Monroe
'Come Fly With Me'	Frank Sinatra
'Wise Woman Blues'	Dinah Washington
'Mack The Knife'	Bobby Darin
'Let There Be Love'	Peggy Lee
'What Kind Of Fool'	Sammy Davis Jr
'Don't Fence Me In'	Bing Crosby & The Andrews Sisters
'This May Be The Night'	Tony Martin
'What A Night, What A Moon, What A Girl'	Billie Holiday
'Jeepers Creepers'	Louis Armstrong
'I'm In The Mood For Love'	Doris Day
'All Of Me'	Dean Martin
'When My Sugar Walks Down The Street'	Ella Fitzgerald
'I'll Be Seeing You'	Bing Crosby
'Get Your Kicks On Route 66'	Nat 'King' Cole
'On A Slow Boat To China'	Dean Martin
'Careless'	Dinah Shore

'Love Letters'	Perry Como
'I'm Just Wild About Harry'	Alice Faye and Louis Prima
'I've Got You Under My Skin'	Frank Sinatra
'September In The Rain'	Peggy Lee
'Boogie Woogie'	Tommy Dorsey
'Darktown Strutters Ball'	Ella Fitzgerald
'It's Only A Paper Moon'	Nat 'King' Cole
'Singing On A Star'	Bing Crosby
'Misty'	Sarah Vaughan
'Blue Skies'	Dick Haymes
'Take The A Train'	Duke Ellington
'In The Mood'	Glenn Miller

Unsurprisingly, it quickly became apparent that the show wasn't working as well as hoped. In early 2003, with the war in Iraq looming, it was decided to focus on the potentially world-changing conflict in the Middle East rather than Harper's easy listening classics, and he was on his way. Shortly after the out-break of war, a music request show was launched for listeners whose loved ones were involved in the conflict. *Touching Base* was presented by Mike Dickin for an hour during his mid-morning show and many song requests were received from wives and girlfriends who were missing their other halves.

However, Dickin rarely managed to play more than the intro of any song before he moved on to the next request. He would read out the message from a soldier's wife in a very sympathetic, dramatic and heartfelt manner and then announce their chosen song, before interrupting it less than a minute in. The reason for this was due to talkSPORT being allowed to play only a limited amount of music per week, according to its broadcasting licence.

But that didn't stop Dickin from gallantly ploughing on and trying to do justice to all the requests he received – without really playing any of them. In the end, the show – which producers had nicknamed Touching Cloth – was canned for what can only be described as logistical reasons.

Another show that attempted – and made a far better fist – of filling the troublesome Saturday night slot was *The Unexplained* with Howard Hughes, a programme very much in *The X Files* genre, with plenty of discussion about UFOs, aliens, conspiracy theories and the mysteries of the universe. Hughes had been a popular newsreader on Capital Radio, a stalwart of Chris Tarrant's breakfast show, who had a fascination with the whole 'There's Something Out There' movement.

Once again, making the jump from irate football fans debating the intricacies of the offside rule to alleged spaceship sightings was another big leap for listeners to make. However, Hughes managed to keep that slot for more than a year before it was consigned to the great radio scrapheap in the sky.

The wrestling boom among younger sports fans did not go ignored by talkSPORT as *Talk Wrestling* was another show that aired for several months on Saturday nights in the station's early years. Presented by Tommy Boyd, a legend from the station's Talk Radio days who still presented his regular talk shows on the station, and British wrestler Alex Shane, the programme discussed all things grappling and may have sparked a mini revival for the ailing sport in the UK.

With the World Wrestling Federation giving birth to global superstars such as The Rock and The Undertaker in the USA, Britain was lagging far behind but, using the buzz created by his show, Boyd promoted the SWAT (Syndicate Wrestling And Tradition) Revival event at Crystal Palace, which earned rave reviews. The one-off wrestling night was also broadcast live on talkSPORT – a radio first in the UK, as live wrestling had never been heard before in the country.

However, two main problems led to the demise of Talk Wrestling. The sport itself was extremely visual – it was all about large men in colourful outfits throwing each other around a ring, and it didn't necessarily provoke the endless stream of talking points that football did, which would then lead to hours of phone-ins. The other problem was Boyd's speedy exit from talkSPORT Towers. He was dismissed after a caller to his regular talk show threatened to kill members of the Royal Family, just hours after the death of the Queen Mother. Despite this, the wrestling show continued with Shane, but Boyd's enthusiasm and presenting skills were missed and the programme was eventually shelved.

Boyd had also presided over another show called *The Human Zoo*. The idea behind the programme was to field unscreened calls on any subject matter for two hours. It was a broadcasting free-for-all, with talkSPORT turning into some kind of public access radio channel for its duration. Of course, with no operator vetting who was on the phone before putting the listeners on air, chaos reigned, with callers who swore having to be immediately cut off. But, by and large, most contributors wanted a chance to shine. Some read their own poetry or occasionally even sang to showcase their gifts. It was *Britain's Got Talent* but way ahead of its time.

Occasionally, it seemed programmes would be given the green light purely on the basis of their title. *The Final Furlong* was presented by Claire Furlong and Rupert Bell every Friday afternoon. Programme director Parry liked Furlong's feisty nature off-air and thought she would replicate that on-air, giving

Bell both barrels and provoking callers to ring in. The problem was that producer Furlong had no interest in presenting and told Parry she didn't want to do the show. She enjoyed doing a spot of reporting, but that was as far as it went. Parry had other ideas, however, and wore away at her until she finally gave in.

The programme's introduction was pre-recorded over music and Parry oversaw it. Each time Furlong would recite her opening lines, Porky would implore her to be more aggressive and punchier, and on each occasion Furlong would tell him she couldn't do it. After four Fridays, Furlong insisted to Parry that presenting wasn't for her and he finally relented. Despite being set for a six-week run, the show was pulled although, as could sometimes happen at talkSPORT, Bell was never officially told of the decision. Eventually, he started to make other plans on Friday afternoons.

Not all shows that fell by the wayside were that bad, however, and one example was *Football First in Europe*, a weekly evening programme anchored by Adrian Durham, with valuable contributions provided by continental experts Guillem Balague and Gabriele Marcotti. The Spaniard and the Italian quickly became respected football pundits with a growing profile in the UK.

The show focused on the increasingly popular major European leagues, such as La Liga and Serie A, picking out the rising stars of the continental game, many of whom would sooner or later appear in the Premier League. Most notably, the programme enjoyed an excellent relationship with the up and coming Porto manager Jose Mourinho. Recognising the media gifts possessed by the man soon to be known as the 'Special One', Mourinho was asked to make several appearances on the show and always obliged. It's unknown whether Chelsea owner Roman Abramovich was a talkSPORT listener, but the exposure

Mourinho received on the channel could not have harmed his chances of landing the Stamford Bridge job. That, and the little matter of a UEFA Cup and Champions League trophy in consecutive seasons.

Balague also had excellent contacts in Spain, where he was close to a rising managerial star by the name of Rafa Benitez. But management felt that Balague's strong Spanish accent was hard to understand and he was replaced. It was a case of bad timing, because that summer of 2003 David Beckham moved to Real Madrid and Balague's links at the Bernabeu may well have been able to secure regular airtime with the England captain. The show was never the same without the Spanish expert and was eventually pulled from the schedules, although Durham confessed he still missed it: 'Without any doubt, if you talk to people who have been at the station a long time, they will tell you that that was the most substantial show. It was a proper good listen, a proper radio show, a mix between a documentary-style show and talkSPORT. It must be five or six years since it went and people still ask me about it.'

Another talkSPORT show with a tremendous cult following was Keith Arthur's *Fisherman's Blues*, which still runs on early weekend mornings. The angling phone-in hosted by the experienced fisherman always attracted a large audience for that time of the day and regularly featured people who were out on riverbanks trying to catch fish themselves. Occasionally, callers would interrupt whatever fishy subject matter was being discussed to blurt out: 'I've got a bite! I've got a bite!'

Back in the station's very early days, during a time when it was trying to catch as many listeners as possible, talkSPORT used to experiment by splitting frequency transmitters so it could broadcast programming that related to a particular region.

And lo and behold, *The Scottish Football Phone-in* was born, presented by former Manchester United defender Arthur Albiston.

One week, Albiston fielded a call from an irate Hearts fan who was dismayed that his team's goalkeeper Antti Niemi kept missing out on Craig Brown's Scotland squad. The caller was completely oblivious to the fact that Niemi was in fact Finnish and therefore ineligible to play for Scotland:

Caller: For three seasons, Craig Brown's been ignoring Antti Niemi.
Albiston: Antti Niemi?
Caller: Aye, I don't know why he doesn't get a game.
Albiston: For Scotland?
Caller: Aye.
Albiston: He's from Finland.
Caller: He's what?
Albiston: He's Finnish, isn't he?
Caller: He's not finished; he's only 28!
Albiston: Not finished – he's from Finland!
Caller: What do you mean?
Albiston: His nationality is Finnish – he's from Finland.
Caller: Oh, I thought he was Scottish!

The Scottish Football Phone-in did not last long.

Regardless of these hit-and-mostly-miss shows, the ongoing appeal of the station was that you never quite knew what to expect when tuning in. The wild and wacky nature of the broadcaster was starting to resemble something like the translation of a tabloid newspaper into a radio station. talkSPORT also kept its listeners on their toes with its steady diet of addictive phone-in shows fronted by talented and engaging presenters. But sometimes the hosts would be as surprised as the listeners at some of the station's content.

During a brief stint as programme director before Parry took on the job, Paul Chantler was at the helm. He was one of such a large number of programme content supremos that MacKenzie stopped calling them by their names and just began to give them numbers instead for simplicity. Parry had so many different stints in control that he was numbers three, five and seven. Chantler – or number six – brought in a newsreader by the name of Peter Stewart and hailed the appointment, claiming Stewart would revolutionise the newsroom and he wasn't wrong about that.

Stewart was trained to make reading the news sound as engaging and dramatic as possible. He was vastly experienced, having written several published books on the art of broadcasting news and he also penned a regular column in *Radio* magazine.

His voice exhibited all the range of emotions news stories can bring, leaving the listeners in no doubt as to how he felt about them. But his colloquial, chatty and all-round entertaining style did not sit well with Parry. Stewart's most unforgettable moment came on the morning after 9/11 when he opened his first news broadcast with the following introduction: 'Oh my God! That wasn't a dream. It was a nightmare! It wasn't a movie. That was reality. Fifty-eight minutes that shook the world. It means thousands of lives will never be the same again.'

Eventually, when Parry had returned as programme director number seven, he'd had enough of Stewart's idiosyncrasies and brought him to task. Stewart protested that Parry didn't understand where he was coming from, but Porky knew exactly where his colleague was going and that was straight out of talkSPORT Towers. As Stewart himself would have said: 'Oh my God! That wasn't a dream. It was a nightmare.'

The station always attracted top guests from the world of sport and was also starting to attract political heavyweights as well. But whereas listeners tuning in may occasionally have expected to hear the voices of William Hague or Gordon Brown on talkSPORT, few could have imagined they would hear radical Muslim cleric Abu Hamza on their favourite channel. It was James Whale who decided to start giving Hamza a platform on his late-night show by having him on as a guest to contribute to various debates about Islam, a subject that had become far more topical following the 9/11 terror attacks.

Despite Whale going on record as disagreeing with everything Hamza stood for, the cleric first appeared on his show in early February 2003 on the phone and was invited back later that month as a studio guest for a debate alongside religious figures from the Muslim, Christian and Jewish faiths. The publicity surrounding Hamza's appearance on talkSPORT provoked a wave of anger and protests from people enraged that the radical was being allowed to broadcast his hate messages on national radio. The most vociferous opponents of Hamza were mainstream Muslims, who argued he was giving all British Muslims a bad name with his abhorrent views.

When Hamza arrived at the studios, he was met by angry protestors, but the show went ahead nonetheless, with Whale defiantly claiming: 'My programme doesn't shy away from the controversial issues. In fact, if Osama Bin Laden called me tomorrow, I'd ask him what time he could come on.'

In the build-up to Hamza's appearance on the programme, the cleric had asked to hear an advert for the show so he could make sure he wasn't being stitched up by Whale.

The trails at the station were all dreamed up by talkSPORT's crack creative team, led by Peter Gee, and it was his job to play

Hamza the promotional audio package he had created for Whale's show. To tease this particular debate, Gee decided to go down the route of playing Turkish casbah music as a backing track for the voiceover that hailed Hamza as 'the most dangerous man in Britain today'. Hamza phoned in to the Creative department and Gee played him the trailer for the show. Completely unfazed by being described as a danger to society, Hamza merely enquired: 'The belly dancing music – where did you get it? It's very, very good!' Sadly for Hamza, Gee had used production library music and he couldn't recommend a CD for 'the most dangerous man in Britain' to go out and purchase.

In the event, the belly-dancing fan said little on the show. He arrived at talkSPORT Towers flanked by an entourage of around ten men, ranging in age from 80 down to about 15. Most of them hung around outside the studio but, while on air, Hamza was accompanied by two of his colleagues who invariably spoke for him while he nodded in agreement. Despite the controversy, the ploy of having Hamza in the studio gave the station tremendous profile and that was the plan for another venture – talkSPORT TV.

The channel, which was designed to increase brand awareness by having an identity on the Sky platform, was launched in 2004. It featured live pictures of the studio during the drive show. The studio was fitted with two remote cameras filming the hosts talking to the nation in front of a makeshift set. However, all the radio sponsorship deals had to be edited out of the telly broadcasts for regulatory reasons. Often the audio would be silenced when presenters were speaking to their favourite bookmakers who sponsored the radio show. Similarly, when the radio station went to commercial breaks, the TV channel screened a girl reading out listeners' emails or texts from a small stock room in the bowels of talkSPORT Towers.

It may not have been riveting telly, but then this *was* radio. talkSPORT TV will arguably best be remembered for almost knocking out Jason Cundy live on air. During one afternoon show that was being presented by Cundy and Patrick Kinghorn, 'the King' moved his seat to deposit a print-out of an email into a rubbish bin and, in the process, managed to dislodge a huge pillar from the set, which collapsed on top of a rather surprised Cundy, mid-broadcast. Kinghorn immediately started talking to the nation to give his dazed and confused colleague time to wonder what on earth had happened. Anybody listening would never have known, but it made a fabulous spectacle for the viewers watching via Sky.

Cundy actually believed Kinghorn had hit him: 'I thought Pat had gone round the back of me and clonked me. My mouth was just open for seconds, thinking "What the fuck has just happened to me?" You know, you are live on radio and you don't expect something to come clattering round your ears, but fortunately I wasn't hurt. It had knocked my headphones off and I had long hair at the time. It looked like my wig had fallen off as well!' Unfortunately, the satellite channel failed to build a large enough TV audience and the plug was pulled shortly after UTV bought talkSPORT in 2005.

Alongside some of the more unconventional programming and ideas in its first few years, talkSPORT also snapped up the radio broadcasting rights to several other unlikely sports. No station had ever covered live darts before, but that didn't stop talkSPORT stepping up to the oche and going over to Ireland to broadcast the World Grand Prix from Rosslare in County Wexford. Until that point, the Irish seaside resort had been famous only for hosting the filming of the beach scenes in Steven Spielberg's Second World War epic *Saving Private Ryan* –

but talkSPORT was doing its best to put Rosslare back on the map.

Durham was the lucky man who arrived in the sleepy town late one night to find a couple having sex on a car bonnet in the car park of the hotel that was hosting the tournament. With that image imprinted on his brain, he returned the following day and, together with his producer Andrew Hughes, was shown into a small, disused kitchen full of mop buckets from where the broadcasts would be aired.

Instead of sampling the raucous atmosphere of the hall, where thousands of fans were roaring on the darts players, talkSPORT were stuck in a small, dank room with leaking pipes and dripping taps for sound effects. And that room became even smaller when Durham was joined by 'Big' Cliff Lazarenko, a 6ft 5in, 20-stone giant of a darts player, and legendary TV commentator Sid Waddell, who managed to bring the colour and drama of the occasion to life for the listeners.

Sadly, that was the only time live darts was featured, although another pub sport to receive the talkSPORT treatment was pool – the line was drawn at dominoes – as the station covered the Mosconi Cup in its early days. With precious little other live sport available to bid for, talkSPORT cleared the airwaves for eight consecutive hours of international pool. The event, a Ryder Cup-style competition between the best European and American players, was held at Bethnal Green's York Hall, a venue more commonly associated with boxing. Fight fans were not to be disappointed as a scrap broke out among spectators, just three rows behind talkSPORT's arena commentary position. It was another first for the station, as no other media outlet had ever been able to broadcast live pool crowd trouble. The commentary team also unwittingly played a part in the action on the table as their raised voices put players off their shots on more than one occasion and they were asked to tone it down.

Behind the scenes at talkSPORT Towers, staff morale had improved considerably since the dark days after the launch when production teams feared for their jobs on an almost daily basis. The pressures of working in a live environment meant staff still let their hair down and drank as much as they would have done at any time, but it also meant that they were more relaxed in the office when they weren't necessarily in the middle of producing a show. One talkSPORT worker who could definitely afford to relax was Paul Anderson, a freelance radio technician who scooped a multi-million-pound national lottery win.

Incredibly, he decided to continue working for the station, which led to many wind-ups and jokes at his expense. Hawksbee and Jacobs were highly amused by the situation and discussed it at length on their show. Whenever Anderson came into the studio to fix some equipment, they would lampoon him for messing around with a microphone when he had just won a fortune. Rumour had it that Anderson would enjoy extraordinary lunch breaks, on one occasion purchasing a new Mercedes before returning to work.

Other wind-ups were common in the office, but if anybody was going to be the butt of the joke, it was Bovill. One regular source of amusement was to make sure someone was hidden in the studio shortly before Bovill was due to read his extended sports news bulletin, which normally ran to 15 minutes. Usually, it would be Dominic 'Our Man in Japan' McGuinness who would hide under the studio desk and when Bovill began his broadcast, the reporter would seemingly appear from nowhere and shock the sports newsreader by pulling a face. This would normally mean Bovill would go quiet for a second or two during his bulletin before composing himself and starting again.

Another favourite among the office clowns was to move Bovill's chair away just after he had started one of his lengthier bulletins. This meant he would be forced to stand for the full 15 minutes and would usually lead to him chasing the protagonist around the office straight after.

Four years in, and MacKenzie's courageous rebranding and relaunching of Talk Radio into talkSPORT was starting to look remarkably like a stroke of genius. And, with a massive year ahead, including Euro 2004, where, unusually, the station had been allowed to purchase broadcast rights for the first time, things were looking up.

But this was talkSPORT and controversy was never far away. And this time, the station was about to face its biggest-ever crisis as Alan Brazil just couldn't resist the lure of the Cheltenham races . . .

7

You're Fired!

What you have got to remember is I am a bit strange. I don't go to
bed early. I do overindulge, I just love being social. I love going out
and talking to people, I love mixing with people. That's the way I am.

ALAN BRAZIL

For most people, practising what you preach would be considered sound advice. For Alan Brazil, who spent a great deal of
airtime discussing his escapades, it was dangerous.

With the breakfast show still leading from the front in terms
of its success and ratings, Brazil and Mike Parry continued to
live the lives they were forever discussing on air. Late nights and
early mornings were par for the course, although Porky was considerably better at rising in the small hours than his colleague.
As was his way, Brazil would always want to continue the party
slightly longer but, to his credit, he would always be standing at
the end of the night when others had fallen by the wayside.

Occasionally, this would lead to Brazil cutting it very fine –
or being late – for the show's 6am start. His producer, Seb Ewen,
would always know if there was a problem as he would ring
Brazil on his mobile phone before the show to give him an exact

rundown of what was planned for the morning's broadcast. If Brazil's phone went straight to answerphone, he knew the presenter was more than likely on his way in to the studio but in a tunnel where he couldn't receive the call. The problem was when the phone just rang out with no answer, but this rarely happened.

By and large, Brazil would make it in to the studio no matter where he had been the previous evening – even if he came straight in from his night out. In the event of a Brazil no-show, Parry would take over the reins on his own for that morning. If there was enough time, the call would go out to reporter Graham Beecroft at home on the Wirral. His long-suffering wife Marie would answer the call, with Beeky groaning in the background: 'Oh, for fuck's sake Seb!' With a broadcast-quality ISDN phone line in his home, he could team up with Parry at a moment's notice.

Often, Brazil might have needed a trip to the loo or a power nap just before the show started in order to recharge his batteries. Any time up to two minutes past six, which was when the news and sport headlines were completed, the Scot could occasionally be found fast asleep on the couch in the production control room.

The show's introduction music was recorded on a loop, so if necessary it could be played *ad infinitum* and, once the tune had started, Ewen's task was to drag, push or pull Brazil off the couch and in to the studio. The listeners would pick up on Brazil's various states almost instantly. If he was sounding hoarse or half-asleep, texts and emails would come flooding in asking if the presenter had been out partying again. More often than not, by staying tuned the listeners would find out exactly where he had been as, once he warmed up, he would discuss it on air with Porky.

Occasionally, Porky, who was still programme director, would become frustrated with Brazil's timekeeping: 'He might show up late or something, but he didn't do it deliberately. That was just Al's way of running his life. He didn't understand why people would get so upset if he turned up half an hour late.'

Using his charm and sense of humour, Brazil could always talk his way out of trouble anyway, often placating a producer who was giving him a hard time by putting a smile on their face and making them feel like they were part of his gang. The difficulty, of course, was when Brazil failed to show up for the programme altogether – and that's why Cheltenham 2004 provided one of the most controversial moments in talkSPORT's history.

One of the highlights of the talkSPORT calendar has always been the Cheltenham racing festival. Every year, without fail, the breakfast show team would relocate to Gloucestershire for a few days, broadcasting the programme from the course before spending the rest of the day taking in the sights, sounds and smells of one of England's premier race meetings.

Brazil and Porky had been Cheltenham regulars for a number of years before the explosive events that March. The pair would always arrive at the course in plenty of time, the night before the festival's first day. After soaking up the atmosphere, they would broadcast the following morning before going on to spend all day in various different hospitality tents. There they would receive many people's good wishes that would be offered to them, alongside pints of beer and glasses of wine.

The boisterous atmosphere in the Guinness tent meant it was like a second home for the brekkie boys during the festival, with Porky often harassing the Irish band to play songs that he knew so he could belt them out at the top of his voice. And all that would take place before lunchtime.

In the afternoons, Brazil would attempt to beat a path through the crowds to take in some racing from the comfort of a sponsor's box. As a keen gambler and horse racing fan, he usually backed several nags months before the festival and could well have landed a windfall if a couple of them came in. Even by his standards, Brazil would enjoy himself to the full at Cheltenham, and 2004's event was no different.

That year, before arriving at the festival, Brazil was already irked by talkSPORT's decision not to broadcast the breakfast show from the racecourse the day after the festival had ended. With Cheltenham beginning on a Tuesday, Brazil could not see the sense in rushing back to London after Thursday's action for one more show before the weekend. He would much rather have stayed for one more night and aired Friday's show from the course. Management saw things differently, however, as the financial burden of doing the show from Cheltenham had to be taken into consideration, and an extra day meant extra hotel rooms for the presenters and crew.

The plan was to arrive on the Monday evening and leave on Thursday afternoon to avoid traffic and make it back to London in good time for the following morning's show. As an added carrot, former Chelsea chairman Ken Bates was due in the studio on Friday morning for the last hour of the show, and the exchanges between him, Brazil and Parry were always entertaining. Brazil was certainly looking forward to that.

The first two days of the festival passed off the same as any other at the great racecourse, with both Porky and Brazil taking full advantage of everything Cheltenham had to offer. But by the end of Thursday morning's show, Parry was beginning to become anxious, as he wanted to return to the capital more or less immediately.

Brazil was having none of it, insisting they go to the Guinness tent for a drink as they normally would after the broadcast. By now, Porky had taken his breakfast show presenter's hat off and had firmly planted the programme director's mortar board on to his head. He was thinking ahead to the Bates interview the following morning and, knowing Brazil's reputation, was starting to worry. On top of that, he was supposed to be travelling back to London in his co-presenter's car.

The minute Brazil arrived in the Guinness tent, it was quite clear to Porky he would have to make his own way back to the capital. While Parry nursed his first pint of the black stuff, Brazil had nailed one, two and then three in next to no time, surrounded by many of his friends and racing associates. So when Porky remonstrated with him to leave, he refused, telling him that he would see him back in London the following morning. Aside from everything the Guinness tent had to offer, Brazil was determined to stay at Cheltenham for the highlight of the meeting, the Gold Cup, in which Best Mate was attempting to make history with a third straight win.

By that point, Parry had decided to return to London by train and he recalled lecturing Brazil before he left: 'I said to him "Al, I am going now, mate. It is entirely up to you how you get home but remember you have got to be there for six o'clock tomorrow morning. We have been sent down here on trust and we have got to get back and not let the listeners or the station down."'

Brazil had no intention of letting anyone down. He rapidly made arrangements to stay overnight in a nearby village hotel, with the aim of waking up at 3.30am and driving back to London. He stayed at Cheltenham to see Best Mate make history before arriving at his digs for the night.

Brazil began chatting to the proprietor and, in the process of
signing a few menus for him, the innkeeper mentioned that he
supposed the Scot would be popping up the road to see his old
friend Jim Steel. Although Steel and Brazil were from either side
of the great Glaswegian divide, they had both made it as professional footballers. Steel enjoyed a successful career at
Southampton, where he played alongside Brazil's racing buddy
Mick Channon. Through Brazil's other Saints mate Alan Ball,
and Channon, Brazil and Steel had become friendly and they
had played together at golf days around the country. Realising
that he had landed up in a hotel across the road from Steel's pub,
Brazil felt he had to pop in to say hello.

Given that it was also St Patrick's Day, the village pub was
busy and Brazil had the punters on their feet and singing before
he had finished his first glass. In what seemed like no time at all,
the clock had struck 10pm and the Scot finally called it a night,
heading back to his hotel.

To this day, Brazil still swears blind he went to sleep that
night having done everything he could to make sure he would
be up at 3am. He set the alarm on his brand new mobile phone
and, just in case, he also asked the proprietor of the hotel for a
wake-up call at the same time. Either way, at 4.30am Brazil
woke up with a start and instantly entered blind panic mode,
realising he had very little chance of making it back to the
London studios in time for the start of the show. He threw on
some clothes, but suddenly found himself locked in the hotel,
as the front door was firmly bolted and locked with nobody
around to let him out.

A bizarre series of events then followed which began with the
presenter having to scale an 8ft garden wall to leave the hotel.
He then commandeered a milk float that was blocking his car,

driving it down the street and smashing plenty of bottles in the process. By the time he reached the Oxford ring road, it was already 5.30am and he had no chance of making it to the studios by 7am, let alone an hour earlier for the start of the show. His new phone was dead so he was forced to use a pay phone to let his producer know he wasn't going to make it, although he was cut off before he could give a full explanation.

While Brazil was struggling with the phone box, a fuming Parry was back in the studio, preparing to go it alone on that day's breakfast show. Bates came in as planned and the interview went well for talkSPORT, as the former Chelsea chairman was his usual candid self and many of his quotes appeared in national newspapers the following day.

Brazil had already booked the week off after Cheltenham and decided to go skiing in Meribel with his family, although he suspected he hadn't heard the end of his non-appearance for Friday's show.

Naturally, MacKenzie was far from impressed with Brazil's antics. Until that point, he and Parry had concluded that the presenter was unique in that you either accepted the way he operated or you got rid of him – and, given that he was the station's star man, the latter option had never been seriously considered.

All seemed to be going well for Brazil when MacKenzie spoke to Parry after his Friday breakfast show. He berated his programme director for flying solo and refused to listen to Parry when he attempted to interject that he had no choice. Parry couldn't win, but that was the end of the matter. Or so Parry thought until he received a call from MacKenzie the following evening:

'Mike, I haven't heard a fucking word from Brazil.'

'Well, he is going skiing actually, Kelvin.'

'Skiing?'

'He had already booked the week off after Cheltenham, Kelvin.'

'I haven't heard a fucking word.'

'Well, to be honest Kelvin, neither have I.'

'I'm not putting up with it. You ring him and tell him that unless I get a fulsome apology then he is out!'

Parry gulped. And gulped again. Hard. This was the end for Brazil. This was also the end of his and Brazil's breakfast show dream team, their incredibly successful partnership, the public speaking engagements and the roadshows. It was all over. Parry knew there was no way in a month of Sundays – or absent Fridays – that Brazil would apologise. That wasn't his way. He moved on and forgot about his misdemeanours and expected everybody else to do the same.

Realising the futility of the conversation, Parry called Brazil to tell him what MacKenzie had said. The man was not for turning and Porky had no choice but to inform his friend that his services would no longer be required by talkSPORT. Brazil remained philosophical about his demise, believing something else would come up.

Meanwhile, Parry was left with the task of finding a replacement for Brazil as well as dealing with a deluge of complaints from thousands of angry listeners who had texted, emailed and rung the station, demanding the Scot's reinstatement once the news became public. In an attempt to draw a line underneath the affair, talkSPORT very quickly announced the surprise appointment of Parry's new breakfast show co-host, Paul Breen-Turner.

For around a year, Spain-based Breen-Turner had been part

of the breakfast show gang of four. He appeared regularly as the programme's David Beckham correspondent shortly after the superstar footballer had joined Real Madrid. In fact, Breen-Turner had been on the programme and correctly predicted that Beckham would be joining the Spanish giants a couple of months before the move, leading to howls of laughter from Porky and Brazil.

Billed as either the Spanish Playboy, Medallion Man, El Numptie, Pablo, Magnum or occasionally the Paella Fella by Brazil, the irony that Breen-Turner was replacing him could not have been lost on the Scot, as he had introduced him to talkSPORT in the first place.

The pair met when Brazil was doing an outside broadcast in Spain and needed access to an ISDN line to be able to go on air. Breen-Turner was a shareholder and presenter on Spain's English language Spectrum FM at the time, so he allowed talkSPORT to use the station's line and the two became fast friends. That was probably helped by the fact that Brazil stayed on after his show to have a few drinks. He even participated in Breen-Turner's programme after his own show on talkSPORT. The Scot enjoyed himself a little bit too much though, as he missed his flight back to London on that occasion.

Having already lined up Beecroft to fill in temporarily for Brazil, Parry turned his attentions on persuading Breen-Turner to take on the role full time. The Spanish-based DJ had his phone turned off that Sunday morning and when he finally switched it on he saw that he had missed 47 calls from the UK. Before he had time to think about what might be going on, the phone rang and it was Porky, admonishing him for not having had his phone on. When they'd finished rowing about that, Parry stunned Breen-Turner by offering him the breakfast show job on a permanent basis – and the Spanish Playboy took some convincing.

He said: 'It might surprise some people but I didn't accept it straight away. I said that I needed to go away and think about it. Mike was very persistent and he phoned me a couple of times and I still wasn't ready to make a decision. If I am really honest, I didn't really expect to be there long term. I was convinced it was a lovers' tiff and in the back of my mind I thought it would be sorted out.'

Despite being a regular on the show, Breen-Turner had never listened to a full day's talkSPORT output, so was still uncertain exactly what the station stood for. But Parry continued to hound him throughout the day and eventually Breen-Turner agreed to fly to London the following morning, where he watched Porky and Beeky broadcasting before taking over himself the next day as the new regular presenter.

Breen-Turner's hunch was proved right, as Parry had already made moves to bring Brazil back to the station. Porky knew the breakfast show needed Brazil. On top of that, the expected lull in the listeners' demands to reinstate their hero never happened. The emails, texts and phone calls continued at a ferocious rate, creating more pressure on Parry to change his mind. Eventually, Parry persuaded MacKenzie that Brazil had to return.

The breakfast boys were finally reunited in a nondescript basement bar in Liverpool Street. Five bottles of wine later, Brazil, who had adopted a 'playing hard to get' stance, agreed to return. 'I was very lucky,' he recalled. 'There were thousands of emails and texts and that definitely got me my job back.'

By this time, the arrangements to bring Breen-Turner over from Spain had already been made and, the day after watching Parry and Beecroft, he turned up bright and early to the studios to present his first breakfast show. Medallion Man was full of beans and raring to go, excited for his first day in his new plum job. But as soon as he arrived, Parry beckoned him over for a quiet word.

'I'm afraid Alan's coming back to the station next week.'

'But I haven't even presented a show yet!'

'Yeah, but we've had thousands of emails and texts supporting Al. But I still want you to do the remaining four days of this week.'

Considering his options, Breen-Turner, who had kept an open mind throughout the saga and had only travelled to London with hand luggage, decided it wouldn't be a bad idea to do the shows anyway. He was proved right, as the following year he would land a regular presenting role on the drivetime show alongside new signing Rodney Marsh.

But for now, Breen-Turner had to make way for Brazil who made a triumphant return to talkSPORT Towers the following week to the delight of the listeners, while the Paella Fella returned to the sunshine of Spain. However, any future errant behaviour would hit Brazil hard in the pocket thanks to a new arrangement with management. A fine system was introduced, meaning Brazil would be docked £5,000 for every show he missed.

Far from happy with this new plan, Brazil was confused by what he saw as the mixed messages he was picking up from his employers. On the one hand, management took a dim view of his party lifestyle and the way it would impinge on the radio station. Yet, on the other side of the coin, Brazil saw the station celebrating his boozy antics with hilarious trails produced by Peter Gee and the Creative department. They had a field day with the Scot's Cheltenham performance and came up with the following ditty to the tune of 'Rudolph the Red Nosed Reindeer':

> Brazil the red nosed DJ
> Had a very dodgy clock
> When it was meant to wake him
> It would always bleedin' stop
>
> Leaving his poor mate Porky
> Sitting on his own, quite miffed
> At five to six they'd phone him
> Still at home in bed quite pissed
>
> Blaming it on the weather
> Blow-outs, traffic jams and frost
> Stuck on the Oxford Ring Road
> Snoring in a layby – lost
>
> Then one foggy Winter's morn
> Kelvin called to say
> Brazil, if you're late once more
> We're gonna make you pay
>
> So now every morning
> Up early as a lark
> Brazil the red nosed DJ
> Sleeping in talkSPORT's car park

With trails like that, it was easy to understand Brazil's confusion and this continued to be a bone of contention between him and talkSPORT management for some time. Breen-Turner still made regular appearances on the breakfast show as the Spanish correspondent, and there were no hard feelings with Brazil over his very brief stint as the flagship programme's presenter.

Now, with Porky and Brazil reunited, all seemed well again in the talkSPORT world, but disaster was just around the corner. Sadly for Porky, his days on the breakfast show were numbered. Just before being sent out to broadcast from Portugal for Euro 2004, he began feeling unwell and that was the start of a lengthy period away from the station due to a serious heart condition. He did make it out to the tournament, but as soon as England were knocked out, he returned home and went straight to hospital where he would spend the next seven months fighting for his life.

Ever the professional, Parry sent a message to Brazil to read out on air on his behalf after he was swamped by cards, letters and messages of support from listeners:

'Hello everybody. I'm sorry I have not been able to be in touch directly with the tens and even hundreds of thousands of you who have contacted the station over the last few weeks. To everyone who has either emailed, written or sent me a card, or even conveyed their best wishes while talking live over the air, I have to say a huge "Thank you".

'You have really kept up my spirits. Basically, upon my return from Euro 2004 on the day after England went out of the competition, I was struck down by a dramatic draining of energy and a severe shortage of breath. I was struggling to walk more than a few yards without fear of collapse.

'Yes, I can hear you all saying it now – that wouldn't have been after a lunchtime session in a wine bar with Al by any chance? Well, actually, no. This was one of those life-changing moments when something clearly different is happening to your body.'

Porky went on to explain how half of his heart had stopped working, putting severe pressure on the other half, and that doctors were continuing to carry out tests to find the best way of treating his condition. It turned out that a heart transplant was deemed the best way for Parry to survive and he remained in Harefield Hospital awaiting a life-threatening operation.

Meanwhile, back at talkSPORT, MacKenzie had taken Parry's illness very badly and showed a genuinely compassionate side during one management meeting when talking about Porky's predicament. In the middle of the meeting, in front of all the station's senior staff, he broke down in tears. It was a rare show of human emotion and colleagues were stunned. Bizarrely, once his tears were shed, he continued with the meeting as if nothing had happened.

The radio station required some important changes now that Parry was out of the picture indefinitely. With Porky's agreement, Bill Ridley was installed as the new programme director – it was his third shift in the role – while Beecroft became Brazil's new partner in crime on breakfast.

Brazil wasted little time in creating a character for his new sidekick Beeky, referring to the clean-living lifestyle his co-presenter enjoyed, in direct contrast to Brazil's seat-of-your-pants, hellraising character. Pretty soon, Brazil was painting imaginary pictures of the cheesy mobile disco business Beeky used to run in his younger days and how he would spend endless hours after the show trawling around garden centres. The listeners loved it.

In his own genius way, Brazil had moved on from his jokes about Parry being small, overweight and short-armed to a new target in the shape of the straitlaced Beecroft. Although the pair would never have tales to tell on air of boozy nights out, countless empty bottles of wine and champagne corks popping, listeners were quite happy to be entertained by Brazil teasing Beeky and getting away with it as only he could.

The former football reporter had gone from being woken up in the middle of the night to replace Brazil, to now waking up in the small hours to work alongside him and be the butt of his jokes all morning. But he took it in good spirits, understanding the importance of characters to the show and the tremendous loss the programme had suffered with Parry hospitalised.

Sometimes, Beeky would unwittingly open himself to ridicule and one such example occurred during the Athens Olympics. The station had decided to cover the event from its studio base, with regular updates from Greece and presenters giving almost-live commentary from the events where Britain stood a good chance of winning a medal.

One morning, Brazil and Beeky were mid-chat when the studio TV screens showed the closing stages of a rowing final in which the British boat was well placed. Brazil began to talk about the race as it built to a climax when Beeky interrupted: 'I'll take it from here, Al!' He was, after all, a seasoned reporter for the station and could call a live event far better than his colleague.

With the British boat in line for a medal, Beeky ratcheted up the drama level with his voice screeching as high as it could go, as he informed the millions listening that glory was surely on its way. The presenter was gone now, lost in the event as Britain rowed closer to the finish line and the tension in the air was palpable as the race drew to its conclusion. After a minute of breathless commentary, intense drama and gut-busting effort from the British boat, not to mention Beeky, he announced to the UK that a hard-fought gold could be added to the British medal tally. At that point, the TV pictures immediately cut to an interview as members of the victorious crew chatted about their success as if they'd been teleported from the water to the riverbank in an instant. Unless, of course, the race hadn't been live and was, in fact, a repeat from hours earlier.

Beeky's face paled and Brazil beamed. He had been commentating on an old race, which didn't quite meet the station's aim to cover the Olympics as an 'almost-live' event. The new presenter wasn't allowed to forget that one in a hurry as the rib-poking banter levels soared sky high. There was a completely different sort of chemistry between Brazil and Beeky than there had been with his predecessor, but the same mickey-taking principles applied. Somehow it worked, thanks to Brazil adapting the station's most important programme and moving it on to a new era.

Meanwhile, after spending months in hospital waiting for a transplant, Parry was told by doctors he could instead have a procedure where they would correct his heart through surgery before placing him on a strict regime of tablets, dieting and no work. Eventually, after popping 22 pills a day and shedding a whopping five stone in weight, Parry started to feel stronger and was ready to start work again.

While he was recuperating, he received a stream of emails from MacKenzie, all of which conveyed how much he was looking forward to welcoming Parry back to talkSPORT Towers. But suddenly, just when he was ready to return to the airwaves, Parry received a bombshell when he was told that breakfast would remain the way it was, with Brazil and Beeky in the presenters' chairs.

'I said to Kelvin "I am not sure if this is a very good idea,"' reflected Parry. 'Apart from the fact that I created the show, I created Brazil and the whole format was created by me, I said to him "Never mind me individually, I think it is bad for the station.'"

But the decision had been made to use Parry elsewhere on shows that needed strengthening, which was clearly a back-handed compliment for the presenter. It was the end of an era, but a new dawn – and with it, a new partnership for Porky – was on the horizon.

8

Spliffs, a Fist Fight and a Top Ten Hit

The main thing I recall from it is recording the video and being in a lift with a very scantily clad Michelle Marsh and Lucy Pinder which was a very nice experience – just me and those two. Me and those four!

ADRIAN DURHAM

If every cloud has a silver lining then, for Mike Parry, the double blow of illness and losing the breakfast show after Euro 2004 led him to an unlikely saviour in Andy Townsend.

Needing to lead a less frenetic life once he was discharged from hospital, Porky couldn't work every day, so he was drafted on to the weekend breakfast show where he paired up with the former Chelsea, Aston Villa and Republic of Ireland footballer for the first time.

Townsend had joined the station earlier in the year and talkSPORT had pulled out all the stops for the ex-footballer, who was their biggest-name signing to date. Having already established himself as a reliable, knowledgeable and watchable broadcaster on ITV's football coverage, he made the transition to radio seem easy and, alongside journalist Lee Clayton, he anchored the weekend breakfast show on Sundays.

Clayton was replaced by another ex-pro, Mick Quinn, before Parry joined Townsend in the studio on Saturdays and Sundays. They immediately struck up a good working relationship, with the ex-footballer often having to play the straight man when Parry got carried away with some of his wilder and wackier thought processes that he liked to share with the listeners.

When Parry wasn't discussing the virtues of fitting Formula 1 cars with ejector seats or installing wing mirrors on jockeys' visors, the exchanges between the pair were vibrant, entertaining and intelligent, as Townsend was far from a stereotypically bland ex-footballer.

The pair complemented one another, as Townsend's nose for a story immediately impressed Parry, who had come to the station from a lengthy career in newspapers. Porky was astonished at his colleague's journalistic instinct and ability to draw listeners into the show with his ideas. Working with Brazil for the previous four years, Parry had become used to being part of the Scot's four-hour charm-athon every morning. But, the weekend breakfast shows were run at a different pace and, if anything, Porky had more time to express his views and engage in sporting debate with Townsend. Whether Parry was happier not being ribbed by Brazil is uncertain, but there was still a fair sprinkling of good-natured banter between him and Townsend. Most importantly of all, the pair clicked and listeners were hooked as a result.

Townsend shared his talkSPORT weekend with co-presenting and commentating duties for ITV, which sometimes led to unusual situations where he couldn't be in the studio for the

Sunday show. While working alongside Quinn during the Olympics, Townsend was forced to broadcast the show using an ISDN line in a dark basement room in Plymouth.

With no television in his dungeon studio, Townsend had no way of seeing pictures of the Olympics, so when Britain's cox-less four rowers won gold, it was barely mentioned yet an edict had come down from above that all shows should provide commentary using TV pictures. Young assistant producer Antony D'Angelo was working on the show behind the scenes and, as the station was playing the national anthem to mark the gold medal, MacKenzie came through on the God Line to demand why there was no commentary on the rowing.

D'Angelo froze because he couldn't mention that Townsend was broadcasting from a studio close to hell and that he hadn't been confident of asking Quinn, a football man through and through, to provide rowing commentary.

'I didn't realise we were allowed to . . .' was all D'Angelo could offer in the circumstances, convinced that this wasn't the last word that he would hear from MacKenzie on the matter. Amazingly, it was.

No doubt MacKenzie would have been busying himself with cricket rights in any case as talkSPORT, after their brief hiatus from covering England's overseas Tests the previous winter, had been back in the commentary box in the Caribbean earlier in 2004.

Following his successful battle against cancer, Geoff Boycott had jumped ship to return to the BBC, meaning the talkSPORT team was led by former England skipper Tony Greig, presumably with his trousers on this time. Determined to capitalise on the financial outlay for broadcasting from the Caribbean, MacKenzie ordered a series of promotional adverts to highlight that the series could be heard, ball by ball, on talkSPORT. However, with talkSPORT even the ads could be controversial.

The radio station took out a full-page advertisement in the *Daily Telegraph* that showed three stumps, with the talkSPORT logo across them, being knocked over by a cricket ball. The copy on the ad read: 'Splat, Splat, Spliff. West Indies v England. Live and exclusive radio commentary.'

A solitary *Telegraph* reader who saw the ad took great offence at the use of the word spliff. The reader saw fit to complain to the Advertising Standards Authority on the grounds that the advert was 'irresponsible because it was a reference to drug use, offensive to West Indians and unsuitable for advertising sport, especially if seen by children.'

The ASA upheld part of the complaint. It decided that the advertisement did not suggest all West Indians used cannabis so wouldn't cause offence. However, it also concluded that because it 'could be seen to condone illegal drug-taking and linked cannabis with sport, the advertisement was socially irresponsible.'

Unsurprisingly, MacKenzie was quick to have his say on the ASA decision, quipping: 'The ASA must be smoking something to give this complaint any credence whatsoever.'

He added: 'I am disgusted that the complaint should be upheld and completely refute the idea that the ad is condoning illegal drug-taking and is socially irresponsible. To suggest so is ludicrous.' Ironically, the furore caused by the advertisement generated further publicity for the station's cricket coverage.

Over in the Caribbean, Greig and co-commentator Jack Bannister were having problems entering their Antigua hotel after each night's play. For some reason, the hotel security guard would question them for an age before allowing them into the building. Greig was becoming fed up with this so, on the third night, when the guard kicked off his interrogation by asking his name, Greig replied: 'My name's Michael Holding!'

It seemed that using the name of the revered former West Indian fast bowler was all that was required as the guard saluted the pair and waved them into the hotel, seemingly oblivious to the fact that Holding was black and Greig was white.

Cricket fever was sweeping talkSPORT Towers by now and with a home Ashes series coming up the following summer, top-ranking ECB officials visited the building for a meeting at which it was hoped the station could convince the governing body to accept their bid to cover England's home series as well.

On the day of the meeting, the ECB bigwigs arrived at the studios and would have been somewhat taken aback to find the entire radio station's staff dressed in full cricket whites. If they weren't convinced about the station's love of the sport before the meeting, they would surely be persuaded now. Unfortunately, not everyone was told about the purchase of the cricket kits from Lilywhites and, with all staff forced to wear them, those who had turned up to work wearing dark underwear were cruelly exposed once they had donned the whites. And it wasn't just the men who had to wear the kits either.

Sadly, as inspired as the stunt was, it didn't do the trick and talkSPORT were not able to wrestle the home series rights from the BBC's grasp. Sales director Tim Bleakley was unsurprised that talkSPORT failed to win the bid: 'They had the great and good of the BBC lined up to meet them. The best we could come up with was a large cheque and everybody dressed in cricket whites when they walked into the building.'

The staff would have had fun in defeat and the station also drew plenty of laughs when it sponsored a full day's racing at

Lingfield with races including 'The Alan Brazil St Legend Handicap' and 'The Porky Parry T-Bone Stakes'. But the unquestionable highlight of the day was the 3.20 Bikini Sprint, featuring six glamour models running the course in their skimpiest beachwear.

When questioned whether the bikini race was a politically correct event by the *Daily Telegraph*, programme director Bill Ridley told the newspaper: 'There's no difference between this and the Olympics. Women sprinters practically wear bikinis these days. Nobody has had any objections as far as I know and why would they? It's going to be great fun.'

There was more unconventional marketing activity at the height of the war with RAJAR over ratings in which talkSPORT was determined to show how many listeners were *really* tuning in every week. In a series of advertisements in the trade press, talkSPORT highlighted the differences between itself and commercial rivals Classic and Virgin. 'If radio stations were sausages ...' was the headline on one ad which showed three pictures of different-sized bangers that were meant to represent the size of each station's audience. Naturally, talkSPORT's sausage was the biggest by far. Similar adverts were run with football stadia and then bottoms, in which talkSPORT's behind was a peachy female bum, partially covered by a barely adequate thong. The other stations' bottoms were as hideous and unsightly as could ever be imagined.

These sorts of marketing gimmicks and ploys had become commonplace at talkSPORT. Shortly after 9/11, the station released a viral email cartoon which showed David Beckham bending one of his trademark free kicks straight into the head of Osama bin Laden in his Tora Bora cave hideout. The ball knocked the wanted man's head straight off. After hundreds of thousands of views, the station, under the careful eye of marketing director Calum Macaulay, released a further viral which depicted Victoria Beckham haggling with Sir Alex Ferguson for a new contract. In this cartoon, 'Posh' walked off into the sunset arm-in-arm with Fergie while 'Becks' was left with his toys in a playpen.

On the eve of the 2002 World Cup, in which England had been drawn to face old foes Argentina in the group stages, talkSPORT were also responsible for another piece of animation that sent up Argentine legend Diego Maradona as Jabba the Hut from *Star Wars*.

The cartoon virals were a big hit, but some presenters seemed to get drawn into the slapstick spirit a little too much, as an amazing incident during a drivetime show illustrated. At the time, the 4-7pm slot was being presented by former Ireland international Tony Cascarino and Patrick Kinghorn, who had joined the station from TV racing channel 'At The Races'. A passionate football and racing fan, Kinghorn was never short of an opinion and seldom afraid of voicing his beliefs.

Billed as 'The King and Cas', the pair clashed on air regularly, and their many heated moments left listeners in no doubt that a very real tension existed between them. Cascarino was quite a sensitive character and Kinghorn was always pushing the boundaries in the banter between them, with the former footballer finding it hard to hide his feelings if he was genuinely annoyed.

Cascarino was no angel himself and he was prone to the odd wind-up, as he once played a trick on Sean Dilley, talkSPORT's current affairs producer, on a night out. Dilley, who uses a guide dog due to being partially sighted, fell over a low wall after enjoying several pints of bitter, but only because Cascarino had been adding vodka to his beer.

The presenters' relationship was far from perfect, but nobody realised just how far it had deteriorated until one particular afternoon. During this show, the lads were talking about the footballer Dwight Yorke, who had been seen chatting up two ladies while relaxing at the cricket.

Kinghorn's reaction was to have a dig at Yorke – and indirectly Cascarino – by saying: 'Typical footballer!' to which his co-presenter responded by arguing that he knew Yorke well, as they had played together at Aston Villa, and that he was a good lad, who was just enjoying himself because he was single.

At that time, Kinghorn had just embarked on a new relationship and Cascarino continued by saying: 'Why are you getting jealous? You've just met Nicola!' For some inexplicable reason, Kinghorn then replied to the ex-footballer: 'Forget talking about me. What about you chasing that 21-year-old round the office?'

Cascarino, who had been divorced once and was married again, tried to laugh off the jibe on air, but as soon as the station went to a commercial break, he was positively steaming with anger and confronted his co-host. The pair became involved in a heated exchange, with Cascarino claiming Kinghorn was putting his marriage at risk by saying something so ridiculous.

The scene was unfolding in front of producers in the control room, who were watching from behind the window that separated them from the studio. As the presenters argued, D'Angelo suggested to his producer Russell D'Albertanson that he should go into the studio to calm them down. But he stayed put, certain it would blow over, especially as the commercial break was coming to an end and they would be back on air in seconds. He seemed to be right as Kinghorn backed down when they returned from the break: 'I just want to apologise for saying that

Cas has been chasing a 21-year-old round the office,' Kinghorn told listeners, as Cascarino began to calm down. 'She wasn't 21, she was 19!'

A livid Cascarino instantly leaped across the studio desk and punched Kinghorn in the face. As producers went straight to another ad break, the two men were on their feet with the Irishman sprinting around the studio trying to catch a fleeing Kinghorn. They spilled out of the studio and into the control room where a sofa, usually meant for guests waiting to go on air, suddenly became the setting for round two – and the gloves were off.

With Cascarino's hands around his neck, Kinghorn was leaning over the sofa attempting to wriggle free while shocked producers looked on, paralysed by the absurdity of the moment. In an even more surreal twist, Cascarino's former Ireland teammate Ray Houghton, who was in the offices preparing for the evening show, chanced upon the scene and saved the day by storming into the control room and dragging his friend away from a relieved Kinghorn.

As Houghton tried to cool down 6ft 3in Cascarino by repeating 'Calm down, big man!' the show was due back on air and producers had no choice but to play another set of adverts straight off the back of the first batch. There really was no way of explaining the bizarre events to listeners.

Houghton worked his magic and, three minutes later, with the commercials coming to an end, Cascarino and Kinghorn were sitting back in the studio. They both looked red in the face with 'the King' sporting several scratches and cuts, but this was radio so no matter. Incredibly, they continued the show from that point without any hiccups – or punches.

Later that evening, the pair were also due to do a promotional night for EA Sports, which they duly attended, although Kinghorn was beginning to resemble a man who had just gone a couple of rounds with somebody twice his size which, of course, he had.

Cascarino was deeply upset by the incident. Incredibly, in 19 years as a professional footballer nothing like that had ever happened to him either on or off the pitch: 'It was such a mad moment and I regret it enormously,' he said. 'I had never cracked like that before. It was such a surreal experience. I thought it was going way too far to say, on air, that I was chasing a girl around the office when I was married. And it wasn't true!'

Perhaps unsurprisingly, that drivetime pairing did not last much longer, although both men stayed at talkSPORT working across different shows for several more years. And they weren't the only drive presenters to start a ruckus. Presenter Richard Kaufman, in an earlier incarnation of the show, almost became embroiled in a full-scale riot during an outside broadcast from a north London pub before a vital Arsenal v Manchester United title showdown.

The decision was taken to leave the pub, but with nowhere else to go, Kaufman found himself presenting the last 45 minutes of his national radio drivetime show from the least glamorous location imaginable – outside a Highbury kebab shop.

As the station of the fans, talkSPORT would often broadcast alongside them or from venues frequented by football supporters. That policy had been essential to the way major football events had been covered – if the station couldn't get into the stadium then they would be right outside it, speaking to people and picking up the vibrant atmosphere of any big match.

However, with the purchasing of broadcasting rights for Euro

2004, talkSPORT had suddenly been catapulted into the stadia from where commentaries could be based and programmes could be presented. The tournament in Portugal was the first time the station would stand side by side with the BBC and give them a serious run for their money on a level playing field – now that they were finally invited to the party.

Lengthy negotiations with the European Broadcasting Union had been required before talkSPORT's bid to become an official broadcaster of the European Championships was accepted. But the station was not just going to turn up at their first major tournament quietly. Instead, they went to Portugal making as much noise as possible in the shape of their very own hit single 'Come on England'. talkSPORT were approached to make the record by a band called 4-4-2, who had written a cover version of the massive Dexy's Midnight Runners hit 'Come on Eileen'. The project seemed too good to turn down as, at the very worst, the station would receive some free publicity.

So talkSPORT teamed up with 4-4-2 as presenters and producers combined to record the single and a video, which was enhanced by the presence of glamour models Michelle Marsh and Lucy Pinder. The lyrics may not have been that original but they did the job:

(commentary on David Beckham's goal against Greece at Old Trafford)

> Come on England
> Come on England
> Come on England
> Hands up high with a glint in your eye
> And give your all for Eng-er-land

It can't be long now
Like '66 we'll get our kicks, yeah
Bend it (like Beckham) Strike it (like Owen)
Win it all and live forever
Come on England!

CHORUS
One-nil, two-nil, three-nil, four-nil, five!
Keep this country's dream alive

Come on England, Come on England,
At this moment this means everything
We are the best so forget all the rest
'Cos we're singing, Come on England
Come on England

(commentary on one of Owen's hat-trick of goals in the 5-1 win against Germany in Munich)

Listen can you hear?
Score one more you'll hear us roar
And give our all for England
Cross it (like Gerrard) Lob it (like Lampard)
Win it all and live forever
Come on England!

CHORUS
Come on, England To Loo Ray Aye
Come on, England To Loo Ray Aye
Come on, England To Loo Ray Aye
Eng-er-land!

Come on, England To Loo Ray Aye
Come on, England To Loo Ray Aye
Come on, England To Loo Ray Aye
Eng-er-land!

Now we must try hard together to reach our goal
To Ray Loo Ray To Ray Loo Ray Aye

CHORUS
Come on England, Come on England
It's your moment, this means everything
Come on England, Come on England
We're all singing Come On England
England!

The listeners loved it, lapping it up in their thousands and, amazingly, the single rocketed up the UK charts, debuting at the dizzy heights of number two. It was prevented from reaching the top only by Mario Winans and P Diddy's 'I Don't Wanna Know'. The single stayed in the Top 10 for three weeks during the tournament and the talkSPORT team featuring, among others, Mick Quinn and Andy Jacobs, all appeared on ITV's Saturday morning pop show *CD:UK* and the BBC's *Top of the Pops*. The Beeb made sure the rowdy rabble didn't actually make it into the studios to rub shoulders with the 'real' pop stars, as they were filmed on an outdoor stage in front of a huge goal.

That wasn't the case over at ITV however, where the great and good of the station were doing their best impressions of A-list rock 'n' roll stars by hanging out in the green room alongside The Neptunes and Blue. With *CD:UK* going out live early on a Saturday morning, the hospitality bar opened at 6am and several talkSPORT regulars, including Quinn and producers Steve Hodge and Seb Ewen, made sure they were there from the start for some much-needed Dutch courage before going on stage.

Jacobs did his best impression of an embarrassing Dad dancing awkwardly at a wedding, while Quinn and Hodge wrapped their arms around each other and jumped up and down, waving their arms and legs about manically as an audience of 200 teenagers looked on aghast. Of course, being an England song, the proud Scotsman Brazil played no part in it. Adrian Durham sang on the original recording and he was gobsmacked to be part of such a huge hit single: 'If you said to me when I was a kid that I would be number two in the charts, I would have thought "Fuck me! That's it, I can retire. I've made it".'

The single caused some controversy as rival breakfast DJ Christian O'Connell, who worked on XFM, had put together a supergroup called Twisted X, which included members of The Libertines and Supergrass. Their Euro 2004 song, 'Born in England', debuted at only number nine, causing O'Connell to trash talkSPORT's effort on his show as 'nothing original, nothing fresh' and describing the rival station as 'vastly inferior, medium wave, Cabbie Moron FM. . .it's an awful station. They have obviously knee-jerked. It's even got the obligatory clichéd football commentary, just like the rubbish FA one.'

Porky countered on behalf of talkSPORT in a press release in which he said: 'Oh dear, Christian's not sounding very Christian at all – not to us, not to the FA and certainly not to London's cabbies. Never mind, we're happy to let England football fans make up their minds which single they want to make number one.'

Even Kevin Rowland, the lead singer of Dexy's Midnight

Runners, was unhappy with the talkSPORT version, despite having given his blessing for the song to be covered. As usual, talkSPORT were in the firing line but, O'Connell and Rowland aside, the station had prepared for their first major tournament in the best possible way, setting up things nicely for the football side of the equation over in Portugal (the station also attempted a World Cup single in 2006, but 'We're England' failed to make the same impact as the Euro 2004 anthem).

Brazil and Parry took the breakfast show to Lisbon for the duration of the tournament, while reporters including Andy Clarke and Dominic 'Our Man in Japan' McGuinness were stationed across the country to provide the latest from the England camp as well as colour from the rest of the tournament.

Mike Bovill, having returned to the station after backpacking, was based in London, where he produced a mid-morning programme on the tournament. But, three days into the competition, he was despatched to Portugal to report on the disturbances that had been taking place on the Algarve resort of Albufeira. English holidaymakers and football fans had been involved in skirmishes at the resort for a couple of nights and it was decided that talkSPORT needed a man on the ground there.

By the time he flew in, hired a car and drove to the popular resort, it was already midnight, but Bovill thought he had better see if there was any trouble going on in the town centre. The strip of bars that had been the scene for much of the violence was pretty quiet, so talkSPORT's finest had a couple of pints and waited to see if anything kicked off. He wasn't to be disappointed.

At about 2am, a chair was thrown, leading to a stand-off between the police and a large group of England fans. Eventually,

If radio stations were bottoms, what would they look like?

talkSPORT
6.3m adults

Peachy

Classic FM
5.7m adults

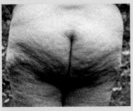

Crikey!

Virgin AM/FM
3.5m adults

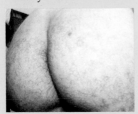

Hmmm

talkSPORT 1089/1053 am

The UK's biggest commercial radio station*

*Source: GfK National Broadcast Media Survey, Oct 13th 2003–Jan 11th 2004. Adults figures based on weekly reach

PURE GENI-ARSE: A classic example of *talkSPORT*'s unconventional marketing under the Kelvin MacKenzie regime. Adverts like these appeared in the trade press in 2004. Another in the series featured sausages...

BREAKFAST BUDDIES: Alan Brazil and Mike Parry's breakfast show started in 2001 and may well have saved the station as listeners flocked to 1089 to hear the pair's amusing banter and tales from their nights out on the town.

ROOM FOR A LITTLE 'UN: Paul Hawksbee (right) and Andy Jacobs (left) have hosted a series of top sporting names on their show including former NFL star William 'The Fridge' Perry.

HEART OF GOLD: After his brush with death, Mike Parry completed the Great North Run in 2007 with his broadcasting partner Andy Townsend (left) and raised £9,000 for Harefield Hospital.

IRON MIC: One of the most bizarre days in *talkSPORT* history saw Mike Tyson visit the studios in 2005 to talk to Rodney Marsh (left) and Paul Breen-Turner (right). It was the former boxer and his 15-strong entourage's off-air antics that shocked producer Jon Norman.

RULING THE (AIR)WAVES: (l to r) Alan Brazil, Graham Beecroft and Mike Bovill take to the waters on Australia's Gold Coast ahead of the 2006/07 Ashes.

BEST MATES: The emotion was palpable as George Best gave what turned out to be his last ever public interview to old friend Rodney Marsh on the drive show with Paul Breen-Turner in 2005.

WORLD CUP WONDERS: The commentary and reporting team in Berlin's *Olympiastadion* before the 2006 World Cup Final – (l to r) Mike Parry, Mike Bovill, Ray Houghton, Alvin Martin and Jim Proudfoot. The tournament was a great triumph for the station and was the first time *talkSPORT* had been an official FIFA broadcaster.

TOP OF THE POPS: James Whale (left) and Rodney Marsh belt out *talkSPORT*'s World Cup 2006 record *We're England*. The track wasn't as big a hit as Euro 2004 single *Come on England* which reached number two in the charts.

WE ARE THE CHAMPIONS: Paul Breen-Turner pops the champagne cork as (l to r) Rodney Marsh, former *Apprentice* contestant James Max and Adrian Durham celebrate drive beating breakfast in the inaugural match between the two shows in 2006.

TOP CAT: George Galloway, complete with trademark cigar, on the football pitch before the breakfast v drive game in 2007, proving he's a team player even though his views may not be shared by many – or any – of his fellow presenters.

FIVE-SPA TREATMENT: Alan Brazil and Ronnie Irani brush up on the latest sports news in the papers as they prepare to broadcast the breakfast show from Champneys in 2008.

PILLOW TALK: Adrian Durham (left) and Ian Wright (er, right) during a drive show live from Leicester Square in 2008. Outside broadcasts mean presenters have to be quick-witted and full of energy as you can see from this picture.

YES, PRIME MINISTER: Just before Gordon Brown (right) goes on air in 2009, Faye Carruthers (left) reads the news, Ian "The Moose" Abrahams waits in the background to read the sports headlines while producer Dennie Morris (crouching) makes sure the PM's technical equipment is in full working order.

KNOW WHAT I MEAN, RONNIE?
Frank Bruno puts Ronnie Irani through his paces at Champneys in 2009. Irani's good intentions turned to nought when Alan Brazil dragged his co-presenter out of the health resort and into the pub.

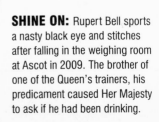

SHINE ON: Rupert Bell sports a nasty black eye and stitches after falling in the weighing room at Ascot in 2009. The brother of one of the Queen's trainers, his predicament caused Her Majesty to ask if he had been drinking.

ROCK 'N' ROLL: Noel Gallagher (left) and Russell Brand (right) don't look thrilled to be at *talkSPORT* Towers but luckily they cheered up on air as their one-off show in 2009 proved to be a massive hit for the station.

police started meting out their own form of justice on anybody they thought was causing trouble, so Bovill called through to the studio to give a live report.

As he was describing the scene of watching a young Englishman taking a beating from the police, he received a tap on the shoulder. While still broadcasting, Bovill turned around and received a whack across the back of his legs from a riot policeman's baton. Slipping straight into his west London roots mid-broadcast, he exclaimed: 'All right sunshine, I'm moving, I'm moving!'

Bovill beat a hasty retreat while continuing to describe the trouble, which eventually subsided, and he recalled how he could not shrug that incident off for the rest of the tournament. 'Instead of being remembered for being the on-the-spot reporter in the middle of an England football riot, they managed to cut that little clip and play it in on a loop for the next two weeks of the tournament. When I got back to the office everyone was going "All right sunshine, all right sunshine!"'

When reporters weren't being attacked by over-enthusiastic Portuguese riot police, live coverage of the tournament was a runaway success for the station – much like the hit single. Fresh from the Cheltenham debacle, Brazil enjoyed himself in the sunshine, but was far more conscientious about his timekeeping. The Scot was accompanied by his family in Lisbon, while Porky was feeling the effects of his as yet undiagnosed heart problems so laid off the drink.

On most days after the breakfast show, Brazil could be found sitting by the hotel swimming pool, supping some of the local brew, Super Bock. Occasionally, he would disappear to the Algarve for a round of golf, but always under strict instructions from Parry to return in time for the following morning's programme. And, with a three-hour drive to the course, if that meant playing 18 holes, relaxing with a drink or two, having a kip then driving back to Lisbon at 2am, then Brazil did it.

Not that he had become a saint overnight. One afternoon, several members of the talkSPORT team were taken out on a boat for a Carlsberg-promoted broadcast and nobody held back on the free booze on offer. At one point, with the boat cruising down Lisbon's River Tagus, Brazil was broadcasting to the nation with a glass in his hand and no top on. This was Euro 2004, talkSPORT-style.

The main difference for the station's reporters was that official broadcaster status meant far better access to players. With that came more pressure to deliver, whereas in previous tournaments there had been minimal expectation because of the absence of accreditation. However, the small talkSPORT team were still aware that the odds were stacked against them when faced with taking on the might of the BBC, who arrived at the tournament in their hundreds.

Despite their ubiquitous presence, it's highly doubtful that any of the Beeb's number would have equalled the performance of talkSPORT's Clarke, who surpassed himself early one morning with a live broadcast on the breakfast show. The reporter had been out drinking all night, finally leaving the last bar at around 5.30am before staggering off to bed. An hour later, he received a call from London asking if he would be able to come on air for a ten-minute chat on the latest from the tournament. Although he was fully aware that he was still far from sober, Clarke told producers that he would do it.

What followed can only be described as car-crash radio as Clarke went live to the nation and babbled incoherently to a bemused audience of millions. He made no sense whatsoever, desperately trying to string sentences together, but never getting anywhere close to doing so. Here is how it unravelled:

> Brazil: Five minutes to eight o'clock, over to Portugal. I don't know what city he's in, it could be Porto but probably Lisbon – Andy Clarke, morning Andy!
>
> Clarke: Morning fellas!
>
> Brazil: Whereabouts are you, pal?
>
> Clarke (slurring): Er, about sunny Lisbon, just er, overlooking the pool. It's, er, it's all gone a little bit quiet over here, I must admit, because basically since England left town ... the erm, the ... edge has gone off the tournament to be honest.
>
> Parry: Edge has gone off the tournament has it?
>
> Clarke: It has really. I mean the England fans when they came over in their thousands for the France game and the two other games, for Switzerland in Coimbra and for Croatia ... down in ...
>
> Parry: Late night last night, Andy, was it?
>
> Clarke: Not particularly, Mike, not particularly, no. I'm a professional, obviously, so I was up in good time to do this slot on your show.
>
> Parry: I didn't ask you how early you got up, I just asked you how late you went to bed!
>
> Brazil: Ha, ha, ha!

Clarke then managed to stumble his way to discussing that night's semi-final between Greece and the Czech Republic with the Eastern Europeans highly rated by the clearly suffering reporter.

Clarke: Erm, and I think with Baros and Jan Koller up front, I
　　wouldn't bet against them, to be honest, because the thing is,
　　the thing about them is . . .

Parry: Yeah. . .

Clarke: Whether . . . If they're struggling, to be honest, they can
　　always, they can always resort to route one with er, with the
　　big Koller up front . . .

Parry: It's a terrible struggle!

Parry and Brazil both knew full well that Clarke was struggling
and deliberately kept the interview going long after it should
have been brought to an end. Looking back, the reporter admitted he was lucky to keep his job: 'I was still drunk but I thought
"I'm invincible, no problem!" And my performance was terrible.
After about 20 seconds, you'd be able to tell I was drunk. In
other places, I'd almost certainly have been sacked. Drinking's
not a badge of honour, but we all did it.'

Incredibly, his rambling and stuttering performance earned
him instant legendary status among the loyal listeners, who
loved every second of his unintentional starring role in that
morning's show. Emails and texts flooded in, hailing him a
genius and superstar of the airwaves. Some even demanded that
he should be given more airtime.

Within that incident undoubtedly lay the key to the remarkable success of the commercial radio station that was now
regularly reaching more than 2.3 million listeners every week.
Here was a reporter, clearly still drunk from a big night out,
manfully trying to sound sober and do his job, but failing mis-
erably. Many of the station's male followers would clearly have
been in the same situation in their working lives once or twice,
because they were only human after all.

The appeal of any radio station lies in how much it manages to stay in touch with its listeners, and talkSPORT couldn't have done any better with its unique style that left the audience feeling like they were part of something special. And the best part of this tone that talkSPORT had created was that it was utterly impossible to replicate. The station was thriving.

9

Late-Night Rants and XXX-Rated Romps

After seven minutes I realised I was talking to someone who had never in their life done comedy. I think she worked as a childminder but somehow she got booked in. This was a stand-up feature that was meant to include the likes of Ricky Gervais and Ross Noble.

IAN COLLINS

The originality of talkSPORT was further enhanced when the sun went down, darkness set in and the night shift took over the airwaves. In the small hours, the station's reputation for bedlam was taken to a whole new level.

Reporters occasionally calling in drunk and presenters turning up hungover during the day were just starters on the menu of controversy and mayhem that typified the schedules between 10pm and 6am on talkSPORT. Nowhere was the station more anarchic and unpredictable than in its late-night output.

Standing at the helm of late-night proceedings was James Whale, a veteran of the airwaves who had first shot to fame on local radio before a successful stint on late-night telly made him a household name. Whale's talkSPORT show made a habit of going as close to the bone as possible and was not without its controversial moments. Other than extensive set-up work to book the wildest and wackiest guests for the show, there was never a huge amount of preparation in the hours immediately before the programme went on air. The improvised tone was a hit with the listeners, who loved to tune in purely because they never knew what was going to happen next.

One evening, legendary US porn star Ron Jeremy arrived at talkSPORT Towers for Whale's show. But he didn't turn up alone. Being a porn star, he was accompanied by two aspiring British 'actresses' who were on hand to tend to him whenever he required their help. This led to unprecedented scenes on the deserted production floor as Jeremy brazenly enjoyed himself with his lady friends both before and after the show. It was just as well that anybody arriving for work the next morning wouldn't have known what had happened on, or around, the desks at which they worked. Jeremy's presence and shenanigans left Whale dumbfounded – which was a rarity in itself.

The sexual theme was continued by the visit of another two female porn stars who specialised in lesbian roles. They were obviously method actors as they sat in the studio while demonstrating the many different uses of a sex toy live on air. All of this was happening as one of the ladies was perched on the very same chair that Porky Parry would be sitting on just a few hours later for the breakfast show.

Anything went on Whale's show as there was no set format. In an experimental cookery section on the programme once, Whale attempted to cook the perfect fry-up in the studio to demonstrate British culinary delights at their best. In the process of frying, the studio's smoke alarms were set off and, within minutes, the fire brigade had arrived. The show was not taken off air on this occasion, but the firemen were far from pleased when they found out why they had been called out to the studios.

Sometimes, there were emergencies of a different kind on the show, such as when a guest urgently needed something to eat, forcing Asher 'Ash' Gould out on to the streets of Waterloo in search of a kebab. This would have been all well and good under normal circumstances but, at the time, Ash was the only person in the control room producing the show, meaning he had to leave Whale to broadcast alone. He did take a phone with him and stayed in touch with the on-air presenter the whole time he was gone.

Aside from porn stars and fry-ups, the late show also attracted its fair share of unusual guests. One evening, a defrocked Irish Catholic priest dressed in a kilt came on the programme to talk about bible prophecies. His views and character were certainly unusual and this was confirmed a few months later when millions of TV viewers saw the same kilted man, Neil Horan, run on to the track during the British Grand Prix at Silverstone, holding a placard which read: 'Read the Bible – the Bible is always right.' He might have had a point, but Formula 1 fans wouldn't have agreed as he caused the race to be delayed that day before being arrested and charged with aggravated trespass.

On another occasion, Heather Mills was a guest on Whale's show, way before Paul McCartney had become synonymous with her name. Glamour girl Mills agreed to take part in an on-air boob test in which Ash squeezed one of McCartney's future wife's breasts in the name of science.

One person who regularly attempted to be a surprise guest on Whale's show, but rarely succeeded, was Parry. After a few drinks, Porky used to demand to go on the late-night show as he was a good friend of Whale's. More often than not, Ash would refuse Porky permission to go on air, which was a difficult task as he was talking to his boss – Parry was still the programme director at that stage.

On those occasions, Parry would eventually phone back and thank Ash for not putting him on air, realising it would have been inappropriate. Once, however, Parry did manage to get past Ash after being particularly persistent and appeared on Whale's show in a slightly inebriated state. After a chat and a sing-song – in which Porky serenaded the host with 'I belong to Whaley' – he was off, but an anonymous spy delivered a tape of Parry's performance straight on to MacKenzie's desk the following morning. The boss was scathing of his programme director and castigated him for behaving in an unprofessional manner.

A tipsy Parry would have been the least of the late-night staff's worries when compared to the evening an intruder broke in to the studios. Shortly before Whale's show was due on air, there was a knock on the production floor door. Anybody coming into the building would have already been buzzed in downstairs, so Ash wasn't too worried when he opened the door.

A strange man resembling a shorter and stockier version of Samuel L Jackson entered the room to see Whale sitting on the sofa. The intruder followed the presenter into the control room while Ash went to enlist the help of a 30-stone trucker friend of overnight presenter Mike Mendoza, who was in the studio next door. Fat Jackson was asking some strange questions, so Mendoza's friend suggested they go outside and he went along willingly. A couple of minutes later, the trucker returned to the studio rubbing his jaw, moaning: 'He punched me! He punched me!' Police were called and the intruder was arrested but no charges were brought, as all involved preferred to just move on from the strange incident.

Mike Dickin was another stalwart of the late-night airwaves. When he was no longer working on the mid-morning current affairs programme, the West Countryman reverted to working on late-night or overnight weekend shows. Dickin was a big bear of a man who enjoyed cult status on talkSPORT. Having worked on BBC Radio 4, LBC and Capital Radio before joining Talk Radio, he was a vastly experienced broadcaster and his curmudgeonly manner was instantly played upon by talkSPORT, who billed him as 'Britain's Angriest Man'.

Dickin was a campaigning presenter who loathed political correctness and regularly became exasperated at how 21st century Britain had gone to the dogs. Topics he covered most often included the unnecessary war on motorists in the form of parking and speeding fines, the rise of yob culture in Britain and the lawlessness that was pervading British society.

Off-air, he was the closest thing talkSPORT had to a rock 'n' roll star – excluding Brazil, although he gave the Scot a pretty good run for his money. If anything, Dickin was the English Brazil, with a healthy appetite for booze. The difference was that the drink could sometimes have an effect on him, whereas Brazil would still be standing under almost any circumstances.

While Dickin was presenting the mid-morning show, he would have to stay overnight in London, which he disliked because he was always more comfortable with his family in his home town of Bodmin in Cornwall. To show his dislike for the capital and his thirst for country life, he would go on the occasional all-day bender.

On one such romp, Dickin spent all afternoon consuming

way more than his fair share of wine before eventually return-ing to the office, for no particular reason, where he decamped to an off-air studio. Later that evening, one of the late-night show producers was going through the routine of setting up the studio and checking the microphones were working. He sensed something wasn't right in the studio and, as he stood over the mixer desk, he felt his foot touch a large presence and looked down to receive the fright of his life. Under the desk he could see a huddled heap of a man – it was Dickin and he wasn't moving.

The producer burst out of the studio screaming: 'Fucking hell! Mike Dickin is dead! Dickin is dead!' While another pro-ducer called an ambulance, the few members of staff who were still in the building raced into the off-air studio to see what all the commotion was about and found Dickin still slumped under the mixer.

Suddenly, amid the noise of the panicked voices, the great, big bear of a man began to stir. He emerged from under the desk angrier than ever before and sporting a raging hangover. The producers were quickly back on the phone to the ambu-lance: 'Sorry, there's been a slight over-reaction to a situation in the office. We thought someone was dead.' Within minutes, the dead man was staggering back to his hotel room for the night.

When he went back to presenting the overnight shows, Dickin insisted that he wanted to broadcast the show from Bodmin. This presented logistical problems for talkSPORT, as Dickin's family home was so remote that there was no ISDN line he could use to go on air.

A solution was found as the station located a doctor's surgery in Bodmin that had a basement with an ISDN connection fitted. After talkSPORT came to an agreement with the doctor to use his premises, Dickin was allowed to air his shows from the surgery basement.

One morning, talkSPORT received a phone call from an extremely irate Cornish doctor who was complaining that his surgery's brand new white leather sofa had biro scrawled all over it, while the building's smoke alarm had been disconnected. Dickin, a keen smoker, had been up to his tricks again.

Having made himself very much at home in the surgery basement, on one evening Dickin became a little too comfortable there. Having clearly had a drink or two during the day, the presenter arrived in the makeshift studio around 20 minutes before his show was due to begin at 10pm. Dickin was also taking medication at the time and the combined effect of the pills and alcohol did him few favours.

He spoke into the microphone to ask Ash, who was manning the control room desk, what had been lined up for the show that night. Back in London, Ash detailed what was planned for the programme, including topics for discussion and special guests. Rounding up the schedule for the show, he said: 'So is that OK, Mike?'

Cue silence from Bodmin.

'Mike, are you there?'

The deafening sound of more silence filled the line.

'Mike, can you hear me? Mike? Mike?'

There was still no response, although Ash was certain he could make out the unmistakeable sound of snoring coming down the line. As a last resort, Ash removed his headphones and placed them next to the microphone to create an ear-drum shattering, shrill feedback sound, but even that could not disturb Dickin's peaceful snoring tones.

Gripped by panic, the producer managed to contact

overnight presenter Mike Mendoza, who was drafted in as an emergency replacement for the snoring Dickin. As Mendoza began the show from a broadcast quality line at his Sussex home, Ash called programme director Bill Ridley to tell him what had happened. The programme director contacted Dickin's son, who raced down to the surgery and hammered on the door in an attempt to wake his father. Eventually, police arrived on the scene to smash down the door, which finally woke up Dickin.

'What's wrong, are we on the air?' he mumbled as he stirred from his power nap. He still seemed keen to go live to the nation, but with Mendoza having already started the show, it was an early night for Dickin.

Mendoza's midweek overnight shows also became the stuff of legend in the talkSPORT office, as much for what happened off air as on. Having worked for overseas broadcasters and then LBC for many years, the man whose biggest claim to fame was being Peter Sellers' cousin joined talkSPORT in 2004.

He used to arrive at the office several hours before his show began and would catch up on his sleep by snoozing on one of the sofas. He then warmed up for the programme by flicking through the office TV channels. At that time, talkSPORT used to receive many foreign stations to pick up live football matches that wouldn't otherwise have been available and, more often than not, one of these outlets would turn into a XXX-rated channel after midnight. Mendoza's favourite trick was to change the channel on every TV in the office – from the plasmas on the walls to the small portables on the desks – to a porn channel, so the production office resembled an old-fashioned television rental shop that specialised in skin flicks.

Mendoza's fun couldn't last forever, though, as a female staffer arriving early for her shift was horrified at the sight that greeted her and complained to management. An email was sent to all staff making clear that the televisions were not for entertainment purposes:

> The viewing of x-rated material on our TVs is prohibited. The televisions in this building are there solely for monitoring news and sport.
>
> Bill Ridley
> Programme Director

That would have come as a nasty shock to Mendoza, but not as much of a surprise as when he looked up into the control room during an overnight show to find his technical operator fast asleep. Overnight programmes were just a two-man operation, with the presenter in the studio and a tech-op in the gallery, manning the phones, going to commercial breaks and producing the show.

On this particular night, Mendoza's technical operator had taken advantage of a free mobile cocktail bar, which had been set up at talkSPORT Towers by a leading drinks brand, before returning to the studios for his shift. Unfortunately, the booze had caught up with him and, after hitting several wrong buttons at the start of his shift, he began to feel drowsy as he sat in the control room. Before long, he had fallen fast asleep and when Mendoza looked through the window, he could see he was suddenly on his own.

Without his tech-op, Mendoza could not go to a commercial break and was forced to continue broadcasting indefinitely until his assistant woke from his stupor. With little option other than going off air to do the job himself, Mendoza decided to let his listeners in on what was happening. He encouraged them to ring in and scream 'Wake up!' down the phone lines in an attempt to rouse the tech-op. All these calls had to be taken unscreened in the studio, but it did make for compelling radio as the quest to wake the tech-op became an epic segment in the show.

Eventually, he did wake up and was horrified to find he had been asleep on the job, much to Mendoza's amusement and, no doubt, relief as he could finally go to an ad break and take a well-earned rest.

The overnight phone-operator's lot was never an easy one. Like all radio stations, there were all manner of weird and wonderful callers who used to regularly ring up talkSPORT late at night. One particular lonely old dear would phone the station approximately every 20 minutes for a quick chat with whoever was on duty. The caller would ask if the phone operator was all right and tell him she was just listening to the show. Then, at about 2am, she would ring back again and say: 'Just to let you know, I am going to bed now!'

The other unfaltering hero of the overnight airwaves at the station was Ian Collins, who remains talkSPORT's longest serving presenter, having joined the station way back in its early Talk Radio days. His long-running show, *Ian Collins & The Creatures of the Night*, was broadcast on both versions of the station and became cult listening for night owls across the country.

As always with talkSPORT, the show was liable to endure the odd disaster and one evening, all the phone lines went down which, for an overnight phone-in show that heavily relied on listeners' contributions, was far from ideal. With the station not yet fully conversant with the idea of its audience emailing or texting in their thoughts at this time, the entire programme took the form of a discussion between Collins and his studio cohorts, telling their life stories and generally fooling around. The following night, when the phones *were* working, everyone who rang in asked if they could repeat the previous night's format from then on.

Collins was also big on laughs and regularly attracted top names from the world of comedy to appear for a chat and a giggle. Over the years, the likes of Lee Mack and Ross Noble had graced the talkSPORT studios with their presence, but on one night, the comic who appeared on air with Collins wasn't all she was cracked up to be.

A junior researcher had managed to track down an up-and-coming new comedienne on the internet and booked her to join Collins in the studio that night. When she arrived in the studio and Collins started asking her about where she had been gigging recently and what new material she was working on, it was quite clear she had no idea what was going on. In slightly broken English, she began to explain why she liked comedy and which comedians she found funny.

After a few minutes of increasingly bizarre radio, Collins deduced this woman was certainly not a comedienne. She was, in fact, a childminder from Dartford who had a website that listed one of her interests as comedy. Somehow, through some internet search engine confusion, she had been asked to come on the show and make the nation laugh.

As night turned into day, talkSPORT continued to speak to its listeners like no other radio station in the country. Very soon, however, huge changes were on the way, with a power struggle at the very top of the company signalling the end of MacKenzie's reign and a new beginning for the station.

10

MacKenzie Gets His Marching Orders

I may be leaving but I'm still walking away with £7 million, so fuck you!

KELVIN MACKENZIE

Kelvin MacKenzie was never going to leave talkSPORT quietly. The station was his baby and, as 2005 dawned over Hatfields, the boss still had big plans to take it to the next level. But within six months, MacKenzie was exiting the building for the last time – although not before a monumental struggle in which he tried just about every trick in the book to remain in power.

MacKenzie's official title was chairman and chief executive of The Wireless Group, a consortium that had initially bought a 63 per cent controlling stake in Talk Radio back in 1998. The main backers were Rupert Murdoch's News Corporation, which owned 30 per cent and US conglomerate Liberty Media, which owned around 25 per cent. MacKenzie himself owned 7 per cent of the new company.

In addition to Talk Radio, The Wireless Group purchased

two major UK radio companies in 1999. The Radio
Partnership, including the six regional stations it operated, was
snapped up for £38.9 million, while the Independent Radio
Group and its five stations was bought for £32.5 million.

Shortly after the relaunch of The Wireless Group's flagship
national station talkSPORT, the company was floated on the
London Stock Exchange, but a year later the group had run into
financial difficulty. With debts rising, the decision was taken to
sell regional stations Scot FM, Kingdom and Wave 105 for a
total of £45 million.

The company, which eventually rebuilt a portfolio of 16 local
radio stations across the UK, never made serious money. Indeed,
since 1995, Talk Radio, which then became talkSPORT, had
managed to lose close to £80 million, although almost half of
that had come in the days before The Wireless Group takeover.
Nevertheless, by the end of 2004, Murdoch and Liberty Media
chairman John Malone had reportedly had enough of their venture into UK radio.

MacKenzie saw this as his golden opportunity to purchase
the business himself in a management buyout, which would
take the company private, if he could convince venture capi-
talists to stump up enough cash. The problem was that each
time he was close to convincing a firm to come on board, something went wrong with the negotiations and he was forced to
start again.

After failing to receive backing from private equity companies
Veronis Suhler Stevenson and CVC, MacKenzie was left high
and dry as The Wireless Group board had little choice but to
instruct investment bank Goldman Sachs to find buyers for a
quick sell. While potential bidders for the group were considering their options, the boss had not given up and attempted to

gain new backing from venture capitalist firm 3i. But after that collaboration failed to materialise, UTV, the Northern Irish television giants, stepped in with a bid of £96.9 million, which was accepted by the board.

The entire deal was thrashed out and completed within three weeks and talkSPORT suddenly had new owners, while MacKenzie could only look on from his new position on the sidelines.

Shortly before the takeover had been completed, RAJAR listening figures had put talkSPORT ahead of bitter commercial rivals Virgin Radio for the first time, with a weekly reach of 2.5 million against 2.4 million. But, for MacKenzie, that counted for nothing – other than pride. Additionally, as a 7 per cent shareholder, MacKenzie was certainly not going to leave empty-handed, but he still found it hard to live with the fact that he was no longer running the station.

Immediately after the deal was finalised, he rang UTV chief John McCann to ask if he could use a small meeting room in talkSPORT Towers as an office, because otherwise he would have nowhere else to work from. He asked for it on a temporary basis, just while he found himself some office space elsewhere. McCann told him he had no objection to that, but MacKenzie would have to ask Scott Taunton, who had been put in charge of the whole UTV radio project and would be running operations from the talkSPORT offices on a day-to-day basis.

MacKenzie and Taunton spoke, and the new talkSPORT boss was most accommodating. Instead of saying MacKenzie could use the meeting room as an office, he invited him to remain in his own office for a couple of weeks. In the meantime, Taunton would use the meeting room instead, while he got to grips with his new surroundings.

Amazingly, during those two weeks, MacKenzie strutted around the building as if the UTV takeover was a bad dream. He would still hold management meetings – sometimes with Taunton in the room. Eventually, two weeks had come and gone and MacKenzie was still there. A bemused Taunton went to see the former boss, who told him he wasn't leaving until he had his cheque. He wasn't talking about the cool £7 million that he had collected from the takeover, because that had already been covered. MacKenzie meant getting paid for the notice period to which he was entitled, according to his contract and he also wanted to come to a deal over his company car.

Shortly before the buyout, the company had spent £75,000 on the swanky Mercedes CL500 in which MacKenzie travelled to and from work. He cheekily offered Taunton £15,000 for the car, but the uncompromising Australian businessman refused. He suggested the car was worth £50,000 and MacKenzie could either buy it for that sum or sell it back to the company for the same figure. Begrudgingly, MacKenzie agreed to buy it for that money.

With financial director Keith Sadler, managing director Mike Franklin and MacKenzie's son Ashley, head of sales, all out the door, Taunton was already juggling tricky financial issues without having to deal with trying to evict the former boss from the building. So, having done his best to resolve the outstanding contract and car issues, he marched into MacKenzie's office – which was rightfully his – with a cheque that cleared up all remaining business between them. He handed him the cheque, saying he should now have everything he needed, only for MacKenzie to look up at him with a smirk on his face and say: 'What about my road tax?'

Taunton did his best not to become too wound up by the

situation and calmly said: 'I understand you don't want to leave talkSPORT but, equally, we're done Kelvin. That's it.'

'I told you, I'm not leaving!' replied MacKenzie.

'Look, because you clearly don't want to leave, why don't you ring your press buddies and get them to come downstairs and I'll call the cops and I'll get the cops to escort you from the building? It'll look like you've gone kicking and screaming!' suggested Taunton.

MacKenzie stared at Taunton as the cogs in his ever-sharp and perpetually alert brain turned over and over. He stood up slowly, still holding Taunton's gaze and said: 'Fuck you!'

And with that, MacKenzie walked out of Taunton's office and out of talkSPORT Towers for the last time. It was the end of an era.

But not before the outgoing boss had enjoyed his leaving do, which gave him the chance to say goodbye to his loyal and hardworking staff – not that anyone would have known he felt that way from the memorable rap he performed that night. A collaboration between MacKenzie and Gee's creative team, the hip-hop ditty was a fitting way for the talkSPORT founder to bow out. Lyrics included:

Well, back in the day, back in ninety eight
I bought a big station that wasn't doing great
A million a month they were losing back then
So I changed it to sport – just like ESPN!

It was called talkSPORT – my radio dream
I bolted it together with a motley team

We pick our presenters from the Yellow Pages
Then fire them and re-hire them with cut-down wages

The studios all stink of booze from frequent nightly benders
The production team and tech-ops look like young offenders

Shake my hand once when you meet me first
Don't take it too easy – fear the worst
If I shake your hand twice – ask me what for
I'll be too fucking busy when you're thrown out the door

To the dim-witted chumps who said we couldn't do it
Eat some humble pie; just sit right down and chew it
And if your name is RAJAR – here's my little rhyme
Stick your diaries up where the sun don't shine

Yes, I'm the K-Mac – the big Mac-daddy
You'll get a P45 if I'm not happy
My time at the top hasn't yet expired
So I got you here tonight to tell you 'YOU'RE FIRED!'

talkSPORT staff quickly discovered that Taunton and UTV's approach was quite different to MacKenzie's. When UTV first acquired the company, they weren't quite sure what to make of talkSPORT, which had a reputation for being radio's *enfant terrible*. Some felt it was possible that, having borrowed so much money to fund the deal, they might even consider a quick sale of the national commercial speech station to plough cash back into their local radio operations instead. But, very soon, the Northern Ireland-based company would come to appreciate the station as the jewel in their crown of media outlets.

The initial policy with which Taunton approached talkSPORT was one of consistency, to allow the audience to become familiar with the programming. In the past, drastic changes had been made – there had been no fewer than eight different drivetime shows in the previous two years alone. Taunton would never make changes for the sake of it and believed the talkSPORT audience needed time to build relationships with presenters and programming.

Another policy would be the abandonment of covering the football World Cup or European Championships 'off-tube'. From that point on, those events would be done properly with full accreditation and broadcast rights – or not at all. The days of sound effects and commentators holed up in studios or hotel rooms were over. That way, Taunton believed a much more trusting relationship with listeners and, lucratively, advertisers would be built over time.

All those intentions were fine, but Taunton's first week in the job proved to be anything but straightforward. On his first day, with security tight all over Britain due to the G8 summit in Edinburgh, the station received a phone call saying there was a bomb in the building. talkSPORT Towers had to be immediately evacuated, taking the station temporarily off air. In ten years based in Belfast with UTV, Taunton had never once had to deal with a bomb evacuation. A few days later came the terrible events of 7 July, when London's transport network was attacked by terrorists, leading to the deaths of 52 people. That resulted in talkSPORT switching its sporting agenda to reporting hard news for days.

On the sporting front, the Ashes series was about to get underway and Taunton's beloved Aussies would relinquish the crown they had held for 16 years, leading to much ribbing from the predominantly English talkSPORT staff.

The first major piece of business conducted under the UTV era was the signing of former footballer Rodney Marsh, who agreed to join the station to become the latest and most famous presenter of the drivetime show. The former QPR, Fulham and Manchester City maverick had been working on TV for Sky Sports, but was sacked after making an innocent, but poorly judged, quip about the South-East Asian tsunami of Christmas 2004. After waiting a few months for the dust to settle, Marsh joined talkSPORT. His co-presenter was none other than Paul Breen-Turner, the man with the shortest ever breakfast show tenure in radio history.

On the back of the tsunami incident, Marsh had come to the station with a controversial reputation, but in many ways he was perfect for radio. He was opinionated, passionate and fiercely individual, refusing to follow consensus views on any subject. Of course, while that would make for good radio, it would also mean producers had a tough time in handling a character who had had allowances made for him during his playing career decades earlier.

Breen-Turner had been presenting the drive show for a couple of months with different partners and he was finally awarded a more permanent contract when Marsh arrived and they were paired together. They had met only once before, at a Champions League tie in Barcelona, but they soon hit it off, with Marsh making fun of Breen-Turner for his Spanish lothario personality and Breen-Turner happy to play the foil for his colleague. They also began socialising together after the show, which could only have helped their on-air relationship. Marsh recalled: 'He would send me up and I would send him up. Listeners would love it as we would go round and round about different topics. I just found it very, very funny – it was more entertainment than it was sport.'

The seeds were being sown for drive to rival breakfast in

terms of creating a personality-driven show with Marsh at the helm. However, what the ex-footballer certainly didn't want was for the programme to be a replica of the successful breakfast formula pioneered by Brazil and Parry. He was determined that his programme would be a unique, standalone radio show unlike any other on the station or even across the dial. This was all well and good in theory, but Marsh's tendencies to go off-piste were causing problems.

Encouraged by management to be himself and say exactly what he was feeling, even going into his personal life, Marsh took this as a green light to do exactly as he pleased while on air. Despite having sat through production meetings in which he would agree with the plans for the show, minutes into a programme, Marsh could easily announce to the nation that he wanted to talk about something completely different. This would leave Breen-Turner looking perplexed and often appealing for help to producers in the gallery. With guests having been painstakingly researched and booked to discuss the agreed topic, Breen-Turner and producers would have a job on their hands just trying to steer the show back to the original plan in the face of Marsh's U-turns.

There was something of the child about Marsh, as he used to be amused by foolish things, although occasionally he would come up with something that would leave an entire room roaring with laughter. The production team coined names for Marsh according to his different moods, as they never knew which version would arrive at the office. When Marsh was behaving badly or apathetically he was known as Bubba. When Bubba was sitting in a production meeting, ideas would be run past him and he would dismissively just say 'next!' after each one as if he wasn't interested.

Another side of Marsh was the bored or depressed version who was simply known as Rodney. When Rodney emerged, anything could happen as he was frighteningly honest. Once, Breen-Turner asked him on air if he'd had a good weekend and he replied: 'Well, I was down on the coast this weekend and I thought about suicide again. Ultimately I would have to say I am very depressed right now, Paul, and if there are any psychiatrists or people listening could they call me and give me some advice?'

Breen-Turner would raise his hands to the ceiling and look into the producers' eyes through the glass divider, pleading for assistance as Marsh didn't leave him with many places to go after an outburst like that. Usually, he would have to ignore Marsh, completely change the subject and say something along the lines of how the Aston Villa manager was under increasing pressure according to the papers. This bizarre carry-on between the two presenters was akin to some kind of post-modern scripted comedy, except this was live radio.

When Marsh was in an enthusiastic mood he revealed what producers took to be the third side of his personality, known as Earl. Funny, effusive and keen, Earl was a radio natural, a real raconteur of the airwaves who would reveal anecdote after anecdote to a captivated audience. Sometimes, Earl, Bubba and Rodney might all turn up on the same day. Producers would call Marsh on his way to the studio to run some ideas past him to which he'd respond: 'No, no, no, no!' Then, just an hour or two later, the very same topics would be warmly received with: 'I love it, I love it!'

The listeners loved it too, despite the awkward moments Marsh could provide. Perhaps it was because of those moments. This was a man who could just as easily discuss the battle to avoid relegation from the top flight as he could talk about the time he had to pull a squirrel out of his dog's mouth only for the canine to bite the bushy-tailed rodent's head off.

On a whim, Marsh would tell listeners he'd been to a fantastic chippie the previous night and he wanted to know what their favourite fast food outlets were and within seconds, emails would be flying in hailing The Dragon in Newark for its outstanding chow mein. For Breen-Turner this meant that he could never fully relax on air. Whereas working with Brazil or Parry, he felt in safe hands, with Marsh he never really knew where the show was going next.

Once, Marsh had been over to his co-presenter's flat, where Breen-Turner had been boasting about how he had fobbed the TV licence people off by pretending he didn't live there. On the following day's show, Marsh innocently asked Breen-Turner if he had bought his TV licence yet, and tears of laughter rolled down the ex-footballer's face as he watched his colleague stutter and squirm his way out of trouble.

But, despite this, Breen-Turner relished the challenge as well as Marsh's company and was pleased – if a little surprised – to learn that ratings for the slot had improved. The old Marsh magic was working as was testified by the record 4,500 emails received in the talkSPORT inbox during one particular show.

The undoubted highlight of the pair's first six months broadcasting together was the appearance in the studio of football legend George Best, a good friend of Marsh's. As a well-connected individual, Marsh had made an instant impact at talkSPORT when he managed to attract England cricketer Andrew 'Freddie' Flintoff to the show the day after England's nail-biting two-run win over Australia in the 2005 Ashes. But the Best coup topped that for the sad reason that it was to be the last interview he gave before illness finally took his life just weeks later.

There were only two people about whom Marsh ever spoke highly or with reverence, both ex-footballers. One was England's World Cup winning captain Bobby Moore and the other was Best, his former team-mate at Fulham. With Moore having already passed away, Best was the only living man who Marsh put on a pedestal, so he was understandably delighted and moved when his friend joined him in the studio for an hour. The legend's agent had told Marsh: 'He'll only do it for you Marshy, but he'll do it!'

Previously, talkSPORT's efforts in covering Best's struggle with alcoholism had been tainted by an unfortunate breakfast show phone-in a few years before. Brazil and Parry had asked callers to ring in with their views on whether Best deserved the new liver he had received after a transplant.

'And the best call,' they told listeners, 'will win a crate of John Smith's!'

When he appeared in the talkSPORT Towers car park, the Northern Irishman was a pale shadow of his former self, his face drawn and his skin discoloured. He was met by assistant producer Jon Norman, whose task it was to look after the frail former football genius for the afternoon. Best was carrying two bottles of water with him and, looking unsteady on his feet, Norman instinctively put an arm around the former European Footballer of the Year.

Best's general state was a shock to everybody in the building, as Norman brought him up to the studio floor. Even Marsh was quite taken aback by how much his friend had deteriorated, but he hid his feelings until 15 minutes into the interview when a commercial break was taken and Best started coughing and spluttering. Both Breen-Turner and Marsh suggested they should call time on the interview at that moment, but Best was determined to stick it out and stay on air for his allotted hour. So the three of them continued to discuss Best's playing days and play a song or two while, in between, the Manchester United legend also took calls from listeners, some of whom phoned in to the station in tears.

It was arguably the most moving interview talkSPORT had run up to that point. A terminally ill hero to millions live on air, reflecting on his career and life to one of his closest friends in football in the full knowledge this could well be his final public interview. Indeed, Marsh raised the subject of mortality when he asked Best: 'Sometimes everybody thinks about dying. What would you want people to think of you?'

'I know what they will think,' Best replied. 'They will forget all the rubbish when I'm gone and they will remember the football. It is as simple as that and I don't give a toss about everything else. As long as they remember the football. And if only one person thinks I was the best player in the world that will do for me. Because that's what it was all about as far as I'm concerned.'

Breen-Turner believed Best must have known that he wouldn't get another chance to talk in public again, as he sensed the legend used the interview as a chance to bid farewell to his fans. 'It was upsetting,' the presenter recalled. 'But in a way, I am glad he did it and I am glad he did it with us. Rod had played with him, Rod knew him and we weren't trying to stitch him up. This was giving him a chance to tell his story and, listening back to the interview, it was almost his chance to say goodbye. It was almost as if he knew he wouldn't be doing any more interviews after that one.'

Sadly, that turned out to be the case, as Best was admitted to hospital shortly after his talkSPORT appearance and, in a cruel irony, Norman was the man sent to report on his condition from outside the hospital. In the last few days before Best passed away, Norman would be stationed outside London's Cromwell Hospital from 5.30am until the evening, giving updates on the scene as crowds of well-wishers came to bring flowers and messages of support.

This time, there was no way back for Best and Britain's most talented footballer was never to emerge from hospital. This was massive news across the country, and the globe, but particularly for the station, whose football-mad listeners wanted to have their chance to express their emotions, pay tribute and offer their condolences at the sad news. The station also covered Best's funeral, which was held in Belfast soon after.

As Marsh carried on making himself part of the talkSPORT furniture under the new owners, several other presenters were welcoming the new regime with open arms.

After a number of no-shows, relations between Brazil and The Wireless Group had become increasingly strained and were heading for breaking point until the sudden takeover. Brazil found UTV and Taunton to be more approachable and any problems were quickly ironed out so he could get on with the important business of presenting the breakfast show – and arriving at the studio in time to do so.

There was good news on another front when talkSPORT picked up a rare Sony radio award for Station Sound – a tribute to the dedicated work of Peter Gee and the Creative department for giving the station its unique tone through humorous trails and promos that actively made fun of the presenters.

The station had never been afraid to laugh at itself and the genius of the Creative team was to pick up on talkSPORT's own frailties and translate them into all the trails and sweepers (inserts that are played at the beginning or end of a commercial break) in order to identify with their audience. It was the task of Gee and his troops to write and record trails and introductions for all the shows, as well as conjuring up a consistent image for the station that was present in all its output from breakfast right through to the overnight show.

Since the first days of talkSPORT, Gee and his colleague Jonathan Young constantly pushed the boundaries and made fun of everyone and everything that the station had to offer. On one occasion in the early days, the team had attempted to record a trail with breakfast presenter Gary Newbon, who told them he was up for anything and that they shouldn't worry about making fun of him.

Halfway through recording a version of the hip-hop classic 'Rapper's Delight' that had been written especially for him to promote the show – hip-hop had been chosen for its ironic value, as Newbon was possibly the person least connected with that musical genre in Britain – the presenter decided he didn't like the trail at all:

'I said a hip hop, a hippy to the hippy to the hip hip hop. You don't stop? It didn't say this in my bloody contract when I joined bloody talkSPORT mate.

'You take it to the bang bang boogle. Is that it? What's all that about? Yeah, I don't want to do that. I'll do a lot of things but I ain't doing that.'

At that point, Newbon had had enough and left Creative's studio, thinking that was the end of the matter and they would have to come up with something else for him. Yet, Gee was delighted with this half-finished version and simply made the trail using all Newbon's protestations for added humour value and the jingle went to air to the amusement of millions of listeners.

But Newbon, who drove a Rolls-Royce with the number plate GN1, was absolutely furious. Looking back on the incident, he said: 'I've never been prepared to lower my standards for the sake of a gimmick. I have got a vague recollection of it and I thought "I'm not going to do this, that's not what I'm here for." I don't see why I should prostitute my career for something I didn't believe in.'

Newbon phoned Parry, who was in the middle of one of his stints as programme director, and told him he was resigning in protest at the trail and the way it made fun of him. Parry immediately went up to see the Creative mob and told them the jingle had to be taken off air immediately, as Newbon was up in arms about it. Gee duly obliged and removed the trail from the schedule. Three hours later, MacKenzie was on the phone to Gee: 'Why's that trail gone?'

'Oh, Mike called us and told us to take it off the air.'

'Fucking put it back on!'

'OK, but the thing is, Gary is quite upset about it.'

'Fucking great! Job done!'

Gee had no choice but to put the trail back into the schedule. The early station messaging was often self-deprecating, with jingles celebrating the fact that talkSPORT had no rights to cover football, but did it anyway with 'knocked off commentary, watched on a stolen telly that was jacked up in the corner of the studio'.

During his time in charge, MacKenzie would always back his

Creative team over their more controversial ditties, encouraging their anarchic spirit. Gee and the gang knew how blokes inter-acted in social situations. They engaged in banter, never passing up an opportunity to take the piss out of each other, find a weakness in their friends and then bring it up time and again. And that's exactly how they would trail all the presenters – by mercilessly ribbing them.

Brazil would always get it in the neck for being a *bon viveur* and tardy type of bloke; Durham would be the ginger, annoy-ing bloke; Parry would be the short-arse, annoying bloke; and Whale would be the bald bloke.

MacKenzie held a special candle for the Creative team, per-suading them to push their piss-taking to the limits, occasionally stepping way overboard in the process. When they came up with 'Brazil the Red Nosed Reindeer' after the Cheltenham fiasco, MacKenzie insisted that the line 'snoring in a layby – pissed' should be included and played on the radio. Gee and Young – who by then had also been joined by Liz Brace – thought the line had been crossed and replaced the word 'pissed' with the sound of a can opening, so it was reminiscent of a 'swish' noise.

When he heard it again, the boss demanded to know why the words had been changed and they explained that they just couldn't swear on a trail that would be going on air during the day.

'*I* will tell you what you can do. It goes back in,' were MacKenzie's final words on the subject.

The former boss often dreamed up new themes for the sta-tion's promotional output. One afternoon in talkSPORT's early days, Young received a phone call summoning him to see MacKenzie. Things took a turn for the bizarre when he entered the latter's office and noticed a Roman shield propped up against the sofa. As he walked around the corner to MacKenzie's desk, Young was baffled to see him leaning over his computer dressed in a full Roman gladiator's outfit.

'Tell you what, *Gladiator* – have you seen it?' asked MacKenzie. 'Saw it last night. Bloody brilliant film.'

It turned out that the previous evening, MacKenzie had been interviewed and photographed for the *Financial Times* supplement. Instead of a straightforward picture, he had decided to dress up as Russell Crowe from the Hollywood blockbuster, with the concept being that he was scything through the radio industry. He was so enamoured with the idea that he had donned the outfit at work, after deciding that all talkSPORT promotional output should now be themed around the film. Young, breathing a sigh of relief that he wasn't about to be scythed himself, returned to his desk to begin work on rewriting all the station's sound and imaging.

Away from Russell Crowe and *Gladiator*, as the star of the station, Brazil would normally attract most of the mickey-taking on Creative's trails – and he did himself no favours with his antics and dodgy timekeeping. Writing his trails was like having a ball in front of an open goal that Gee couldn't fail to stick away into an unguarded net.

One night, Gee and Brazil were holed up in a local boozer and in a moment of guilt, Gee said: 'Alan, you know we are only taking the piss and if you ever have a problem ...' but before Gee could even finish his sentence, Brazil interrupted: 'If I have ever got a fucking problem, I will come and kick your fucking door down!'

What helped Gee and Young immensely was, strangely, their dispassion for all things sport. That might sound unusual for a dedicated sports radio station, but it worked because it meant that trails were more likely to pick up on the humorous side of sport than the geeky, anorak or statistical approach. And it worked so well because talkSPORT could never compete with the BBC in terms of resources or rights, but they could more than match their rivals in the entertainment and fun stakes.

The best example of this jovial approach came through all the station announcements and introductions for which Creative used the same voiceover artist, who became known as Mr talkSPORT simply because his voice was synonymous with the station.

He was Steven Hartley, an actor who has previously appeared in several films as well as *EastEnders* and *The Bill*. He was soon contributing ideas of his own and adding to scripts that Gee had written. Hartley was chosen as he was very much like 'the bloke in the pub that you don't know, but if you wanted an ideal bloke in the pub it was him,' according to Gee. His character was smart and witty, but he was also as hard as nails so people kept their distance. Hartley perfected this persona to a tee so much that Gee actually received an email asking who Hartley was and that he sounded like a bouncer standing on the door of a nightclub. 'I knew then we had the right person for the station image,' said Gee.

It was Hartley who voiced the legendary sweepers that are still being updated to this very day. Before returning to a programme, listeners would hear Hartley's voice say something like: 'talkSPORT: the radio station which puts its speeding points on its wife's licence!'

And these little gems could also be topical, such as the listeners' firm favourite: 'talkSPORT: the radio station which didn't go and see *Brokeback Mountain*!'

These sweepers helped to give the station an identity, almost breathing life into it and giving it a character. This personification of talkSPORT was extended further in the sweepers in which Hartley would add his own little comments: 'talkSPORT: the radio station which wonders why you don't get bras that open at the front!' That would have sufficed, but Hartley then offered: 'That would've saved me a lot of hassle over the years.'

The actor would regularly be recognised in public places – not by his face but from his voice: 'When I'm in the back of a cab, drivers always say to me "Oh, you're the bloke off talkSPORT." It happens a lot,' he said.

Hartley's social life even helped shape the personification of the radio station when the stories he would tell Gee and the team about the south-east London pub where he drank would make it to air on trails. The pub was full of characters and villains and, after chatting with Hartley one day, the team came up with another classic sweeper: 'talkSPORT: the radio station that's storing a couple of things in the garage for its mate Danny down the pub!'

Hartley would never be afraid to add his own sense of humour to any trails he was voicing and, as soon as Marsh joined the station, he decided to have some fun: 'Every time I used to say Rodney Marsh, I used to say it as if I was Del-boy so I said "Rod-er-nee" and it used to drive Rodney Marsh round the fucking twist!'

Marsh regularly complained to Gee that his name was being mispronounced but, until the day he would eventually leave the station, the ex-footballer's name was always broadcast as Rod-er-nee in every talkSPORT trail – all thanks to Hartley.

The Sony silver award for talkSPORT's Creative department was richly deserved. Not only because of the superb work this small team had done in setting the tone of the station, but also because commercial radio stations found Sony awards extremely hard to come by.

With the wealth of the resources available to the BBC, their stations traditionally dominated the Sony gongs, yet the Creative team excelled themselves, leaving the judges with no choice. It was the start of a rich spell of recognition for the department, which scooped two Sony silvers and a bronze in three consecutive years, helping to put talkSPORT firmly on the map.

This unconventional, bastard child of a radio station was here to stay and, under new owners, the future was looking brighter than ever before.

11

Hi-Jinks in Oz and Terror In the UK

I think I came off air at 10pm. I felt stunned and astonished. I remember standing at the bar at whatever hotel I was in, watching the telly and thinking to myself 'The world will never be the same again.'

MIKE PARRY

Alan Brazil perched on a seat in the shade as he soaked up the sounds and smells of Melbourne's Yarra Valley wine region. He was in Domaine Chandon, founded by the world-famous French champagne house, and as he protected himself from the heat of the early afternoon sun, he breathed in a smell he would never forget. The Shiraz grapes were being pressed and the scent invaded Brazil's nostrils, giving him one of the most pleasant sensory experiences of his life. He swigged, he spat and he swallowed – he was in vineyard heaven.

Hours later, Brazil was back in the studio with just minutes to go until his breakfast show was due to go on air. It was 4pm local time and talkSPORT were in Melbourne for the 2006

Commonwealth Games, only this time the tables had been turned. Where was his co-presenter Graham 'Beeky' Beecroft?

The talkSPORT team had visited the vineyard before the day's show and normally, Brazil would have been the odds-on favourite to be the biggest casualty, with Beeky impatiently waiting in the studio for *him*. As the clock ticked towards the hour, there was still no sign of Beeky. Brazil was relishing the moment, after almost two years of being lectured about his timekeeping by his colleague.

This was payback time for the veteran of too many Cheltenhams and Open golf championships to mention. At least, it would have been revenge until Beeky, who had disappeared for a sleep after making a drowsy return from Yarra Valley, turned up at the very last moment to take his seat in the studio. Brazil had to admire his style, having so often parked his own behind on the studio chair with seconds remaining – or even seconds too late.

The show began and another day had dawned for talkSPORT's millions of listeners back in the UK, who were becoming accustomed to hearing their favourite programmes coming from a whole host of new locations under the new owners.

Brazil's reputation for enjoying a party was just as well known to the new management regime as it had been to the old, but an element of trust had now been established. That was the theory, but Brazil never worked in theory. He was always more of a practice kind of man.

The Melbourne trip hadn't started auspiciously for the Scot, who had managed to miss his flight to Australia from Heathrow. The Games started soon after the Cheltenham festival, so when Beeky left the Gloucestershire course after the Gold Cup, he went straight to Heathrow airport for a flight on which he and Brazil had both been booked. But he made the long trip Down Under alone because Brazil had been 'held up' at Cheltenham. Eventually, new flights had to be arranged for the Scot and he managed to join up with the rest of the team in time for the first Melbourne show a couple of days later.

Broadcasting the breakfast show from 4-8pm suited Brazil far better than the unearthly hours at which he had to go on air while in London. Breakfast sports newsreader Ian Abrahams – or The Moose – had also joined the team in Melbourne to report on the Commonwealth Games. Just like Beeky and Porky before him, Abrahams' nickname had stuck firmly, and Brazil had created another character for his show. The Moose was a relentless target of on-air ridicule by Brazil, who would often throw pens, scrunched-up paper or anything else he could find at him while he was reading the sports news.

The nickname had come about a few years earlier when Brazil had arrived for a show to be greeted by a wildly enthusiastic Abrahams, talking about the previous night's football. Always bouncy in the early hours, Abrahams buzzed around Brazil's head like an errant wasp, repeatedly asking him if he had seen the match and what he had made of it. Brazil, a little surly at that time of the morning, asked Abrahams to leave him alone. Pretty soon, he was telling him where to go in stronger language and when Abrahams would not relent, Brazil finally snapped: 'Will you just fuck off? And do you know what, you look like a moose!'

Abrahams thought nothing of it, fully used to being in Brazil's firing line every morning, and when he went into the studio to read the 6.30am bulletin (he also read the news back then) he greeted Brazil during an ad break, but the presenter offered nothing in response. The red studio light went on and Brazil looked up and said: 'It's 6.30 and here with the news headlines is The Moose.' Abrahams looked at him and Brazil held his gaze. The Moose realised he had no choice but to read the news and sport and deal with the consequences of being called The Moose later. The following hour also saw him introduced as The Moose and on it went. Brazil had given birth to The Moose that morning and there was to be no stopping his creation.

From that point, Ian Abrahams ceased to exist. He was referred to as The Moose every time he was on air, whether he was reading the news or reporting from a match. And listeners loved it too. When Abrahams was seen out and about with his talkSPORT microphone, people would immediately recognise his voice: 'You're The Moose!' was the most common phrase he would hear wherever he went.

Building on the personality and character that had been created, The Moose was sent out to add colour to sporting events and never failed to make an impact on air – although sometimes the impact was made on him.

Once, reporting from a meeting at Lingfield racecourse, Moose was interviewing *Soccer AM* presenter Helen Chamberlain, a feisty character who was never afraid to give as good as she got. She was attempting to make a few wisecracks during the interview, but The Moose consistently interrupted every single joke because the conversation wasn't going the way he wanted. But he had bitten off way more than he could chew, as Chamberlain thumped him live on air, to his and the listeners' amazement.

The Moose was also quick to make his mark in Melbourne. While setting up a live report from the city, he chose a picturesque park in front of one of the area's top hotel/casinos where security was always tight. The Moose took out his satellite link, a weird-looking contraption with wires emerging from it, and placed it on a wall overlooking a river. With just moments to go until he was on air, Moose was approached by two policemen who wanted to know what he was doing and, more importantly, what this worrying looking gadget was. Moose quickly explained who he was and that he was about to go live to London, but the policemen looked at him dubiously and requested to see some identification.

Unfortunately, Moose's wallet was in the safe in his hotel room and when he was asked which hotel he was in, he drew a rather untimely blank and could only tell the police that it was an old building with an indoor swimming pool. With their suspicions well and truly aroused, the coppers radioed back to their superiors and were told to keep an eye on The Moose, who invited them to stay and watch his broadcast, although not to stand too close as it might put him off.

Whether they thought he was a madman who spent the next five minutes talking to himself or believed he really was The Moose, the Aussie police left talkSPORT's finest to it as they must have decided he was not a major security threat after all.

Of course, the reason why Moose was setting up his equipment in the middle of a park was because, despite their presence in Melbourne, talkSPORT still had no accreditation to be inside the stadium that was hosting the Commonwealth Games track and field events. The closest that the talkSPORT team got to any of the action was a boat trip along the River Yarra, which took them past the stadium. The women's marathon frontrunners sped past Beeky one morning, but that was as good as it got.

A few months later, the breakfast show team were back in Australia, this time for the start of England's winter Ashes tour. With the first Test being staged in Brisbane and the flagship show sponsored by Gold Coast tourism, two and two were quickly added together and a week of shows live from Australia's east coast was arranged.

There was still a fair amount of paranoia about Brazil, with the main concern being that he would enjoy himself a little bit too much before the programme's 4pm start. To that end, assistant programme director Steve Hodge was sent out to oversee the outside broadcast and he spent most of his time stalking the station's breakfast star. Brazil, who was given a chauffeur-driven limousine for the duration of the trip, would take the car out to other hotels, bars and restaurants to wile away the hours before the show. As if by complete coincidence, Hodge would walk in to whichever hotel bar Brazil had found and say something like: 'Fancy seeing you here, Al?' before discussing that day's show with the presenter.

Day trips were also organised in an attempt to keep Brazil and trouble as far away from each other as possible. The team went surfing one morning but Brazil decided he was better off as a spectator; while, on another trip, Beeky learned how to play the didgeridoo. But Hodge needn't have worried too much as Brazil was accompanied to the Gold Coast by his wife and youngest daughter, meaning he was far less likely to go walkabout and the trip was a great success.

A year earlier, Brazil, Beeky and The Moose had travelled halfway across the world to broadcast from Singapore ahead of the International Olympic Committee's announcement on which city would be hosting the 2012 Games. With London one of the favourites alongside Paris, the station decided to base the breakfast show in the Far East to capture the excitement and drama of the IOC's decision.

The differences between Brazil and Beeky were never more obvious than on their first-class flight over to Singapore, which the Scot hailed as his best ever travelling experience. Shortly into the journey, Beeky disappeared into the toilets and emerged with his pyjamas on – bright blue overalls which made him look like a Kwik Fit mechanic. Brazil asked him what he was playing at and Beeky announced his intentions to eat his dinner then go to sleep for the rest of the flight. An incredulous Brazil, who was already supping a glass from his first bottle of champagne, said: 'What? This is first class! Look at the movie channel, there are over 500 movies. There's Dom Perignon from the bar. You're having a laugh!'

So Beeky and Brazil tucked into their starters of smoked salmon and prawns before indulging in steaks and a magnificent cheesecake for dessert. Before long, Beeky said good night to Brazil and spent the rest of the journey fast asleep in the comfort of his first-class bed. Brazil was appalled and beckoned a stewardess over to him: 'If you see me dozing, please will you wake me up?' asked the Scot.

'Why?'

'I'll tell you why. Dom Perignon and all those movies!'

Brazil had started that particular trip exactly as he had intended it to go on, and the Dom Perignon on the plane was soon replaced by Singapore Slings on the sun loungers alongside the hotel swimming pool. Very much a man of travel and culture, Brazil's philosophy in life was to always adopt a 'When in Rome . . .' approach, especially when it came to alcohol. So what else could he have possibly poured down his gullet while he was in the country? On the first day sitting by the hotel pool, he tipped his panama hat in the direction of the waiter, who immediately rushed over to his sun bed: 'I would like two Singapore Slings . . .'

'OK, no problem,' said the waiter.

'. . . every half an hour,' continued Brazil.

The waiter looked confused, so Brazil had to spell it out to him again in no uncertain terms. Beeky would never forget the look on the waiter's face: 'The waiter had never heard anything like it. He headed towards the bar staring at his pad and scratching his head. Al just chuckled and leant back on his sunbed!'

The waiter had certainly not come across anybody like talkSPORT's breakfast show presenter before, and the Singapore Slings just kept coming and coming. Brazil soon tired of the gin and cherry brandy cocktails, however, and he was back to one of his more traditional tipples on the flight home, when he managed to consume so much red wine that the Singapore Airlines flight ran out.

Due to the time difference in the Far East, the show was on air between 1pm and 5pm local time, which certainly gave the team enough time to go out and sample all the local entertainment before sleeping off any hangovers the following day. The studio was set up in producer Matt Smith's room and Brazil made sure the hotel manager was on side for the duration of their stay and understood their needs. Those needs included several cans of beer delivered to the studio from 1pm every day. Brazil would regularly double the amount of cans he had asked for the previous day and by the time he was broadcasting the final show of the trip, ten cans of Heineken had joined him in the studio with Beeky.

After the shows, a few glasses of wine were enjoyed in the hotel bar before the gang headed out to sample the local nightlife. On one evening, some of them visited the infamous Orchard Towers to see what all the fuss was about. A four-storey building that was a shopping arcade by day, turned into a bar and nightclub haven at night in which hundreds of women paraded around wearing as little as possible. This earned the place the unforgettable nickname 'Four Floors of Whores'.

The party continued once the Olympic decision had been announced and London was awarded the Games. Brazil was on full throttle, making fun of the French for missing out and letting all the listeners know what a good time they were all having in 'Steamy' Singapore as he had decided to christen it. At least one member of talkSPORT's breakfast crew managed to gatecrash the London bid team's official victory party that night.

But tragically, the jovial atmosphere was suddenly soured by the 7 July London bombings, which resulted in the outside broadcast being taken off air so that the latest news could be reported from the multiple terrorist attacks that had struck the capital back home. The station's normal daily output was completely overhauled and replaced by constantly updated breaking news about the bombings with reporters sent all over the capital to bring listeners the latest information. talkSPORT had suddenly become talkNEWS, but the switch was necessary given the terribly sad events of that day.

What the 7 July bombings taught talkSPORT staff and listeners was that here was a radio station that was far more than a blokes' football phone-in channel, frequented by ex-professional footballers. Programme director Bill Ridley took control of the situation. As an ex-newspaper editor with decades of experience working in the UK and the USA, Ridley was the perfect person to oversee the 24-hour breaking news operation that followed.

From the moment that Ian Collins, who was presenting the 10am-1pm show, had come to see him to discuss what was initially reported as power surges on several London Underground lines, Ridley was a calm presence, directing operations as the production floor became a newsroom.

Ridley ensured that reporters were sent out to each public transport location where bombs had gone off. Producers, set-up staff and others stepped up to the plate to cover the atrocities, due to the difficulty of contacting people as mobile phone networks were inefficient after the bombs.

Jon Norman had arrived at work on a friend's bicycle and he was soon sent straight back out on it to the scene of the Liverpool Street attack before heading on to Russell Square to report on the bus bombings there. Other reporters were sent out on hired bikes, while those who hadn't yet made it into work were diverted straight to the incident locations rather than struggling in to the office with the whole transport network having been shut down.

As the full scale of the horrors emerged, Collins, Whale, Parry, Durham and, later, Collins again performed heroically behind the studio microphones. They updated the nation on exactly what was happening, took calls from concerned listeners and spoke to expert guests who had been lined up via the superb contacts books of production staff.

There was a rawness about talkSPORT's 7/7 coverage. Tuning in made listeners part of something compelling and it was very hard to switch off, particularly with so many different developing stories. With the two regular current affairs slots (in the morning and from 10pm-6am), the station was easily able to swap its sports cap for its news hat. And with everybody mucking in, as has always been the talkSPORT way, the coverage was a match for anything else that was on the airwaves that fateful day.

The station may not have had hundreds of staff at its disposal like the BBC, but the extraordinary collective effort from a small but dedicated and talented editorial staff meant that, once again, talkSPORT was punching way above its weight. As all other regular sports shows were cancelled, each team of producers and their assistants were able to assist the ongoing breaking news show that stayed on air long into the following day. By the time the coverage had gone right around the clock twice, talkSPORT had truly come of age.

It was a very similar set of circumstances to four years earlier when the 11 September attacks on the USA changed the world and also matured talkSPORT more than any other event beforehand. The difference between the two was that the London bombings happened on the station's doorstep, whereas with 9/11 the station was totally dependent on television screens in the studio to help keep listeners updated.

Within minutes, talkSPORT switched from its afternoon show to take the Sky News audio feed, while Parry raced around the office, trying to line up terrorism experts and preparing to go on air himself. Shortly after, Parry took to the airwaves to update talkSPORT listeners on an amazing and tragic story that seemed to go far beyond the realms of possibility. Using his intimate knowledge of New York and Washington, Parry was able to describe what was happening to captivated listeners.

The programme director stayed on air until 10pm, despite having started his day in the office at 4am to prepare for the breakfast show. And, after a night in a nearby hotel, he was back on air for breakfast the following morning when the 9/11 coverage rolled on. In those days, with the station still treading on uncertain ground and fighting to make an impact, this was groundbreaking radio that had a dramatic impact on how talkSPORT was perceived.

With the knowledge and confidence that they could handle the biggest breaking news stories, the station was never afraid to cancel regular programming and enter a live news format – but this was talkSPORT and sometimes they just got it wrong.

On one occasion, a couple of years after the Asian tsunami which claimed hundreds of thousands of lives, reports had been coming in on the wires that a new monster wave was heading for a remote Japanese port. Following an earthquake that had measured 8.1 on the Richter Scale in the nearby Kuril Islands, mainland Japan was now supposedly under threat from waves which were forecast to be up to two metres high.

Sky News had gone into overdrive on the possibility of another Asian tsunami, with reporters stationed in Japan and regular pictures of the coastline that was preparing to bear the brunt of the battering. Taking a lead from the 24-hour news channel, talkSPORT decided to stop normal programming and go into full breaking news mode, which meant Hawksbee and Jacobs suddenly became Hawksbee and Parry.

The waves began to crash into Nemuro port on Hokkaido island, but the TV pictures showed that what had been forecast to be a tsunami looked a great deal more like the tide coming in at Whitley Bay. Nevertheless, Parry decided to make the incident as dramatic as possible, describing how these ferocious six-feet waves were battering Japan when, all the time, the TV pictures were not doing Porky's account justice.

As Jacobs strolled around the production floor wondering why on earth he wasn't on air with Hawksbee broadcasting their normal show, the listeners, who were also watching the telly, were quick to point out to the station that this was no tsunami. Among the comments on the emails that were sent in were 'I've seen bigger waves in my cup of tea!' and 'The soup I had for my lunch is more ferocious than that!'

'It was ridiculous, really,' recalled Jacobs. 'This particular day, Bill Ridley completely overreacted to what turned out to be, basically, a wave!'

It wasn't long before Jacobs had returned to his rightful place in the studio alongside Hawksbee and normal programming had been resumed. This was clearly a story that would make as little impact on the world as those waves had on the Japanese port.

Thankfully, after the horrors of the London bombings, it was one of those rare occasions when talkSPORT would have been glad a potentially tragic story turned out to be a red herring.

12

The Truth Behind the Beckham and Tyson Exclusives

A guy kept popping his head in between us, making sure the questions were OK. They were all dressed like New York mafia. I was a little bit on edge; I found them very intimidating.

RODNEY MARSH

When the station wasn't dealing with breaking news, talkSPORT could sometimes make the news instead – especially when huge names from the sporting world appeared on-air as guests.

In the last decade, there has been no bigger sporting name than the former England football captain David Beckham, and he has appeared on the station a number of times. Once, when Adrian Durham was sent out to La Manga to cover an England training camp, the presenter managed to secure some exclusive time with Beckham. But best of all was in October 2005, when Beckham was a guest on Mike Parry and Andy Townsend's *Weekend Sports Breakfast* show one Sunday morning. The day before, Beckham had been sent off for England at Old Trafford, but his team-mates had still held on to beat Austria 1-0 and qualify for the following summer's World Cup finals in Germany. Porky was straight on the phone to the FA, requesting an interview with the England skipper for the next morning's show.

With Beckham staying under the Football Association's jurisdiction only until he was due to leave the England squad after breakfast on Sunday, it was crucial that the FA could ask him to do the interview before he left Manchester's Lowry Hotel. Parry received a call in the early hours of Sunday morning confirming that Beckham would do the interview, although he had gone above and beyond what was required by agreeing to speak to talkSPORT after he had left the England squad.

Later that morning, Beckham was driving his family down the motorway from Manchester to their Beckingham Palace home in Sawbridgeworth, Hertfordshire. Victoria, or 'Posh', was in the front seat alongside him, while Brooklyn, Romeo and Cruz were in the back of the silver Bentley. At the appointed time, Beckham pulled in to a service station car park, got out of the car and, while leaning on the roof, called talkSPORT on the number with which Parry had supplied the FA.

Naturally, Porky and Townsend were delighted to welcome the England captain onto their show and equally excited at the effort he had gone to for the station and the listeners. Aware that talkSPORT was known as the listening choice for many of England's dedicated, loyal and long-suffering fans, Beckham made the most of the opportunity. He paid tribute to the national team's supporters, thanking them for their efforts and saying England couldn't have reached the World Cup without them. In all, he was on air for 15 minutes, and the interview was picked up by many other media outlets, helping the station to some free publicity at the same time.

If Beckham was the biggest name of the last decade, then controversial former boxer Mike Tyson must have been one of the world's most infamous sportsmen of the last 25 years. His appearance at talkSPORT Towers as a guest on Rodney Marsh and Paul Breen-Turner's drivetime show in November 2005 is still talked about in the office to this very day, due to its bizarre nature and the chaos surrounding it.

It all began when the station received a phone call from a south London promoter who purported to be behind a series of UK speaking engagements featuring Tyson. He wanted Tyson to make an appearance on talkSPORT to help publicise these talks and, naturally, the station were all for it. However, with arrangements still uncertain and senior management dubious about whether the interview would ever happen, it was decided not to advertise or trail the Tyson appearance, just in case.

The day before the scheduled interview, station staff were informed that Tyson was still happy to come to the studios, but that before the show he wanted to eat in the swanky Oxo Tower restaurant nearby. This wouldn't have been a problem but for the fact that Tyson wanted to eat at 4pm – before going on the show – at which time the restaurant would have been closed. Fortunately, Breen-Turner happened to know the restaurant's chef fairly well and stepped in to convince his friend to open the dining room especially for Tyson.

The following day, Tyson, accompanied by a formidable entourage of 15 burly minders and associates all dressed in dark suits with dark shirts, arrived at the Oxo Tower as arranged. A waiter showed them to their very large table in the otherwise deserted restaurant and asked Tyson what he wanted to eat, handing him a menu.

The former boxer barely glanced at the menu before requesting a bowl of spaghetti with a steak in the middle. When the chef heard what Tyson had ordered, he threw a Gordon Ramsay-style strop and refused even to entertain the idea of preparing such a monstrosity of a dish in his kitchen. Eventually, after carefully worded, diplomatic negotiations between the waiter, the chef and the restaurant's management, one of the finest bowls of spaghetti and steak in culinary history was put before Tyson.

At this point, Jon Norman arrived at the restaurant as, just as when Best came to talkSPORT, he had been assigned the duties of looking after Tyson and bringing him to the studios – although when he walked in and saw the rugby team of minders and a scantily clad, young blonde he did wonder if Tyson really needed looking after.

The strange entourage was made up of American friends of the former boxer, several former fighters who had moved into security – including three Irishmen with whom Norman struck up some conversation – a few other hangers-on and the girl, who was none other than Aisleyne Horgan-Wallace, soon to find fame in the 2006 series of *Big Brother*. Norman, like everyone else, had no idea who she was at the time, but she and Tyson seemed to be an item, although they barely spoke. Norman joined the ex-fighter's table and faced an uncomfortable half-hour as Tyson chomped down his steak à la spaghetti.

The former world heavyweight champion finally finished his meal and, almost as one, the entire crew rose to leave the restaurant and headed to the lifts. The Irish minders beckoned Norman into the lift with Tyson and Horgan-Wallace, on the grounds that he knew where he was going, and they were joined by another two security men as well as an American friend of

Tyson's, who appeared to be carrying a gun – or 'packing' as it's known on the streets.

The lift doors closed, Tyson started snogging the face off Horgan-Wallace while the American who was 'packing' turned to look at Norman and asked him who he was. Norman replied that he was Jon from talkSPORT.

'Oh yeah!' said the American, who turned to Tyson and added: 'Hey Mike! This is the guy I was telling you about. He has been badmouthing you all through the meal!'

Silence filled the lift. Tyson stopped kissing the blonde and fixed a wild-eyed gaze on Norman, who remembered seeing his life flashing before his eyes: 'I knew he was joking,' said Norman. 'But I just made this sound, kind of laugh, kind of fear, not really knowing what to do. And Tyson looked like he had been on the old beta-blockers or Valium.' Luckily, the lift doors opened not a minute too soon for Norman.

As Norman was about to lead the entourage to talkSPORT Towers, a security guard told him: 'If any gangsters turn up, if they have got guns, if there are any problems, leave it to us.' There were no gangsters and soon enough, Norman was in the talkSPORT lift with Tyson and Horgan-Wallace. Despite not exchanging a word at any time, the pair began hungrily eating each other's faces again – the boxer and the blonde that is.

Eventually, Norman led Tyson, the blonde and the 15 minders onto the production floor. This was the biggest entourage seen at talkSPORT since Abu Hamza had been a guest on Whale's show – the boxer wasn't in great company there – and the whole office came to a standstill.

Love him or hate him, Tyson generated a reaction that few other sportsmen can match and there was pandemonium in the studios as the guests made themselves at home. Mobile phones were ringing, huge, muscle-bound men were pacing up and down while a tattoo-faced former boxer surveyed the scene before him.

Tyson was shown into the studio to meet Breen-Turner and Marsh, but there was no way he was going in there alone. No fewer than six minders accompanied him, immediately causing the presenters to panic. They were going to have to interview the former boxer under the noses of his bodyguards.

Two burly men stood behind each presenter while the other two paced up and down on the squeaky studio floorboards, sometimes talking into mobile phones. In these circumstances, it was never going to be award-winning radio and Breen-Turner admitted afterwards how intimidated he and Marsh had felt: 'I had two bodyguards on me who were about 6ft 8in each and Rod had two on his side, and then we had Tyson in the middle,' recalled Breen-Turner. 'I remember thinking to myself "He could probably deal with Rod and me on his own, he doesn't need these bruisers with him." It was the most ridiculous thing you have ever seen. And it was a difficult interview. Rod didn't like it; it was the only time I have really seen him appearing to be a little intimidated.'

Tyson was no more than two feet away from Marsh, yet every time the former footballer asked him a question, a minder managed to get his head into the space between them to eyeball Marsh and put him even further on edge.

To his credit, Breen-Turner still asked Tyson about the incident in which he had bitten a chunk out of Evander Holyfield's ear during a world title fight, despite the death looks coming from the security men. Marsh, a big fight fan, discussed boxers of old with Tyson and was surprised how well Iron Mike knew his history, including all the boxers' nicknames.

With all the background noise from the minders' pacing and

snarling, this was the best the drivetime pairing could have done and the spectacle was soon over, but not before Tyson had posed for photos with Breen-Turner and Marsh. All that time, Horgan-Wallace had been sitting alone on one of the production floor sofas. But she was soon back in action as she had to return to the ground floor in the lift with Tyson and Norman, who would never forget that afternoon: 'It was a bizarre episode, the most surreal day I have ever had.'

The only other person to have come close to matching Tyson for an entourage – apart from Abu Hamza – was Don King, the smooth-talking, flamboyant boxing promoter. His arrival with four cars caused the street outside the studios to be closed. Another former world heavyweight champion to grace the talkSPORT studios was George Foreman. This time, there was no entourage and certainly no snogging in the lifts with a future *Big Brother* contestant. Foreman appeared on the Hawksbee and Jacobs show, ostensibly to promote the range of cooking grills that carried his name.

H&J decided it would be a good idea to use the grills in the studio to cook some steaks, so they covered up the smoke alarms (something that Whale had failed to do when cooking a fry-up in the studio) and duly shared some fine meat and boxing chat with Foreman. The following year, the former boxer returned to talkSPORT Towers as he was promoting his brand new 'Lean Mean Boiling Machine'. Hoping for a repeat of the previous year's meal and chat with Foreman, Jacobs turned up for the show with some dumplings that had been specially prepared by his Chinese daughter-in-law. The idea was to steam them in Foreman's new machine. However, as it turned out, the 'Lean Mean Boiling Machine' was just a glorified kettle and the dumplings went uneaten.

Foreman was one of a series of top names to appear on the Hawksbee & Jacobs show – the stability of the squeaky studio chairs was once tested by 22-stone eighties American footballer William 'The Fridge' Perry.

Sir Garfield – or Garry to his friends – Sobers once joined the pair in the studio to talk cricket. Jacobs had perfected his Sobers impression, featuring the casual strut and the collar up, to a tee and as the legend was leaving the studio, the presenter followed behind, mimicking him perfectly. At that moment, sensing something was up, Sobers turned around and just caught sight of what Jacobs was doing, much to everyone's amusement.

Before that, Brian Clough was possibly H&J's biggest guest. During a commercial break, the legendary manager started to tell them a story about a European away match. Half way through the anecdote, the show came back on air again, but Hawksbee just let Clough continue with the tale rather than interrupt him.

Completely unaware that he was talking live to the nation, Clough continued: 'So I turned round and I said to that fella "You can fuck off!"' Luckily, Hawksbee was able to use the 'dump' button which meant listeners wouldn't have heard Clough's aberration (talkSPORT operates on a seven-second delay and the dump button is regularly used to ensure callers are instantly edited if they swear or say anything inappropriate).

If Beckham was football's legend and Tyson was boxing's biggest name then, apart from Tiger Woods, there is no bigger star in the world of golf than Jack Nicklaus, the winner of a record 18 major titles. Thanks to the sterling efforts of correspondent Bob Bubka, who was watching the action at the 2005 Open from St Andrews, Nicklaus was also interviewed live on talkSPORT.

It was the second day of the Open and the golfing legend was playing his last ever competitive round in the great championship that he had won three times. As he walked up to the 18th green, some 50,000 people lined both sides of the fairway in unprecedented, emotional scenes. Bubka was waiting on the edge of the green and commentated as 65-year-old Nicklaus signed off in style with a birdie.

As the golfing great made his way through the crowds, Bubka quickly interviewed Nicklaus's wife, son and then finally, the legend himself – all live on talkSPORT. It was a magnificent few minutes of broadcasting that really captured the sentiment of the occasion and showed how far the station had come.

Another big name to grace the airwaves was Sir Alan Sugar. The entrepreneur had arrived at talkSPORT Towers looking rather dapper one afternoon. It was the start of the first-ever UK series of *The Apprentice* and Sugar was there to publicise his show. Perched on a sofa waiting patiently to be called into the studio, Sugar's arrival had coincided with a rather unfortunate incident in the infamous talkSPORT kitchen.

Normally frequented by mice, rats and most other living parasites, the kitchen that afternoon was also playing host to a large pile of dog sick as Brandy, current affairs producer Sean Dilley's guide dog, had managed to vomit all over its floor.

With the kitchen opposite the sofa on which Sugar was sitting, he only had to look to his right to survey the carnage. At that moment, a production assistant approached Sugar and offered him a cup of tea. He glanced to his right, as piles of sick were hastily being cleared from the kitchen floor, and said: 'No, you're all right.'

Fortunately, Sugar still went ahead with the interview, which is more than can be said for Michael Winner, the film director and food critic. He was due to appear as a newspaper reviewer on James Whale's Sunday afternoon show, but when he arrived at talkSPORT Towers there was nobody on the door to let him in.

On evenings and weekends, the talkSPORT door was usually manned by head of security Alec Gradinsky, a Danny DeVito lookalike who stands no more than five feet tall – even with the raised platform shoes he wears. When he was sitting at the reception desk, he operated a strictly no-nonsense admission policy, unless he knew who they were or they possessed a fob to let themselves in. All talkSPORT employees were issued with magnetic fobs that opened doors around the building, including the front entrance. Gradinsky's policy was quite simple. If you didn't have a fob, you weren't getting in. No exceptions.

When comedian Rory Bremner turned up at the radio station one evening to do a slot on the late-night show, Gradinsky decided not to let him in as he didn't know who he was. Far worse was when Dennie Morris, a talkSPORT producer, was mugged down the road from the building by two hammer-wielding yobs one evening. He sprinted back to the office to call the police and started hammering his fists against the door in a clearly distressed state. Gradinsky sat behind the desk completely unmoved: 'Alec! Alec! Let me in, I've been mugged!' screamed Morris, only for Gradinsky to come back with: 'Where's yer fob?' before finally taking pity and allowing Morris to come in and call the police.

talkSPORT's first line of defence took no prisoners and was more than a match for the likes of Winner. At that time, however, Gradinsky had plodded off on one of his numerous security rounds where he would walk around every floor of the building, checking everything was in order. He would take his time, opening doors, closing doors, closing windows and securing all exits and entrances.

While he was doing his rounds, anybody trying to enter the building would have either had to contact somebody on the production floor to come down and open the door for them or wait until Gradinsky returned. Winner was one of those who had to wait until he returned and his patience was running out.

After hammering on the door for what seemed like an eternity, but was in fact about ten minutes, an extremely riled Winner was eventually let in to the building by former footballer Mick Quinn, who was just leaving talkSPORT Towers after finishing his show. He told Winner that Whale was waiting for him upstairs and that he should go on up but, by now, the film director was incandescent with rage: 'Are you sure? I have been bloody waiting here for half an hour! I have a good mind to go home!' he bellowed at Quinn.

'Hey, don't take it out on me, Michael. I have just done a show and I'm knackered and want to go home myself.'

'But you work for this station, don't you? This is an absolute disgrace. I have never been so insulted in all my life!' spluttered an exasperated Winner.

At that time, Winner was appearing in a series of TV insurance adverts in which his catchphrase was 'Calm down dear, it's only a commercial!' The irony was not lost on Quinn, who, chuckling to himself, used the catchphrase back on the film director.

But Winner didn't calm down. By this stage, he had stormed out of the building he had spent so long trying to enter, refusing to appear on Whale's show. Quinn couldn't help but be amused by Winner's ranting: 'As a millionaire, he is used to being ushered here, there and everywhere. But as we know, that just doesn't happen at talkSPORT. You have got a map and a compass and you have got to find your way to whatever studio you are going to!'

Moments after Winner had walked off in a huff, Gradinsky finished his latest security round and returned to his seat at the reception desk, completely oblivious to the drama he had helped to create. Winner did eventually appear on the Whale show on another occasion, but only after the talkSPORT presenter had called him to apologise for the incident.

But that was talkSPORT: the radio station where anything could happen at any given moment – and usually did. And that was especially the case now that two new heavyweight political presenters were about to join the fun.

13

Clash of the Titans – On and Off the Pitch

This geezer was so uncoordinated. He kicked the shit out of me on the pitch and then I saw him putting it on my missus!

IAN WRIGHT

When talkSPORT announced the signings of presenters George Galloway and Jon Gaunt, billing them as two political heavy-weights, nobody actually expected them to come to blows. Yet, amazingly, they very nearly did.

It would have been hard to find two men more diametrically opposed politically to front the station's current affairs slots. It was no surprise that they had little time for each other's view of the world. What *was* a surprise, however, was that they seemed to have little time for Voltaire's famous liberal doctrine of 'I dis-approve of what you say, but I will defend to the death your right to say it'. Less philosophically, they were going to sort out their differences with a good old-fashioned fist fight until station bosses stepped in.

Galloway had been first to come on board the good ship

talkSPORT in March 2006. His public profile grew considerably from his appearance on the TV show *Celebrity Big Brother*. However, Sean Dilley, talkSPORT's senior current affairs producer, had suggested bringing Galloway on board the previous year after his famous oratorical masterclass in front of a US Senate permanent sub-committee, but his recommendation had fallen on deaf ears.

Although Galloway had entered the reality TV show as a controversial figure, because of his extreme political views and a well-publicised meeting with Saddam Hussein, his performances on the show won him many new fans as he showed a different, lighter side to his passionate personality. The highlight came when he acted as a cat with actress Rula Lenska, pretending to lap up milk out of her hands and burying his head in her lap.

The trails and jingles on his show played on this somewhat cringeworthy incident and showed that Galloway was certainly not afraid to make fun of himself. The voiceover hailed him as 'The purr-secuted cat of chat! Catch Pussycat George on talkSPORT!', while in the background, Galloway added: 'I'm your pussycat doll!' Eventually, Galloway's theme tune and nickname became 'Top Cat' from the popular sixties cartoon.

Tying up the deal to bring Galloway to the station was far from easy. Not only did talkSPORT want to employ a serving Member of Parliament to host an opinion-based phone-in, but they wanted to employ someone who was known to be an outspoken critic of the government. All radio shows have to ensure they abide by the media watchdog Ofcom's rules about 'due impartiality' on political matters. So Galloway couldn't present a Respect Party Political Broadcast every week as that would have broken those rules.

However, the rules do allow a presenter to express strong

views on air as long as contrary opinions are not excluded. So Galloway was free to present his shows on Friday and Saturday nights, as long as he stayed loyal to the Ofcom guidelines.

Once he was in the building there was no stopping him. Galloway was the only talkSPORT presenter who didn't require a chair, broadcasting every show on his feet as if he was addressing the nation from his soapbox. As soon as he arrived in the studio, he would raise the flexible microphone bracket to its highest point so it would be level with his mouth while he was on his feet. Come 10pm, he was standing and delivering, but only after he had embedded his rosary beads firmly into the palm of his hand. A devout Catholic, Galloway always rolled the beads around in his hand while broadcasting.

A natural orator, the erudite Glaswegian took to radio with the same ease as one of his fellow MPs might fiddle their expenses. His show quickly built a huge following for a programme that was going out late on weekend evenings. Galloway had as many fans as he had enemies, but the great success of his show was that they all tuned in. With his uncompromising views on topics such as the Middle East and communism, the phone lines would often be jammed with people either wanting to congratulate or berate him. Love him or loathe him, it was superb radio and talkSPORT had never known a show like it.

The only thing Galloway couldn't do on air while he was pacing up and down the studio making his points was suck on the expensive cigars that had become as synonymous with him as his alternative politics. Instead, he would rush out to the fire escape staircase during news breaks to take a few precious drags before speeding back to the studio to resume broadcasting.

Although the politician would broadcast alone in the studio, he was always accompanied by Kevin Ovenden, his silent assistant, who would provide any information he required during a show by passing him handwritten notes. Ovenden, or 'my good friend Kevin' as Galloway referred to him on air, was like a walking internet search engine and invaluable to Top Cat.

Galloway was an outspoken critic of the Israeli government and Zionism and would seldom miss an opportunity to turn a debate into a phone-in on what he would describe as the 'oppressive Israeli occupation of Palestine'. The amazing thing about Galloway's show was that he would attract calls from Zionists and anti-Zionists alike. Both sides became avid listeners, even though he invariably nailed his colours firmly to the Palestinian mast.

From a management point of view, Galloway's signing had been a masterstroke. Although he'd made several appearances on James Whale's show, it was still seen as a major surprise in the radio industry when the station announced that the controversial Glaswegian was joining their ranks. Certainly his views were in marked contrast to those of his fellow non-sport presenters.

A less surprising signing was Jon Gaunt, who joined the station two months later in May 2006 to present a daily mid-morning programme. The winner of multiple Sony Radio Awards during his time with BBC Three Counties Radio, Gaunt was the closest thing to a shock jock to appear on the 1089 frequency since the early days of Talk Radio. It's fair to say his politics were slightly to the right of centre and he arrived with the reputation of being the 'Biggest Mouth in Britain'. Gaunt also wrote a weekly political column for the *Sun*, so instantly understood the tabloid style of the radio station.

Gaunt's broadcasting style was unequivocally loud and proud. It was in-your-face, energetic and shouty radio where he called the shots and listeners phoned in to agree with him. Anybody with an alternative viewpoint was given airtime, but would usually be shouted down by Gaunt sooner rather than later. It wasn't for the faint-hearted, but he quickly raised a loyal army of listeners who flocked to hear their hero telling it how it was.

Galloway and Gaunt clearly listened to each other's shows as, soon after his arrival at talkSPORT Towers, Gaunt began goading his colleague about his views on the Middle East and the wars in Iraq and Afghanistan. Galloway would subsequently respond to Gaunt's goading, giving back as good as he got until one week when Gaunt labelled Galloway a coward. For the Glaswegian, that was a step too far.

The following Friday night, Galloway stood in the studio and delivered a stern ultimatum to Gaunt, announcing on air: 'I did hear Jon Gaunt call me a coward. So, at 11.08 and 22 seconds let me say this. Gaunt, I am challenging you to five rounds in the ring at York Hall with a referee of your choice on a date of your choice – that will give you some time to get rid of the... well, flab. I'm challenging you to a fight. Do you understand me?

'I'm slapping you across the face with a glove here. With a Gaunt-let if you like. And I'm challenging you to see who is the coward. So Mr Gaunt, you are hereby challenged, live on radio, to see who the coward is. Five rounds. York Hall. We'll charge for tickets and we'll donate the proceeds to a charity of your choice. Let's see who the coward is, Gaunty? The gauntlet is thrown down.'

As a boxer in his youth, it was an understandably confident challenge that Galloway issued and the listeners were thrilled at the possibility of the two men clashing in the ring. Emails, texts and phone calls came flooding in to the station about the proposed fight. Unfortunately for the listeners, the radio station didn't think it was such a good idea for two of their presenters to settle their differences with a fight. All talk of the bout was banned on air from that point onwards, while Galloway and Gaunt's mutual goading was also toned right down in an attempt to defuse the situation.

Galloway later found another presenter to fall out with, following a brief appearance on the drivetime show when Tony Blair was coming towards the end of his reign as prime minister. Adrian Durham described his colleague as a 'mate' of Iraqi dictator Saddam Hussein and all hell broke loose.

'You, whose name I do not even know, have defamed me!' cried Galloway as Durham's face turned redder than his hair. The politician continued to rant at Durham before putting the phone down in disgust, although the two would later make up and appear together on other shows.

One of the undoubted highlights of Galloway's talkSPORT tenure to date was the 2008 US election results night when Barack Obama was voted in as the country's first black president. talkSPORT decided to broadcast a US election special to mark the momentous occasion and Galloway was among the team who were keeping tabs on all the incoming results. As it became clear that Obama was going to triumph, it all became too much for Galloway, who broke down in tears live on air as he was so caught up in the emotion of the moment that had the potential to change the world.

Change on a far smaller scale was also in the air at talkSPORT back in the summer of 2006 when it was announced that Paul Breen-Turner would be leaving the drivetime show he had been presenting with Rodney Marsh. Their on-air relationship had hit something of a wall, and management decided that their star name needed a different co-presenter to work with. For its first six months, the programme was extraordinarily successful as

Breen-Turner and Marsh's entertaining personalities kept listeners glued to their radios. Often, the pair would spend vast parts of the show just trying to score points off each other with good-natured banter and wind ups which proved to be a hit with their audience.

But Marsh felt his pairing with Breen-Turner had taken the show as far as it could go and if it was going to grow further, a change of presenter might be necessary – and it wasn't going to be *him* stepping down to make way for fresh blood.

Breen-Turner's contract was up for renewal and when he returned from a holiday in the Caribbean, the decision was taken that he would part company with the station. While he was naturally upset at losing his job, it also came as something of a relief as the broadcaster had been leading an extremely hectic working life.

When drivetime finished for the week on a Friday, he would jet back to Spain to work as a commentator for worldwide English language TV feeds of La Liga matches. That would see him broadcasting in Madrid for both Saturday and Sunday's matches before flying back to London on Monday morning in time for his first talkSPORT show of the week. At one stage, Breen-Turner went six months without a day off, so he was philosophical about the news of his departure, seeing it as a chance to have a well-earned break and take in the forthcoming World Cup from a more relaxed perspective.

For talkSPORT, Germany 2006 was anything but relaxed. The tournament was the station's largest-ever operation, as 20 staff were sent out to central Europe to cover the event. That was a paltry number compared to the hundreds of employees the BBC would have sent to Germany, but it still represented a massive undertaking for the commercial station.

Leading the way for talkSPORT was Marsh. Despite Alan Brazil still being seen as the star of the station, talkSPORT were firmly behind England and the breakfast show presenter was a proud Scot. That meant Marsh was pushed to the fore as the face of talkSPORT for the duration of the tournament. For the 35 days that the station was based in Germany before, during and after the World Cup, Marsh was on air for every single one. Often, he would be broadcasting in his capacity as a match summariser or he would co-present phone-ins after England games, as hundreds of callers came on to air their views about their national team.

At other times, Marsh would be co-presenting the drivetime show from Germany with his new broadcasting partner, Adrian Durham. The former evening show frontman had been well briefed about Marsh, learning about his penchant for taking a show in a completely different direction at a stroke. But he was pleasantly surprised by the former footballer as they immediately struck up an excellent working relationship during the tournament. Marsh was engaging and entertaining, clearly inspired by being so close to the action at the world's greatest sporting event. The pair hit it off so well that Marsh even suggested they should consider putting on a series of roadshows for talkSPORT fans when they returned to the UK.

But Marsh was still prone to his more surreal moments. During one afternoon show with Durham, which was being broadcast from the Berlin hotel room that was also doubling as talkSPORT's studio, he rose from his chair during a commercial break. Nothing seemed out of the ordinary as Marsh made his way to the window overlooking the German capital. He was simply stretching his legs, which was quite a common thing for presenters to do mid-broadcast. What wasn't so common was for a presenter to undo his trousers mid-stretch and lift forward the elastic of his underpants. Marsh stood by the window, holding open his trousers and pants for a few moments, and then quickly put himself back together.

'What are you doing?' asked a bemused Durham.

'Just getting some air on them,' replied Marsh, who then returned to his seat and continued broadcasting as if nothing had happened. It was an extremely hot day in Berlin – and the weather stayed like that for most of the tournament – which might have explained Marsh's actions. That, and as an ex-footballer, he was fairly comfortable to be in various states of undress in front of total strangers. Durham was mystified by the stunt: 'I thought "fuck me!" But that's the kind of oddball he was.'

Funnily enough, Marsh wasn't the only talkSPORT presenter to reveal a hidden part of his anatomy during the World Cup. While filming a video diary for a talkSPORT World Cup DVD, Durham decided to say his piece from the comfort of his hotel bed. He set up a video camera – which all presenters had been given to use for the DVD – at the end of the bed and then lay on his stomach with his head a few inches from the lens. He gave his verdict on the day's World Cup action before shutting the camera down for the night.

Thinking only his head was in shot, Durham hadn't bothered to clothe himself before recording. And nor had he watched back the footage of his performance. That's why when the DVD editor played Durham's video back he received a nasty shock as there, right in the background throughout the film, was the drivetime presenter's naked arse. Needless to say, the video was never put on the main DVD film, although it did make it on to the 'extras' section.

The extraordinary naked theme continued in Germany with

The Moose the next to remove all of his clothes. The reporter was out and about in Munich in the English Gardens, a huge public park in the centre of the city. Part of the park was sectioned off for nudists and Moose thought it would be a good idea to discuss how the World Cup was shaping up from the point of view of German naturists. In an item that was made for radio, talkSPORT's intrepid reporter spoke to a naked German woman while removing every piece of his own clothing and making her describe what he was doing for the benefit of the listeners back in the UK.

When they weren't removing their clothes, several of talkSPORT's finest managed to lose the mobile phones that had been bought for them especially for the tournament – Durham's was flushed down a toilet, while fellow presenter Patrick Kinghorn's was run over. The money-saving idea of purchasing German phones and SIM cards for the team soon backfired as more money was spent on replacing the lost ones than would have been paid if they had continued using their UK mobiles.

After almost four weeks at the tournament, during which Mike Parry had behaved himself and barely touched a drop of alcohol, he decided he fancied a proper night out. Accompanied by Alvin Martin, Porky made merry and returned to the hotel in high spirits where he encountered a group of Australian fans. Having been to see Australia play earlier in the tournament, mainly because their star player was Tim Cahill, one of his Everton heroes, Porky decided to goad the Aussies, telling them that Cahill was the only decent player they had and that the team would be nothing without him. The fans from Down Under were not impressed by Parry's drunken shenanigans and became quite aggressive with the talkSPORT man until 6ft 1in former West Ham centre-back

Martin stepped in to save the day – as he had done so often in his career.

The station's World Cup broadcasts were a roaring success. Under Scott Taunton's stewardship, talkSPORT had taken on a tournament in its most professional and wide-ranging manner to date, and sponsors had formed a long and orderly queue to work together with the station, bringing in vital revenue. They may have had fewer personnel than the BBC would take to a weekend away covering a music festival, but pooling all their resources together for 35 days, talkSPORT once again managed to produce outstanding radio.

When they returned to broadcasting back in the UK, like all the stars of the World Cup, attention quickly turned towards the new football season and talkSPORT had strengthened their squad with a couple of new signings.

In August 2006, former TV presenter Terry Christian was announced as the new host of the Saturday evening football phone-in. After fronting cult Channel 4 show *The Word* in the early nineties, Manchester United fan Christian had continued to work across the media, including various stints on radio. He was drafted in to work alongside Mick Quinn, a proud Liverpool fan, and the pair clashed regularly, given the rivalry between their clubs.

Naturally, the listeners loved hearing Quinn and Christian exchanging banter. Christian was no shrinking violet and would often wind up callers, especially if they were seen to be having a go at his favourite team. Quinn became genuinely annoyed at Christian's amazing tendency to turn all phone-in topics round to talk about his favourite team: 'With Terry, you could talk about the snow in Alaska or the Dead Sea and it would come round to Manchester United again!' said the prolific striker.

Also joining the station at the same time was Kelly Dalglish, who arrived in a blaze of publicity as talkSPORT's first-ever female presenter (despite the fact that Claire Furlong presented four episodes of *The Final Furlong* alongside Rupert Bell). The daughter of Liverpool and Scotland legend Kenny, she had already impressed while working for Sky Sports and she joined the station to present the Monday night *Kick Off* show alongside Jason Cundy and European football expert Gabriele Marcotti. Dalglish's arrival was a big deal for talkSPORT. The station brand had been built on a male-dominated environment and the only female voices heard on talkSPORT belonged to sports stars or newsreaders. To bring in a female presenter was a bold step and showed how the station was maturing.

Dalglish was well aware of the difference she was set to make at talkSPORT and was determined to mix it with the big boys and hold her own. However, her first shows were difficult experiences for her. Cundy and Marcotti hardly allowed the new presenter to get a word in edgeways between their very loud and very male voices. But Dalglish was a quick learner and was soon trading blows with her colleagues as the three developed a strong relationship.

One aspect of working with Cundy that Dalglish had to become accustomed to was the amount of food the ex-footballer would put away of an evening. Cundy had a formidable appetite and would often come into the studio armed with a takeaway noodle dish that he would munch on during the show. Once, when he was co-presenting with Kinghorn shortly after lunch, Cundy even managed to belch into a microphone immediately after a commercial break for which he had to apologise profusely. Many of his talkSPORT colleagues still joke that it was the most sensible thing to have come out of his mouth throughout his time at the station.

Once she was settled into her new role, the one aspect of presenting that used to fill Dalglish with the most fear was handing over to James Whale at the end of the programme. Whale would always come in and pretend he knew nothing about football, muttering things like: 'Who's this Beckham character then?' Dalglish, well aware that Whale had a reputation for controversy, would always worry that he would say something inflammatory while it was still her show and land them in trouble:

'Whether it was him [Whale] or George Galloway – and you couldn't get two much more chippier people, of course – you would be in the studio with Jason and Gab and it was all really lovely, and you are kind of chatting away and it is all quite friendly. Suddenly one of these little timebombs would come in and you'd think "Please God, don't say anything until ten o'clock when it is actually your show!"'

As well as she did, Dalglish stayed only one full season at the station as she joined TV outfit Setanta Sports the following year and that meant committing to working with them for their Monday night football matches instead of doing her talkSPORT show.

New signings aside, it was still very much business as usual for the radio station after the success of the World Cup, and that meant the focus was still heavily on the breakfast show. And Brazil in particular. After keeping a low profile during the World Cup, the Scot embraced the new season with his usual gusto.

One Thursday morning, he was running late for the programme after a particularly heavy night at a charity gig. That week he was co-presenting with Mick Quinn, as Beeky was on holiday. Quinn held the fort for the first half-hour, during which there were floods of calls, emails and texts from listeners outraged by a shocking incident from the previous night's match between Manchester City and Portsmouth. In that game, City's Ben Thatcher had clattered into Pompey's Pedro Mendes, knocking him unconscious and putting him in hospital. It was an undeniably horrific challenge that had no place on a football pitch and talkSPORT listeners were up in arms about it.

When a rather hungover Brazil arrived in the studio, Quinn quickly briefed him on what had happened the previous night, as Brazil hadn't seen the incident, and how the listeners were calling for Thatcher to receive a tough punishment. Brazil waded straight into the debate by telling the nation that football was a man's game and that it wasn't for namby-pamby types. He argued that of course there would be harsh tackles, but players had to just get on with the game as that was part and parcel of the physical side of football.

If Mendes had been listening from his hospital bed, it's fair to say he might have asked Brazil how he was supposed to have got on with the game while unconscious the previous evening. And the listeners took their hero to task for his outrageous view of the incident – which he still hadn't seen. The phone lines lit up and the switchboard jammed as callers queued up to tell Brazil he wasn't talking sense.

Fortunately, the show then went to a break for the news. At this point, Brazil was watching the studio TV monitors which were showing footage of the Thatcher challenge. The incident was shown half a dozen times from different angles and at different speeds and on each occasion Brazil's jaw dropped lower. This was no ordinary bad tackle and the breakfast show presenter realised his 'it's a physical game' line was badly wide of the mark.

When he went back on air after the news, Brazil's approach to the incident was far more conciliatory as he started the process of some of the finest backtracking ever heard on radio. By the time he had dealt with several more angry callers, a battered and bruised Brazil turned to Quinn and jokingly asked him if there was any wine in the fridge as he could do with half a glass. It had been quite a morning and it was only 7.30am.

There were still occasions when Brazil wouldn't make it in to the studio at all. However, as his previous regular stand-in Beeky was now his co-presenter, a new last-minute, ask-no-questions, deputy presenter had to be found to field calls at all hours of the night from desperate producers. Step forward, Ian Danter.

The Birmingham-based broadcaster had worked across various shows for talkSPORT, including a regular Sunday afternoon presenting gig, as well as providing football reports and matchday commentaries. A versatile character, Danter was as comfortable debating weighty football issues as he was talking about current affairs, and that flexibility meant he was used right across the talkSPORT schedule. In fact, he remains the only talkSPORT presenter who has worked on every single time slot, right around the clock.

Usually, Danter's mobile phone would ring any time after 5am. Keeping his eyes shut while trying to locate the ringing phone with one hand, Danter would eventually put it to his ear and emit a grunt. One of the breakfast producers would ask if he was able to fill in for Brazil.

'What time is it?' would somehow emerge from a combination of Danter's still half-asleep brain and mouth.

'5.15'

'Fuck!'

With the advantage of having a broadcast-quality ISDN line

at home, Danter wouldn't have to go far to co-present the show. A quick shower, followed by rapidly absorbing the morning's agenda and the show's running order, and Danter would be ready to begin, sitting at home with his headphones on at a time when he had been planning to be fast asleep.

He soon learned to sleep with one eye open as he never knew when he might receive *that* phone call. The amount of notice he was given varied. Sometimes, if Brazil knew he wasn't going to make it in the next day, he would call a producer at around midnight to let them know he had a sore throat and wasn't feeling up to it. On those occasions, Danter's phone would ring just as he was going to bed. Instead of setting his alarm for 7am or 8am like most people, he would then re-set it for 3am, grab a couple of hours' sleep before dashing down the motorway to make it to talkSPORT Towers by 5am in time to prepare for the show. That was the more relaxed way of standing in for Brazil, far more civilised than a 5.15am wake-up call out of the blue.

There was also one morning where Danter broke the world record for receiving the shortest possible notice for being a Brazil stand-in. It was 5.57am and someone was needed to partner Beeky, albeit with three minutes' notice.

Danter's phone rang. It was the usual conversation, but when he asked the producer the time and was told it was 5.57am he sat bolt upright in bed in a panic. He threw some water on his face, slung on a dressing gown and raced to turn on his radio equipment. He put on his headphones and listened to the sports headlines so he had some kind of rough idea of what topics might be up for discussion during the first hour of the show. And suddenly he was on air – although this time, with a new world record tucked safely under his dressing gown belt.

Danter's heroic stand-ins quickly made him something of a

hero within the talkSPORT office, and if producers ever took pity on him, they would sometimes call on Jason Cundy to fill in for Brazil instead. If the call came early enough, Cundy would race in to the studios from his Hampshire home. But the former footballer's lack of an ISDN line at home meant that in any emergency situation, it would be Danter who always got the nod.

Cundy and Danter, the station's two very own firefighters, teamed up with Alvin Martin every Sunday afternoon for a live show looking at the weekend's football which led to one incident that none of them would ever forget.

Away from talkSPORT, Danter's other passion is music and he is a drummer for the world's longest-running Kiss tribute band, Dressed To Kill. Danter and band colleagues took their work seriously, gigging across the UK regularly and spending hours caking themselves in make-up to emulate Gene Simmons and the boys as accurately as possible.

One Saturday night, Danter and his band were playing in Stourbridge, one of their regular venues. After the gig, the band all had pizza and the talkSPORT man remembered thinking that the onions didn't quite taste right. The following day he was on air in the studio alongside Martin and Cundy when he started to feel decidedly queasy. There was no doubt in his mind that he was about to throw up – he just had to find a way to do it as discreetly as possible so the listeners wouldn't know.

Danter asked Cundy a question and, as the ex-footballer was answering, the presenter could feel the bile rising up inside him so he hopped out of his seat and vomited into the studio dustbin as quietly as possible, but with less accuracy than might be ideal. Any extremely alert listeners may have just heard the sound of the puke hitting the bottom of the bin, but the show continued with Cundy attempting to answer the question as if nothing out of the ordinary had happened. Martin just looked on in disbelief.

There was no way Danter could continue and he never made it back to his microphone, with Cundy having to take on presenting duties – possibly the first time that one stand-in was standing in for another stand-in – while his colleague rushed to the toilets to make a further series of deposits. Eventually, Cundy announced to the listeners that Danter wasn't feeling well and would be unable to return to the studio. But that wasn't the end of the ordeal for Danter's co-presenters, as Cundy recalled:

'I had to take the reins and present the show after that, but the smell was pretty horrific,' he said.

'We had to get air spray and the cleaners had to come in. The doors were left open so we were doing a live show with all the doors open to try to ventilate the studio because it stank of vomit!'

Danter's alter ego as a member of Dressed To Kill inadvertently caused him another problem on talkSPORT after a gig in Glasgow. While driving back to the Midlands from Scotland overnight, the presenter's car broke down somewhere near Carlisle at 1.30am. The following day he was due to be reporting for the station at Nottingham Forest, but with only a few updates required over the course of the match, it wouldn't have been the end of the world if he was a little tired.

After being towed by three different rescue trucks through the night, Danter eventually rolled back into Birmingham at 8.30am. It was far from perfect, but if he grabbed a few hours' sleep he wouldn't have had too much trouble broadcasting updates and goal flashes from the City Ground. But then his phone rang and a very different equation suddenly presented itself. The station's leading commentator Nigel Pearson was unwell so talkSPORT had asked their favourite stand-in to replace him. That day, Pearson was scheduled to commentate on the full 90 minutes of Aston Villa v West Ham.

The good news for Danter was that he no longer had to leave Birmingham that day, as Villa were based in the city. The bad news was that after an 11-hour journey home through the night with no sleep, he now had to broadcast a live Premier League commentary to millions of listeners for which he had done absolutely no preparation. And the game he was covering was at the home ground of the team he despised, as he was a lifelong Birmingham City fan. Disappearing into the nearest phone box to change into his Superman gear, Danter somehow summoned up the energy to cram some stats into his head and nipped over to Villa Park in time for the game.

Danter's early-morning phone calls were still the exception rather than the rule and Brazil continued to thrive on the station's flagship programme. The two biggest shows on any radio station are breakfast and drive, and often there would be friendly rivalry between the two programmes. This was very much the case at talkSPORT, especially when Marsh joined the station and upped the ante as far as the drivetime show was concerned.

One morning, Brazil found a sparkling new pair of Puma trainers in the studio and, on a whim, decided to give them away to one of his listeners as a prize. Later that day, Marsh was back in talkSPORT Towers for the afternoon show and couldn't find his trainers anywhere. It turned out that the previous day, England rugby international Steve Thompson had been a guest on Marsh's show and had given the shoes to the ex-footballer as a gift. Unfortunately, they were the wrong size so Marsh had left them in the studio overnight, hoping to exchange them the next day. When somebody in the office pointed out to him that Brazil had given away a pair of trainers on the breakfast show that morning, Marsh wasn't best pleased but still saw the funny side of it.

Later that day, Marsh used the airwaves to let the listeners know what Brazil had done and ramped up the rivalry between the shows by declaring drive to be far better in all aspects. The following morning, Brazil escalated the tension between the pro-grammes by attempting to give away one of Marsh's unwashed coffee mugs as a prize, prompting the drive presenter to raise the stakes higher: 'We were slagging each other off on the air which was quite funny,' chuckled Marsh.

'Everybody got into it. Live on drivetime I said: "The break-fast lot are a bunch of wusses who are not up to the challenge. We'll play them at five-a-side football any time, anywhere." Bill Ridley jumped all over it. He loved the idea and they've been doing it ever since.'

Unlike the proposed Galloway and Gaunt fight at York Hall, this was one rivalry that management were prepared to support, quickly realising the huge potential of having the two shows' ex-footballers going head-to-head on the football pitch. What started out as a friendly game between producers and presenters suddenly emerged into something massive, as many other ex-pros, who also worked for the station, were drafted in to play in the match. Thanks to a pair of trainers and some dirty coffee mugs, the annual talkSPORT Breakfast v Drive football match was born.

Over the years, talkSPORT presenters and former professional players including Ian Wright, Tony Cascarino, Jason Cundy, Alvin Martin, Ray Houghton, Mick Quinn, Don Hutchison, Ray Parlour, Marsh and Brazil would play in the fixture in which there was still plenty of professional pride at stake. Martin and former Irish footballing god Houghton were two spring-heeled veterans whose class always shone through in these matches, which were never anything less than fiercely competitive.

The game usually took place on a weekday afternoon during the Hawksbee and Jacobs show, so the pair decamped to the roof of talkSPORT Towers, giving them a bird's eye view of the five-a-side pitch across the road from the building. Joining H&J on the roof was the matchday commentator, either Pearson or Danter, while reporters would be pitchside, providing listeners with on-the-spot interviews with the players. The station couldn't have organised a more professional production had the World Cup final been played on the pitch opposite the studios.

Brazil played in the first two fixtures, but the back problem that curtailed his career has prevented him from participating since. That, and the fact that there was usually a break of about four hours between the end of the breakfast show and kick-off, meaning the lure of the pub may have been too great.

Memorably, the first year saw Galloway take part and he played with his trademark cigar in his mouth, which was certainly something none of the ex-professionals had seen before. But Marsh was the star of that inaugural fixture, belying his age and all the years he was giving away to his opponents with a memorable performance capped with a peach of a goal to lead the drive show to the first of three consecutive victories.

The Moose, whose sporting prowess included defeats to Beeky on the track and in the pool, as well as being beaten by a dalek during the London marathon, was truly fired up when called upon the following year. Sharing a pitch with Ian Wright, who had just joined the station, proved too much for the sports newsreader, who lunged in on the former England striker's dodgy ankle.

Wright still winces when recalling the incident: 'This geezer was so uncoordinated and he gave me a kick on my ankle. I didn't know him from Adam. In the end, it was fine. He apologised. My missus Nancy came to that game and, afterwards, Moose was standing watching with no top on. He came up behind Nancy with his naked torso and put his arm against the fence, leant over her and said something like "So are you enjoying the game?" And when she told me that, I just burst out laughing. I thought "Does he want me to fight him or something?" He kicked the shit out of me on the pitch and then he's putting it on my missus!'

Shortly after that incident, the Arsenal legend would have enjoyed seeing Moose being stunned by a fierce shot that slammed into him, straight between the legs during a stint in goal. After another defeat, the breakfast team complained bitterly about the disadvantage of having been awake since 4.30am and not kicking off until 2pm, while their opponents could enjoy a far more leisurely approach to the match. There was nothing that could be done about that and drive continued to dominate until the 2009 fixture, in which breakfast recruited their best side yet.

Recently retired professionals Parlour and Hutchison, alongside Cundy and Perry Groves, all starred for breakfast – who had Brazil's new co-presenter Ronnie Irani in goal but could find no place for The Moose. Their opponents fielded an injured Wright, Durham, Quinn, Cascarino and Bobby Gould, who had last been able to call himself a *recently* retired pro when his opponents were still at junior school. The match went to a penalty shoot-out, leading to a memorable moment when Cascarino gathered his team-mates into a huddle to see who would take the spot-kicks.

The former Ireland international had famously scored in his country's dramatic shoot-out win against Romania in the last 16 of the 1990 World Cup so was understandably confident about his chances of scoring in the talkSPORT match. As he looked into the eyes of Wright, Durham and Quinn, he said: 'How many of you have taken a penalty at the World Cup?'

Knowing the answer before he had asked the question, Cascarino took in the blank response and put himself forward for the job. After that, there was only ever going to be one outcome and the Irishman's spot-kick was duly saved by Irani, diving to his left, as he had done for every previous penalty due to his dodgy right knee. That proved to be the difference, although Quinn also managed to embarrass himself by dinking his penalty against the crossbar, with Irani having already committed to his customary left-sided dive.

The drought was over. The breakfast team and Brazil, who was on the pitch to motivate rather than play, had tasted victory for the first time since giving away Marsh's trainers. The event had grown bigger every year, with hundreds of spectators gathering to watch the match and bringing Hatfields to a standstill. Sponsors such as Mars had even come on board to endorse the match as the build-up to the game always started weeks before, with presenters discussing it on their shows, attempting to land a few early psychological blows.

With the first staging of the breakfast v drive fixture, the World Cup and Galloway and Gaunt coming on board, 2006 had been a remarkable year for the station, but it ended in tragedy. On 18 December, Mike Dickin died in a car crash. The presenter had been driving near his home on the A30 near Bodmin when he was involved in a six-car pile-up. He was airlifted to hospital but was pronounced dead soon after.

His death had an enormous impact on the station's staff and the listeners, so the tributes flooded in. A book of condolences was opened up on the talkSPORT website (before being passed on to his wife), while obituaries appeared in many national newspapers. Whale, who was possibly closest to Dickin at the station, aired a special three-hour tribute show to his colleague three days later.

Whenever listeners who called in to Dickin's show began by asking him: 'Hello Mike, how are you?' the presenter had a habit of always answering with the same line: 'My health is not in question.' It was due only to his hunger for debate and desire to hurry on with the show's chosen discussion topics that he had coined the phrase but, over the years, it stuck.

Sadly, as he no doubt would have pointed out himself, his health *was* no longer in question and the airwaves were a poorer place without him.

14

Wright Man For the Job

Wrighty's one of the greatest signings the station has made. He's one of the lads, down to earth, funny and good company. He cares. He really does. When you work with someone that closely and that often and they actually care about you, it's quite rare. It's touching really.

ADRIAN DURHAM

'What's the most amazing thing you have seen on a football pitch?' asked Adrian Durham from the talkSPORT studios.

It was one of those open-ended phone-in topics that would normally lead to hundreds of emails and calls from listeners sharing their amusing experiences of being fans or Sunday morning players. But no sooner had Durham finished his sentence, he was interrupted by his co-presenter Rodney Marsh, who was sitting just to his right in studio two.

Like an eager schoolboy, Marsh raised his hand and blurted out: 'Oh! Oh! Oh! Stop it right there. I have got the most amazing thing and nobody is going to be able to top this.'

Durham turned to him expectantly while the producers in the control room all looked in to the studio to hear and watch Marsh deliver his story. The mercurial ex-footballer had some amazing tales from his playing days, having appeared alongside some of the game's greatest players, so this would be a belter.

'When I was in America, I was playing in a game and this guy who had scored a goal was celebrating,' said Marsh. 'He stopped celebrating then somebody with a gun jumped out of the crowd, chased him around the pitch and shot him dead!'

If a record had been playing in the background, it would have made that awful scratchy sound and ground to a halt. As it was, Durham and the producers sat open-mouthed wondering what on earth to say next. Even if the story were true, it did not leave the show with many other places to go during a phone-in with the question 'what's the most amazing thing you've ever seen on a football pitch?'

Marsh's habit of behaving as unpredictably as possible on air had struck again, leaving Durham with no choice but to say: 'You are absolutely right, Rodney. Nobody is going to be able to top that so we'll be back after this,' and the show went to an early commercial break.

The incident was typical of Marsh's maverick style after he had returned from the World Cup and resumed his drivetime partnership with Durham. After the glamour, colour and excitement of being part of the greatest show on earth over in Germany, Marsh had seemed distracted, if not just bored, once his day-to-day talkSPORT life had resumed back in London.

Despite having had his workload reduced from five afternoons a week to four, after a meeting with programme director Bill Ridley whom he knew was always extremely supportive of him, Marsh was still unhappy. His overwhelming passion to try to turn the drive show into a standalone programme built around his quirky personality was leading him into situations where he would act in an increasingly bizarre manner. Once, while discussing an amazing 4-4 draw from the previous night, Marsh decided he was no longer interested in that and instead invited listeners to ring in with their thoughts on whether Sharia law would work in the UK.

There were times when Durham would become totally exasperated with his colleague. One such occasion was when Marsh had claimed he wasn't aware that they were supposed to be discussing the topic of 'football matches that turned out to be far better than you'd expected'. Live on air, Marsh said he didn't remember having agreed to talk about that subject in the pre-show meeting. Durham, with nowhere left to turn, resorted to saying: 'Right, hands up. Did we say in the meeting that we were doing this topic?'

All hands in the control room were raised. Marsh still claimed he didn't remember, so Durham removed his headphones and folded his arms, leaving the ex-footballer to ask, not for the first time: 'Are there any psychiatrists listening to the show because I think I might be having a breakdown?'

Another time, Durham was forced into boycott mode when Marsh revealed he hadn't seen the previous night's match the pair were supposed to be discussing. He said: 'I didn't see the game as I was out on the lash and, do you know what, Ade, I am actually feeling quite depressed right now.' After another Marsh plea for help, Durham sat in silence again, leaving the ex-footballer to fill the remaining two minutes until the break with a monologue about his psychological state.

The relationship between Durham and Marsh was close to breaking point by this stage, with both men equally disillusioned about where the show was going. Marsh's odd tangents would always draw a response from the listeners, but that wasn't necessarily the reaction that Durham and the producers were looking for. 'The unique brilliance he sometimes brought to the show was often outweighed by the garbage,' recalled Durham. 'Sometimes he could be hilarious and engaging and other times he could be so infuriating.'

Marsh, on the other hand, believed there was something of a personality clash between Durham and himself: 'If I could have done one day a week with Adrian Durham, I'd have done it for the rest of my life,' said Marsh. 'I agreed to do four days. I'll be perfectly honest, our personalities clashed on a personal and professional level. We were very similar in one way, and diametrically opposed in another. I think Adrian Durham is one of the best technical professional presenters around, though.

'It was argumentative for the sake of being argumentative,' continued the former footballer. 'I should have been much more of a leader, I should have made an issue of all this, but frankly four days a week of doing the same thing every day – i.e. copying the breakfast show – wasn't me. So I went to see Bill Ridley again, who was sensational, and I said that I just couldn't work under these guidelines. Reluctantly, we both agreed to sever our ties. It was a bit emotional really. I'd only been there two and a half years.'

In Marsh's view, listeners could switch on the radio on any afternoon and the show would sound exactly the same as the previous day. Of course, it was that consistency and familiarity that many radio stations craved, but Marsh saw that as a negative.

After more than two years at the station, the footballing legend, a maverick genius both on air and on the pitch, was history. The search was on for a big-name replacement. Marsh was one of the few presenters who made their own decision to leave, rather than being forced out. A unique character, Marsh's time at talkSPORT was summed up by Ridley in a press release which simply said: 'Rodney Marsh is a one-off. There is only one of him and now he's off!'

But if listeners thought drivetime's reputation for controversy had diminished with Marsh's departure, they were about to find out that that was far from the case.

Mick Quinn was Durham's interim co-presenter at the time and, one afternoon, the pair were discussing the early international retirement of Liverpool footballer Jamie Carragher. The defender had come to the decision after repeatedly missing out on selection for the England team by then manager Steve McClaren. Carragher felt that even when other players were injured whom he perhaps should have replaced, he still wasn't chosen and therefore he was wasting his time. Rather than spending his international weekends warming the substitutes' bench, Carragher had decided to no longer make himself available for selection.

Durham was incensed by this decision for two reasons. Firstly, he felt the timing was poor, because England were in the middle of a difficult qualifying campaign for the European Championships, so he argued that Carragher had let his country down. Secondly, he was also on the defender's back, because he believed McClaren was asking him to fight for his place in the team and his response was to throw in the towel. In Durham's eyes, that made Carragher a bottler.

Quinn and Durham argued the toss at the top of the show, with the ex-footballer coming out in defence of the Liverpool player, whom he also happened to know through mutual friends. The phone lines went red-hot for the first hour of the show as listeners rang in to dismiss Durham's arguments and there was massive support for Carragher. But Durham was sticking to his guns, frequently labelling the footballer a bottler who had no stomach for a fight. As the show broke for the news, Durham was feeling extremely pleased with how the afternoon was going.

But there was one listener who wasn't at all happy with the way the show was going – and that was Carragher himself. The Liverpool star had heard Durham calling him a bottler once too often in that first hour of the programme and decided he could no longer be a passive bystander. So he phoned the station and asked to speak to Quinn about the show. As the programme had gone for a news break, Quinn was in the control room and took the call: 'What is that dickhead going on about me being a bottle job?' exploded Carragher in his broad Scouse accent. 'I will fucking get his arse to the training ground and we will see who is a bottle job!' he continued.

'Look, Jamie,' said Quinn. 'You can come on the show but you can't swear. I know you are upset but you can't swear.'

'Get me on! Get me on! Get me on!'

Quinn immediately informed everyone in the office that Carragher was about to go on air and the whole production floor began cheering as Durham, once again turning as bright a shade of red as his hair, returned to the studio like a boxer about to enter the ring. The presenter remembered that moment clearly: 'At that point I thought "Oh shit!"' said Durham. 'I really did. It is kind of easy to just sit there talking about someone when they are not there. But when they confront you, you have got to learn to deal with that as well. It doesn't happen very often. I thought "Well, how am I going to handle it? Let's just go for it. It's got to be done; it's great radio. He's got his right to reply."'

The red on-air bulb lit up in the studio and the presenter took a deep breath before telling listeners about his surprise guest:

Durham: Someone has said, if Jamie Carragher called you up what would you say to him? Well, we'll find out, because Jamie Carragher has called up. Jamie's with us on talkSPORT. How are you doing?

Carragher: Yeah, I'm all right. Just on my way to training and listening to your show this afternoon. Normally a good show until you started rabbiting on about me being a bit of a bottler. It'll be interesting to see if you've got any bottle and come down to Anfield or Melwood and say it to me and we'll see what happens.

Durham: I'd say it to your face and I'll say it to you now.

Carragher: Oh would ya mate? Tell you what, come down to Anfield for a Champions League game or whatever and we'll see then, won't we?

Durham: Yeah, we will.

Carragher: You can say other players are better than me, everyone's entitled to their opinion, but don't ever call me a bottler in front of thousands of people that are listening!

Durham: So why are you even thinking about quitting international football?

Carragher: Because there's that many people who he [McClaren] has played ahead of me. It's a game of opinions, but when you're at my age, they're all younger than me and they're all going to improve which maybe I won't at that age. I played in a Champions League final; there's not much more you can do in football. He [McClaren] played Ledley King, who is a top player but he's been injured all season, so how would you feel in my situation? What would you do?

Durham: I'd feel like proving myself and getting a stomach for the fight going and going for it.

Carragher: Proving yourself? I'm 29 and I've been doing it for eight years and obviously I haven't proved it enough. So it's not going to change now is it? It's not as if I just got in the squad and jumped out. So when you talk about proving yourself... And who's the other fella going "Oh he's probably got his contract at Liverpool worth 100 grand a week." Who's he?

Durham: He [Andrew 'Macca' McKenna] reads our sports bulletins.

Carragher: Is that ...

Durham: Hang on, Jamie! He's a football fan, an England fan who's entitled to his opinion.

Carragher: None of yous are more of a football fan than me, so don't try and make out that I'm more interested in money than playing football!

It was an impressive performance from the Liverpool man, who managed to avoid using any expletives and just about kept his temper in check. That was as heated as the interview got, but there remained a great deal of tension bubbling under the surface as Carragher, Durham and Quinn, when he could squeeze a word in, continued their discussion.

The defender, who won 38 caps for his country, made Durham see the situation from his point of view, although he eventually acknowledged that the timing of his announcement could have been a little better. The call lasted the best part of ten minutes and it was captivating radio throughout. He ended the conversation with a repeat of his invitation to Durham:

Durham: Listen, Jamie. Thanks very much for phoning in.

Carragher: I'll see you at Melwood or Anfield for a Champions League game!

Quinn: I'll drag him down there!

Carragher: Make sure he brings his boxing gloves, Quinny!

There was a challenging undertone to Carragher's offer and Durham was immediately under pressure to accept the proposal or risk being labelled a bottler himself. The footballer had very cleverly turned the tables on the talkSPORT presenter, who admitted as much: 'People thought he owned me in the interview, which is great,' said Durham. 'I have no problem with that whatsoever. I think he got a lot of respect from people for coming on and doing what he did, which was brilliant and, as it turns out, the show went on and it was fantastic.'

While Durham was considering Carragher's offer of a trip up north, the story was picked up by all of the following day's national newspapers. Durham's picture was splashed across *The Times* sports pages while the row made the front page of the *Liverpool Echo*, which left the presenter concerned about ever setting foot in the city again. The incident was also well documented on television as talkSPORT had supplied channels, including Sky Sports News, with a recording of the interview.

The saga left Quinn, a proud Liverpudlian, in the awkward position of mediator between Durham and the people of Liverpool. He felt that he had become a Henry Kissinger-style diplomat who was trying to patch up Durham's relationship with the city. Quinn was instrumental in clearing up any residual resentment between Carragher and Durham when he helped set up a meeting between the pair a year after the original spat. With Carragher's open invitation to Durham to visit him in Liverpool still very much on the presenter's mind, it was decided to broadcast a special show with Quinn and Durham going to Merseyside to coincide with the launch of the Liverpool star's autobiography.

Quinn set the whole venture up through a mutual friend of his and Carragher's, with the show coming live from Cafe Sports England, a bar/restaurant owned by the footballer himself. By that stage, Ian Wright had taken over presenting duties alongside Durham and, even though he wasn't going himself, the former Arsenal legend was worried about his colleague's trip to Merseyside, fearing for his safety.

Durham was accompanied up to Liverpool by his producer Steve Morgan and the pair approached the city with a fair amount of trepidation. The man who had given the label of bottler to one of the city's favourite sons was showing his face on Carragher's manor.

Durham had stressed to Morgan that keeping a low profile and not drawing attention to themselves was absolutely paramount. As such, there was to be no talkSPORT branding anywhere in the bar and all the equipment for the broadcast would be set up in the basement of the restaurant well before the presenters arrived. They would do the show, then discreetly leave as quickly as possible in case any angry Liverpool fans were waiting for them outside.

That was all well and good except nobody had told that plan to talkSPORT head technician Neil Sedley. So, when Morgan and Durham arrived, everything was indeed set up and ready for broadcast, but, to their horror, Sedley was parading around in a fluorescent yellow talkSPORT branded jacket! Poor unsuspecting Sedley was told to remove the jacket immediately, with Durham and Morgan fearing that the damage may already have been done. But they needn't have worried as the afternoon in Liverpool couldn't have gone any better.

Durham and Carragher met for the first time since 'Bottlergate' and shook hands to bury the hatchet once and for all – they even posed for photographs for the *Liverpool Echo* both wearing a pair of boxing gloves. In the event, the Liverpool player could not have been more civil and accommodating, appearing as a guest on the show for around an hour and taking calls from listeners. Carragher even handed Durham a Liverpool shirt as a gift that left the presenter bowled over.

When the show finished, Morgan couldn't help but run up to Durham and say: 'Did that really just happen?' such was the success of the venture. Amazingly, Carragher and Durham have since stayed in touch, exchanging texts about football. Durham has even been to Anfield on the back of tickets given to him by the Liverpool star and met up with him in the players' bar after the game.

Three years later, Carragher was actually scheduled to co-present a daily talkSPORT World Cup show with Durham, but a surprise late call-up to the England squad bound for South Africa – alongside a change of heart about his international career – meant the Liverpudlian was unable to honour his commitment to the station.

'I wouldn't say we're mates but we are on good terms,' reflected Durham. 'One of my policies in the job is not to make special friends with footballers. I think it compromises your position too much. But I've got his number and he has come on the show a couple of times.'

A few months later, Durham began his drivetime show by asking listeners if they thought Theo Walcott should walk out of the England Under-21 squad. The Arsenal youngster had been left on the bench by manager Stuart Pearce, despite his obvious talent, and Durham was arguing he may have had a case to turn his back on his country. Two minutes into the show, Durham's mobile phone started buzzing. He had received a text message. It was from Carragher and it read: 'I'm listening.'

talkSPORT was clearly the station of choice for many football personalities as, following on from the Carragher spat, the drivetime show received another unexpected call. Once again, Quinn was sitting in for Wright alongside Durham, when the presenter started laying in to Everton manager David Moyes. The Toffees boss had hit the headlines earlier that day when he stayed silent for almost a minute during a press conference. He had refused to answer questions about an alleged falling-out with his striker Victor Anichebe and each time he was pressed on the matter, he rolled his eyes and kept his mouth firmly shut.

Durham decided this was unacceptable and that Moyes should have been forced to answer those questions. His argument was that the media help to plough huge amounts of money into the Premier League, so managers should always play ball and answer reporters' questions fully rather than ducking any issues.

Listening in to this broadside was the Everton manager himself, driving home from the training ground. Like Carragher before him, he called in to the station and explained to Durham his reasons for his silence and then proceeded to answer every single question that he had avoided earlier. But that was talkSPORT for you.

Unfortunately, it was also talkSPORT when someone claiming to be former Liverpool ace Jan Molby was put on air to speak to the nation. Molby had been trailed to listeners as a guest on that particular show and the hoax was only rumbled when the real Molby rang in during the imposter's interview wanting to know what on earth was happening.

Moyes and Carragher were not the first characters from the football world to confront Durham on air as the presenter had once been taken to task by ex-Wimbledon hardman and Hollywood movie star Vinnie Jones. During a phone-in back in 2002, Durham had called for Dennis Wise to have his contract terminated by his club, Leicester City, without receiving any payment, after the midfielder had thrown a punch at team-mate Callum Davidson and broken his cheekbone. But Jones, a good friend of Wise's, came on air and launched a tirade against Durham, telling the presenter that he couldn't sit in the studio and judge people without knowing the full facts of the story. Two weeks later, Durham's heart began thumping at twice its normal speed when he saw Jones on a train. However, the former Wimbledon player, who had been interviewed by the talkSPORT presenter in the past, failed to notice Durham, who breathed a rather large sigh of relief.

Back in 2006, Durham had settled well into his drive presenter's seat after a rough ride with Marsh. The 4-7pm show had presented problems for the station when the right combination of presenters could not be found. But all that changed on 26 March 2007, the day Ian Wright first walked through the doors of talkSPORT Towers.

The former England striker was the man the drivetime show had been waiting for. One of the greatest signings talkSPORT had ever made, Wright settled into life at the station very quickly. His personal, cheeky and informal style was a perfect fit for talkSPORT and he hit it off with Durham straight away. The two soon realised they could entertain listeners with their own banter, usually driven by Wright's personality and sense of humour. Durham knew exactly how to get the best out of Wright, learning when he could push him and when he should be left alone. He knew what buttons to press and the relationship blossomed.

Wright laughed on air and made people laugh on air. He sang, he entertained and he made listeners feel like he was their mate. The former striker was extremely popular in the talkSPORT office, thanks to his personal touch. Within a week, he knew everybody's names from the work experience kid making tea to all the producers and researchers. He was everybody's friend and he made people feel good. He also had the amazing knack of being able to translate those personality traits effortlessly on to the airwaves.

Every presenter would love to pretend to be one of the lads but Wright was the genuine article. On top of that, and thanks to his record-breaking football career, he brought thousands of fans with him to the radio station. His caring attitude was summed up by his relationship with Durham, to whom he would regularly send text messages late at night if he sensed he had been down about something during the day.

But Wright had been shocked the first time he tuned in to hear Durham broadcast. His agent had told him that he would be working with Durham – initially for a two-month run which was quickly extended – so he should have a listen. Wright remembered turning the dial to 1089 and hearing Durham belittling the band Snow Patrol: 'The first thing that came out of Durham's mouth was "Snow Patrol? They're garbage!" I thought to myself "Who *is* this guy saying that about people?" But then I realised he was right about certain things. If you think something is rubbish, then say it's rubbish.'

Once they began working together, Wright built up a tremendous amount of respect for his co-presenter, as he realised he had plenty of courage. Anybody who had the balls to call Jamie Carragher a bottler live on air must have had something about them, whether he was right or not. Durham was the man who would say the things he thought, the thoughts other people would be too afraid to articulate and Wright loved that. He also learned a great deal from Durham, as he realised the presenter's reputation among some listeners for picking arguments was unfair – he was just being honest.

Drive producer Morgan had been worried that Wright would be another ex-footballer who would become bored with broadcasting for three hours, four days a week. But he was happy to admit: 'I was proved completely wrong because Wrighty is hard-working and disciplined. I know he buggers about and has a laugh and everything, but at the end of the day he had to graft when he was a footballer and he still has that same temperament. He still has that same mindset, he takes what he does really seriously. He would often pull me to one side and say "How did that sound? Did that work, was that OK?"'

As a player who came to football much later than many of his peers, Wright understood what it meant to graft. The 21-year-old Greenwich Borough striker was all set to continue working as a plasterer, after failing to land a professional contract. Then, three months short of his 22nd birthday, he was offered a deal by Crystal Palace and kicked off a fairytale career in which he eventually became Arsenal's record goalscorer. Although he took his work seriously, Wright was always up to something while off air at talkSPORT Towers. He found it hard just to sit down patiently – especially with a three-hour show looming.

In his early days, he was reprimanded by Ridley for playing football in the office. In one of his over-enthusiastic moments, Wright was whacking a ball around the production floor when he accidentally dislodged one of the ceiling tiles. Ridley had to do his best headmaster impression and invited the former

England international into his office where he said: 'I can't have Ian Wright doing that when I've already told everyone else not to fucking do that!'

Wright put his hands up in the air in surrender and said: 'Bill, it won't happen again.'

The new drivetime star often cycled from his home straight into talkSPORT Towers – not to the cycle parking area in the basement, but right up to the second floor. Wright would ride all the way through the reception, into the lift, then straight from the lift on to the production floor while high-fiving anyone he rode past. Often, if he missed a high-five, he'd have to cycle back out of the door and begin the procedure again. He was a dedicated professional.

The superstar soon had to become familiar with the way talkSPORT operated when it came to outside broadcasts. After working for the BBC for a number of years following his retirement from football, Wright was used to first-class travel and five-star accommodation. But within months of joining talkSPORT, Wright was queuing up with the masses for an easyJet flight out to Milan for the Champions League semi-finals.

Wright was also baffled at how the station would often broadcast shows from bars or hotels rather than from inside the stadium. Before Manchester United's defeat to AC Milan, the drivetime show came live from a hotel room five miles away from the San Siro stadium. The only window in the room was overlooking a building site. Wright had brought Nancy, his other half, along for the trip, expecting it to be something quite different.

Wright thought there was clearly a difference between the working practices of talkSPORT and the BBC, although the commercial station was obviously operating with a far smaller budget than the public-funded Corporation. And he found it all to be one hell of a culture shock.

It worked both ways, however, as Wright also loved working for a broadcaster where he could be himself alongside people whom he considered to be real. At the BBC, Wright resented being looked down upon for not pronouncing every word correctly and for the Corporation's attempts to mould him into somebody he was not. At talkSPORT, Wright was encouraged to go on air, be himself and not worry about what anybody else said. He loved the drive production team too: 'It was refreshing to be around real blokes who support their teams and weren't zooming off down to the Cotswolds once they had finished their shift. They were proper blokes!'

Wright was also given opportunities away from football. As a passionate golf fan and friend of British star Ian Poulter – who was also an Arsenal fan – Wright was sent up to the 2008 Open at Royal Birkdale to broadcast the drivetime show, while Durham joined him via the studio in London. At the time, Wright had just had ankle surgery to correct a long-term problem, meaning he was hobbling around on crutches and also required ice on his ankle as often as possible.

On Day One, Wright's loud and boisterous presenting style drew one or two raised eyebrows from some of the snootier established golf journalists who were sharing the same space in the media centre as the talkSPORT man. The following day he inadvertently caused much more of a stink. Wright's agent spent most of his time running around Birkdale bringing bags of ice to his client, but towards the end of the day, there was a severe shortage. The best his agent could come up with was a bag of frozen prawns, which Wright gratefully placed on his troublesome ankle. Unfortunately, the bag of prawns was left overnight under the media centre desk from where Wright had been broadcasting. The following morning a foul stench filled the media centre, much to the disgust of everyone working there.

Wright's expertise went way beyond sport, as he was also comfortable speaking about social issues. The star was involved in his own projects for children in deprived areas. On one afternoon, Wright and Durham dropped the sporting theme to present a show on gun crime. But never was Wright more serious than the day when one of his sons hit the headlines for the wrong reasons.

Bradley Wright-Phillips, who was a Southampton player at the time, was arrested by police for stealing the contents of handbags from a Southsea nightclub. When Wright went on air the same day the story had broken, he decided he couldn't just bury his head in the sand about the incident: 'I never had anything rehearsed. I said to Adrian "When we go on there, ask me about Bradley." I don't even know how I didn't burst into tears somewhere along the line, because it was cutting me that deep.'

But instead of crying, he delivered some of the most honest and emotional radio talkSPORT listeners had ever heard. Wright bared his soul to the nation, explaining the difficulties of being a father. He spoke from the heart with raw emotion, wondering if he had gone wrong somewhere as a parent. Here is what he said on air:

'The fact is that Bradley, right now, wherever he is, he knows he has majorly messed up now, and he needs to look in the mirror and realise that. If he thinks at one stage to himself "I should have listened to my Dad", then I've done my job. I can't tell him any more, I can't follow him for 24 hours a day.

'If he can't recognise he's in a bad situation then he's going to have to take the consequences of that. I have to stick by him – he's my boy; I want him to do well. But I want him to realise that he's learning the hardest lesson in football, in being a footballer, that anyone can learn – from this day on.

'He knows he shouldn't have been there and no one's going to sit back in the family and say "Yeah but, don't say this." No! Because it's wrong. It's wrong and what I can't forgive him for, he should be thinking about getting in the first team and impressing his new manager. That is what I was saying to him, but now how hard is the lesson going to be? I just wish they'd bloody listen!'

The response from listeners was incredible as other fathers called in to share their experiences. Wright's son Bradley was one of the listeners that day. After the show, he spoke to his father to tell him that what he had said was perfect.

By that stage, Wright and Durham's drivetime show was operating four days a week, from Monday to Thursday. The programme differed from many other talkSPORT shows at the time as it rarely relied upon guests to add their views on any topics. This show was for the listeners, and Wright was more comfortable with that. He believed that once a programme began relying on guests, it would be easy to point out when it was going downhill as the calibre of guest would decrease.

This was the formula for the extremely successful new drive show and presenter partnership that took the station to new heights. With Wright leading the way, the 4-7pm slot was finally rivalling breakfast. But changes were also afoot on the station's flagship show, with new blood waiting in the wings to keep Alan Brazil company in the early hours.

15

It's Chicken For Brekkie and Porky's Up the Pole

After the show, we had a drink at 10.15am. Having a Stella at that time was a real change for me!

RONNIE IRANI

There is only one radio station that would send someone who knew nothing about rugby union to cover the sport's World Cup. Take a bow, talkSPORT.

Mike 'Porky' Parry's workload was back to normal again following his health problems, although he still had to make sure he watched his alcohol intake. That was put severely to the test when he was sent out to France late in 2007 to provide reports and bring home all the colour from rugby's showpiece event.

Parry would be the first to acknowledge that his rugby knowledge 'couldn't fill the back of a postage stamp', but he was in France to pick up reactions from supporters and give listeners an insight into how the tournament was being received by the French. There was nobody better at thrusting a microphone in the faces of unsuspecting fans and, with England being the defending world champions, Porky was as patriotic as usual.

Lending a weight of expertise to proceedings were former England captain Will Carling and Australian legend David Campese, while talkSPORT's Mike Bovill provided all the updates and match reports from the grounds.

With England unexpectedly reaching the final after a poor start to the tournament, talkSPORT's coverage became increasingly popular, as it lacked the stuffiness of the BBC's where the listeners' knowledge of the game was almost assumed. Instead, when football fans became interested in how England were progressing, talkSPORT were able to offer coverage in layman's terms, so people less familiar with the sport could understand what was going on.

It was all a far cry from the previous World Cup, back in 2003 in Australia. Bovill was the only talkSPORT man there, having paid his own way as a backpacker, working for the station on a freelance basis. With no accreditation, he bought his own tickets to all the games and then spent all night queuing for a ticket for the England v Australia final in Sydney.

Having forked out £250 for his ticket, he then received a call from Jim 'Jim'll Fix It' Brown, who told him that the station wanted him to broadcast live from a Sydney bar during the final. Understandably, Bovill, a massive rugby fan, was not best pleased and refused to give up his ticket to what potentially was the greatest sporting night of his life – especially having spent all night queuing for it. The row rumbled on until Bovill appeared on the breakfast show the morning before the final, where programme director Parry asked him to confirm that he would be watching the final from a bar.

Bovill said he wouldn't and the pair became involved in

something of an on-air ding-dong, which was followed by a blazing row after the show in which Bovill refused to give up his ticket under any circumstances. Eventually, another freelancer was found to report from the bar, Bovill went to the game and the rest is history. He even came on air live from the ground after the game, where he and Parry both cried to the nation after watching Jonny Wilkinson kick England to victory.

Back in France four years later, England's defeat in the final at the hands of South Africa was an anti-climax after the drama of Sydney. But talkSPORT had covered the tournament far more professionally in their capacity as official broadcasters. They paid their way to be there, inside the stadia. And, in a similar vein, the station had also just embarked on its most exciting project yet.

Scott Taunton's determination to cover football in an official capacity was rewarded when he signed a deal with the Premier League to make talkSPORT official broadcasting partners of the English top flight. Now, for the first time in the station's history, coverage of Premier League games would be heard across the UK every Saturday afternoon.

Whereas previously the station could talk a good game, Saturday afternoons were always notable for the absence of nationwide top-flight commentary. Adrian Durham did a fantastic job of juggling the latest scores and reports from around the country every week, but even he would have welcomed the new deal, as he could pause for breath during the live commentary.

Nigel Pearson, who had commentated at the World Cup the previous year, was drafted in to be the station's lead commentator and the first broadcast came live from the Reebok Stadium as Bolton Wanderers took on Newcastle United. This was a far more mouthwatering fixture than it looked at first glance, as former Bolton manager Sam Allardyce was taking charge of Newcastle for the first time on his old stomping ground.

It was another milestone for the station and a further levelling of the playing field between the commercial outlet and the all-powerful and resource-heavy BBC. For Pearson, it was a far cry from when he worked for the station in its infancy. He once reported from a Newcastle home match in 2001 where even the local radio stations were turning their noses up at talkSPORT having a place alongside them in the press box.

Alongside the Premier League broadcasting rights – and the arrival of Ian Wright – 2007 also saw a new arrival on the *Alan Brazil Sports Breakfast* as former England and Essex cricketer Ronnie Irani joined the station in September to replace Graham 'Beeky' Beecroft, who returned to reporting in his native north west. Irani struck up a different kind of relationship with Brazil, although the Scot would always revert to his default setting of banter and mickey-taking, eventually settling on the nickname 'Chicken Biryani' – or mostly just 'Chicken' – for his new partner in crime. Brazil had originally tried to call Irani 'Vernon' as he sounded – and looked – not too dissimilar to TV presenter Vernon Kay. That name didn't stick at all, so Brazil went with Chicken.

Irani had already appeared on several talkSPORT shows in the months before he joined the station permanently. He had recorded cricket interviews for the station and even spent a week alongside Paul Hawksbee, filling in for Andy Jacobs. That was during the winter, while Irani wasn't playing cricket and, despite overtures to do more work for the station once the new season was underway, he was back at Essex concentrating on the game he loved. However, within a couple of months, his career was ended by a serious knee injury, which meant he was available for media work again. Bill Ridley moved quickly to tie up a deal to make Irani the new breakfast show co-presenter.

Most seasoned drinkers would find it difficult to keep up with Brazil, but Irani was about to embark on a professional and social relationship with the talkSPORT legend on the back of around five years of barely having touched a drop of the hard stuff. In the early part of his career, Irani boozed with the best of them, from his Essex team-mates to his England colleagues, but as cricket became more professional, the players spent far less time in pubs and bars.

Nevertheless, when the new breakfast pair's first show had finished, Brazil dragged Irani straight to the pub and the former cricketer had a pint in his hand before most people had finished digesting their breakfasts. He admitted the experience was unusual: 'After the show, we had a drink at 10.15am. Having a Stella at that time was a real change for me!'

Life was about to change quite dramatically for Irani, who rose at around 3.30am every morning in his Essex home to be driven into the studio by his driver Dave – even *he* received a nickname from Brazil, as the Scot began calling him Lewis on air, after the Formula One world champion Lewis Hamilton. The early rises were not such a rude awakening for the former cricketer as, in his youth, he had worked in a fruit and veg market where he started his shift at 2.30am. Compared to those days, presenting the breakfast show gave Irani a lie-in.

Irani also had to become used to accompanying Brazil on social engagements for the station. His first experience of the Cheltenham festival was an eye-opener. Brazil quickly schooled his colleague in the ways of the racecourse: champagne during the last hour of the show, followed by the rest of the morning in the Guinness tent. Then, after a spot of lunch, it was time for the racing.

A more relaxed trip away from talkSPORT Towers was the breakfast show's annual sojourn to Tring in Hertfordshire for a week's detox at Champney's health farm. Over the course of their stay, the breakfast presenters would enjoy complimentary treatments at the spa, which led to the bizarre sight of the burly Brazil enjoying a facial as well as a cholesterol test. After a couple of days at the resort one year, Brazil had built up a bit of a thirst, so he and Irani sneaked out of the complex and took a taxi to the nearest pub, three miles up the road.

Stephen Purdew, the spa owner, grew concerned that he couldn't find them anywhere when they were supposed to be enjoying the spa facilities. He repeatedly rang Brazil's mobile phone, but there was no answer. Meanwhile, Brazil and Irani were making merry in the pub and didn't return to the hotel until 10pm. As their taxi pulled up to the gates of the complex, Purdew was waiting for them with a furious look on his face: 'Where have you been? This is bang out of order!' he exploded at them. But his efforts at disciplining Brazil were futile, and when he heard the pair had been in the pub all day, he was soon laughing along with both of them.

Having gone away together to broadcast from various UK destinations, Brazil and Irani also treated themselves to a trip overseas towards the end of 2007, although this was strictly pleasure, not business. Charismatic boxer Ricky Hatton was taking on the highly rated Floyd Mayweather Jr in one of the fights of the decade in Las Vegas, and the breakfast presenters were going on a weekend jolly to watch the bout.

The pair landed at Las Vegas airport all revved up for a superb weekend, only to be greeted with a volley of abuse from a group of Manchester City fans. Hatton is a passionate City supporter and his fights always attracted thousands of fans of the club from the blue half of the city. With Irani being a Manchester United supporting, Lancashire-born cricketer who chose to play for southern county Essex and Brazil an ex-United player, they were easy targets for Hatton's fans.

Brazil immediately felt uncomfortable and said to Irani: 'Chicken, I'm not going to the fight!'

'Al, we've got to go to the fight!'

'No way. If you think I'm going to go there and get pelters from them . . . It's not happening.'

Irani thought a few drinks on the Strip and a stint at one of the casinos might change his colleague's mind. After all, this was the biggest sports event on the planet at that time and tickets were reportedly changing hands for as much as £5,000. But Brazil wasn't for turning. The Scot knew the MGM Grand, which was hosting the fight, would be full of City fans and he had no intention of going anywhere near the place. Instead, the pair holed themselves up in the luxury of the Wynn casino where they proceeded to hit the roulette tables and knock back a lorry-load of drinks.

By the time the fight was about to start, Irani still had a pair of tickets in his pocket and was keen to nip over to the MGM Grand. But Brazil remained adamant that he wouldn't join him. They ordered more drinks, won more than $2,000 between them on the tables and would have had no idea that Hatton was receiving a pasting from Mayweather just up the road.

Having flown more than 5,200 miles to witness the biggest fight of the year, Brazil and Irani returned to London having not seen a single punch thrown in anger. The former cricketer had to be content with watching a recording of the bout from the comfort of his Essex living room later that day.

One talkSPORT presenter who would never have left a ticket unused was Mike Parry. He was given a new role reporting on England away matches at around the same time as the station began its Premier League commentaries. A fiercely passionate, chest-thumping Englishman, Parry considered it a privilege to be able to attend so many of England's internationals in far-flung places from Kazakhstan to Belarus.

Even in his earlier talkSPORT days on outside broadcasts before major matches alongside Brazil, Parry would frequently go to games alone. The Scot would usually pull out at the last minute with a variety of excuses – the fact was he just preferred the comfort of watching football from a hotel bar (particularly if it was an England game).

Parry's new role as the station's roving England reporter provided for a host of new adventures and incidents as he travelled across Europe watching his national side. This was especially the case when travelling to the former Soviet Union, where Parry found that not much had changed despite two decades passing since the collapse of communism. Porky was always accompanied on these trips by producer Matt Smith, who set up the satellite broadcasting equipment to ensure his live link-ups back to the UK ran as smoothly as possible.

On one trip to Belarus, Smith and Parry arrived at the airport in Minsk. Not just satisfied with checking all of Smith's audio equipment in the airport for 45 minutes, the Belarussian officials then drove the talkSPORT pair and all the gear out into the freezing cold night to a remote outhouse on the outskirts of the airport. All this, despite Smith having arrived in the former Eastern Bloc state armed with all the necessary paperwork. It was as if the KGB were still in charge.

Parry was told to wait in the pokey outhouse while Smith had to follow a customs official who was in possession of the radio gear. Walking along a dirt track in the middle of a pitch black night, Smith began to fear the worst. Eventually, after what seemed like an eternity, Smith arrived at a warehouse which was full of shady-looking Belarussians drawing hard on cheap cigarettes.

The customs official told Smith he would have to leave all the radio equipment in this warehouse overnight. Looking around at the rabble of warehouse workers, who were doing their best to look as inefficient, shifty and untrustworthy as possible, Smith asked if there was anything he could do to leave the airport with their equipment that night. Perhaps he could make sure the customs official received a pair of tickets for the game the following night? Unfortunately for Smith, the Belarussian was keen to go to the game but was offering nothing in return, suggesting only that the talkSPORT man should hand out some cash to the warehouse workers to ensure that the radio gear was properly looked after overnight.

With no choice, Smith and Parry had to leave the airport minus all sound gear – and a fair bit of money. The following morning, Porky was forced to appear on the breakfast show via mobile phone while his colleague returned to the airport where he spent another three hours battling to retrieve the station's equipment.

Amazingly, Smith had to go through exactly the same process the following day on the way out of the country. On a 36-hour trip to Belarus, the producer was in the airport for at least 14 hours. And Parry didn't fare much better with his attempts to talk to locals about the game for a radio colour piece. Every time he approached anyone in the street with a microphone in Minsk, they would wave him away with a frightened look in their eyes.

Over in Russia, Parry had more luck, thanks to the recruitment of Igor, a local who spoke the language and helped ease Porky through all the red tape at the airport. With England in Moscow for a crucial European Championship qualifier, Parry was keen to hear what the Russian people thought about the England team and Igor could also assist in that department.

Hovering around the area close to where the England team were based, Porky saw two girls walk past him in tears. Igor approached them to see what the problem was and it turned out that, bizarrely, they were upset that Phil Neville had apparently snubbed them. The Everton midfielder had rushed past the girls, who were part of a scrum of fans hunting for autographs. Unfortunately, Neville hadn't noticed that one of the girls, who declared that she loved the former Manchester United player, was trying to give him a Russian history book as a gift.

When the England players had boarded their coach after training, one of these girls had stood next to it in tears while waving the book in Neville's direction. Fortunately, the girl also spoke a bit of English and gave an interview to Porky, detailing her heartbreak. This surreal story was played out on talkSPORT repeatedly throughout the day, as puzzled British listeners attempted to work out how any young female could have targeted Neville ahead of David Beckham or possibly Frank Lampard. Parry spoke to Everton about the incident and Neville said that he would love to receive the gift, but unfortunately the station lost touch with the girl as she had changed her mobile phone number.

By this stage, Parry was being sent out to report from all the major matches, not just those involving England, and he was in Rome for the 2009 Champions League final between Manchester United and Barcelona. The trip had gone smoothly for Porky until he tried to enter the stadium to watch the match. Parry had milled around the city with the fans and soaked up the pre-match atmosphere in his live link-ups with each talkSPORT show on the day of the final.

Ever the conscientious professional, he arrived at Rome's Olympic Stadium two hours before kick-off. As he approached the specific entrance to the stadium to which his tickets had directed him, two huge gates slammed shut. A red carpet was then laid out along the entire road leading up to those gates in preparation for the arrival of Silvio Berlusconi, the Italian prime minister. Porky asked where he was supposed to enter the stadium and was told to walk just around the corner.

By this stage, several other ticket holders had been denied access at the same recommended entrance and joined Parry in walking the length of one side of the stadium only to be told at each gate to walk a little further down. By the time Parry had reached the end of the stadium, he was becoming a little fed up and asked another official what on earth was going on. After being fobbed off again, Parry spied a set of steps that led down to the stadium and asked a steward if he could use them. Once again, he was turned away and sent further round the arena and up into the surrounding hills.

After walking what seemed like close to a mile, Parry and his gang of exiles looked round and found they were so high above the Olympic Stadium that they could actually see the pitch. Realising he was going to miss the game if the ridiculous charade continued any longer, Parry and his cohorts began to clamber over fences and slide down clay-surfaced sheer-faced drops in the direction of the stadium.

Disaster then struck for Porky: 'I couldn't keep my balance. I catapulted over and was covered in clay and lime and stuff. I cut my elbows, face, everything. I looked a complete mess. They almost wouldn't let me in as I looked like a fucking bag man!'

Finally, after surviving a mini-crush at the turnstile, Parry took his seat just as the teams were walking on to the pitch, despite having arrived at the stadium two hours previously.

The talkSPORT legend had also found himself in Italy back in 2007 for Manchester United's Champions League semi-final against AC Milan. The evening before the match, Porky was stationed outside the hotel as the United team were about to leave for training. With huge crowds having gathered, Parry – who stood 5ft 8¾in in his stockinged feet – was struggling to see the scene he was supposed to be describing in a live report for the drivetime show. He started his broadcast on top of a wall, but even that didn't give him a decent vantage point so he climbed up a flagpole.

As the United bus pulled out of the hotel car park, midfielder Paul Scholes pointed out of the window towards a wild-haired and bearded man, who was dangling from a flagpole with a microphone in his hand. He called over his team-mates and they all began pointing and laughing at the talkSPORT correspondent. Parry witnessed their hilarity but chose not to mention it on air.

The following morning, United's kit man was having a chat with Porky in the team hotel and casually mentioned to him: 'You should have heard Scholesy giving you a bit of stick on the bus last night. He called you a monkey on a stick!'

With a Manchester United player making fun of talkSPORT's finest, one of England's most charismatic and talented footballers joining the radio station and a former England cricketer co-presenting the breakfast show, 2007 had been a quite magnificent year for the station. To cap it all off, talkSPORT swept the board at the annual Arqiva Commercial Radio Awards.

Ridley walked off with the Programmer of the Year gong, the station won a special Gold Award for its efforts over the previous 12 months and also landed a Technical Innovation award for broadcasting World Cup coverage to England fans in Germany via digital radio. And the cherry on top of the icing on the cake came in the shape of the Station of the Year award, which Scott Taunton gratefully received.

It seemed like nothing could stop the runaway success of talkSPORT, even though none of the home nations had qualified for Euro 2008, meaning there would be less advertising revenue and a barren football summer ahead. As it turned out, that was to be the least of the station's problems as its very own *annus horribilis* was about to dawn.

16

How the Mighty Fell

You're a Nazi ... You're just showing yourself up for the ignoramus
you are because you are not even allowing me to finish. You're just
shouting!

JON GAUNT

Programme directors had come and gone at a rapid rate in the
early days of talkSPORT, but a period of stability had kicked in
under Scott Taunton's stewardship. Bill Ridley had been in the
hotseat since Parry's serious illness in 2004, and, by early 2008,
it was time for a change.

Ridley was retiring, although he would remain at talkSPORT
Towers in a consulting capacity, and Taunton had pulled off
something of a coup by persuading Radio 5 Live's managing
editor Moz Dee to join the station. Although he started work as
an actor and appeared in several films and theatre productions,
Dee moved from acting to radio when he joined BBC Coventry
and Warwickshire as a presenter. From there, he was headhunted
by Talk Radio, where he presented sports shows and eventually
became the station's Head of Sport. Shortly before the launch of
talkSPORT, Dee joined Radio 5 Live, where he remained for

nine years. Now, he was returning to the 1089 frequency, although it was the first time he had ever set foot in talkSPORT Towers.

Returning to commercial radio from the BBC was something of a culture shock for Dee. He liked the edginess of talkSPORT as opposed to the more passive listening experience offered by his old station. He was impressed with how talkSPORT had evolved over the eight years since its launch and he knew that 5 Live and other established mainstream channels were starting to imitate the different way in which the station interacted with its listeners.

The main task when he arrived was to make sure everyone in the building realised just how huge the talkSPORT brand had become. Here was a massively successful commercial radio station, but Dee found some people were almost apologetic for the way talkSPORT did things. His vision was to make even more people sit up and take notice of this new major player in broadcasting by making everything the station did 'bigger, bolder and better'. After all, there was always room for improvement.

The first year of his tenure was marked by an aggressive expansion of talkSPORT's talent roster. Suddenly, former footballer Stan Collymore was on the station more or less six days a week, controversial TV presenter Jeremy Kyle was presenting a lunchtime show on his passion for football every Sunday, and former England cricket star Darren Gough also became a regular presenter. Then, in April 2009, talkSPORT shocked the world as Dee persuaded comedian Russell Brand and Oasis frontman Noel Gallagher to present a one-off, exclusive show together.

But before those landmark moments in talkSPORT history, Dee had the unfortunate task of dealing with two huge crises that led to the dismissals of two of the station's biggest names.

James Whale was – and still is – a talkSPORT legend. His cult late-night show was compulsive listening for hundreds of thousands. The programme was so popular that it attracted twice talkSPORT's overall market share for its slot. He may have been slightly egotistical – the night England missed out on a place at Euro 2008 following defeat by Croatia, he threw a hissy fit. It wasn't because his plans for the following summer had been thrown into disarray that led him to throw his toys out of the pram. As a result of England's defeat, an extended fans' phone-in was aired, meaning Whale's show was cancelled and that resulted in the presenter ranting and raving outside the studio – but Whale lived for radio and his talkSPORT show.

That probably explained his reaction better than thinking it was an ego-motivated strop. It was that passion, along with his ability to surprise, to which listeners were addicted – but it was that fervour in his beliefs that led to his downfall one evening.

It was 20 March 2008 and Whale was discussing the forthcoming London mayoral elections on 1 May, in which the two main protagonists were the incumbent Ken Livingstone, the Labour candidate, and Boris Johnson, the Conservative choice. Ofcom's rules regarding broadcasting firmly state that all television and radio output must remain duly impartial. This rule was especially stringent in the run-up to an election.

For some reason, that evening Whale had wound himself up after reading about the prime minister Gordon Brown's endorsement of Livingstone as his preferred candidate. The following live exchange with his producer Asher Gould spelled trouble:

Whale: Now, in the run-up to the mayoral election in London, I don't think we're supposed to show any, any preference one way or the other. But in an interview earlier today, I heard

Ken Livingstone being championed by the prime minister. Gordon Brown said if Londoners didn't vote for Ken Livingstone, if they voted for Boris Johnson, who, by the way, I think would make a fantastic leader of this city. If Boris Johnson was the London mayor, people would have a far better quality of life and would not be ripped off nearly so much, if at all. And for anybody that doesn't vote for Boris, you'll get what you deserve because what you'll get is Ken Livingstone. Now, I'm pretty sure we're not supposed to champion one . . .

Ash: Yeah, you're not allowed to do that.

Whale: But I don't give a stuff. I couldn't care less. If the prime minister feels that he can champion Ken Livingstone, and let's face it, Ken Livingstone has been nothing but a complete and utter tragedy for the capital city. And I know if you're listening in Glasgow or Cardiff or Portsmouth or whatever you're not interested in London. But London is the capital city of this nation and whatever happens in London affects everybody here. And I think, quite frankly, Gordon Brown should be ashamed of himself. If Ken Livingstone wins the next election then, quite frankly, I think people had better, anybody with any kind of intelligence and any kind of I don't know, you know interest in improving themselves, their lives and the lives of others, better leave. I think Ken Livingstone running London again will be a complete tragedy. If you don't walk, you'll be a non-person.

Ash: It's good for some people what he's done.

Whale: No, not good for anyone. Boris Johnson . . .

Ash: If you're a roller blader.

Whale: 'Boris Johnson for Mayor of London' that has to be the mantra. And if the authorities don't like it . . .

Ash: You're not allowed to say that.

Whale: I couldn't give a stuff.

Ash: You can't do, sorry you can't. He's [Boris Johnson] a nice bloke, though; he did the show here when you were off. Really, really, really nice, genuinely nice guy.

Whale: Vote him in.

Ash: You can't say anything about his politics. You're not allowed to.

Whale: Make sure that he's the next Mayor of London . . .

Shortly after that exchange, Whale had the following conversation with a caller:

Whale: I don't think any of us would see much difference at all. I mean, the one little thing that makes me, makes me feel that there is a light at the end of the tunnel, if Boris Johnson gets in as Mayor of London, I think you will see the face of politics change dramatically.

Caller: Well, on a final note, and on that subject, James, I mean Brown's backing Livingstone. Well, that's the kiss of death for Ken then, isn't it?

Whale: Well, I hope so, but I was under the impression that the prime minister should be totally impartial to who became the mayor of our capital city. And since he's not going to be impartial then nor am I. And I think if people don't vote for Boris at the elections, then they've just got themselves to blame if Livingstone gets in for another term. Because if he gets in for another term, he will increase the congestion charge area wider and it will operate longer. And the people of London that drive cars, and they are the majority in my view, will suffer.

Caller: And the only real thing that they've been arguing, I think Brown was arguing for Ken is the amount of people, the increase in the use of public transport. But of course that's no thanks to New Labour; that's because we have had so many new people into the country recently.

Whale: You see, I think Boris would control that. I think Boris would make the place a more fun city to live in. You get, you know like, some of these major cities where the mayor has been a bit of a personality, rather than a tyrant. I think that's what we can look forward to if we get Boris Johnson in as mayor. As long as the prime minister starts promoting Ken Livingstone and he wants a war, he's got it.

If Whale had slipped out an innocent comment about voting for Johnson just once, he may well have kept his talkSPORT job. The problem was the way he repeatedly breached the rules during the course of that evening's show.

talkSPORT had never been fined by Ofcom, but on this occasion the regulator handed the station a whopping penalty of £20,000. Just as tough was the decision that was made regarding Whale's future.

To the man in the street, it was difficult to square the Ofcom rules that sunk Whale with the fact that newspapers are not subject to anything like the same regulation. In fact, on the day of the election – six weeks after Whale's comments were broadcast – London's *Evening Standard* could have led their front page with a screaming headline: 'VOTE FOR BORIS JOHNSON' with no problem at all. But radio and television *are* still bound by the rules, whether they liked them or not and, having broken them, the decision was made to let Whale go.

It was with extremely heavy hearts that management arrived

at that judgement, as they were reluctant to remove a character who had become so synonymous with the radio station. Whale's loyal listeners were up in arms at their hero's dismissal, but the decision had been made and wasn't going to be reversed. It was an acrimonious departure, but time is a great healer. A year later, Whale met Taunton at an industry dinner where they shook hands and put the matter behind them.

Unfortunately, another presenter needed reining in, but for different reasons. Programme director Moz Dee was soon knee-deep in controversy again, just months into his new job, when Jon Gaunt overstepped the mark during an interview with a local councillor. Gaunt's naturally confrontational, shouty style was his trademark and often sparked on-air spats.

But it was an off-air spat that had proved unforgettable, when Gaunt went over to Brussels to broadcast a programme live from the European Parliament. The show itself ran smoothly, but there was a notable off-air exchange between Gaunt and a Finnish MEP by the name of Alexander Stubb. The politician accused Gaunt of being racist and the two became involved in a shouting match in which the talkSPORT man told the MEP to 'Fuck off!' – an embarrassing incident for all concerned. It didn't paint the station in a particularly good light – and neither did his confrontation with the local councillor a year later, in November 2008. That encounter proved to be his last broadcast for the station.

In the days before that interview, Redbridge Council had taken the decision not to allow foster children to be placed in the care of adults who smoked. This was clearly a matter of controversy and was a subject very close to Gaunt's heart, because the presenter had spent time in care as a child. As he saw it, the council were condemning children to stay in care purely because potential foster parents smoked. Gaunt's producers had attempted to arrange an interview with a Redbridge councillor for the day before, but nobody was available. On the day the interview took place, Gaunt's *Sun* column had focused on the story and he had labelled the council as 'health and safety Nazis'.

Here's how the interview panned out:

Gaunt: Let's have a chat with Michael Stark, cabinet member for children's services on Redbridge Council who joins us now. Hello, Michael.

Stark: Hello.

Gaunt: Right, your policy then on fostering and smoking, what is it?

Stark: Well, we intend from 2010 that any foster carers in the London Borough of Redbridge will be non-smokers and there will be exceptions to this, of course, there will always be the exceptions, and the reason for this is because ... cot death, asthma, middle ear disease, pneumonia, bronchitis are illnesses that are increased by smoking.

Gaunt: By passive smoking.

Stark: Yes, by passive smoking, and we also know that Professor Robert West who is a Director of Tobacco Studies at Cancer Research has stated that while fostering is a difficult area and it sounds harsh, I think this ban is a good thing. On balance you have to go with the health of the child.

Gaunt: Right OK, slow down, slow down a bit. You saying it's not a blanket ban?

Stark: Well, there's always exceptions isn't there?

Gaunt: No, is it a blanket ban? Because you mentioned ...

Stark: We will ...

Gaunt: No, hang on a minute, there seems to be a contradiction in what you're saying. It's either a blanket ban or it isn't.

Stark: If only life was so simple, Jon.

Gaunt: Really.

Stark: But it isn't.

Gaunt: Is it not?

Stark: The reality is that we, our foster carers we have now that are smokers, will be encouraged to give up smoking and we will be providing that support.

Gaunt: That's good.

Stark: People we are taking on will be required to be non-smokers.

Gaunt: So no new foster parents will be allowed, let me just clarify?

Stark: Yeah, this is . . .

Gaunt: I haven't finished. No new foster parents will be allowed if they're smokers after 2010, yes?

Stark: There will always be exceptional circumstances, I mean . . .

Gaunt: That is different to what the policy said.

Stark: No, the policy has always said there will be exceptional circumstances.

Gaunt: Well, what would be exceptional circumstances?

Stark: Well, let me give you an example. I was thinking of this coming home on the train the other day. Supposing you on your street knew a child and you were very friendly and sometimes [the child] stayed with you, but you weren't technically related, you were an 'auntie' or an 'uncle', or something like that, and there was some disaster and the family were wiped out in some terrific, awful event. Obviously, a child might want to live [with you]. You'd be willing to take them on and so on. Exceptional situations like that we would obviously look at, of course we would.

Gaunt: I understand that. What about an existing foster parent who doesn't give up smoking and says "Actually, I like having a fag, but I'm not going to smoke in front of the children. I never smoke in the room, I only ever go out of the front door." Why can't they foster?

Stark: Well, we're not going to drag children away from foster parents they are already with.

Gaunt: No, I'm talking post-2010, when your policy comes in to place.

Stark: In the future we won't be using them as foster parents.

Gaunt: OK, so now we're getting to it. So therefore, somebody who says "Yeah, I like a fag. I smoke about 10, 20 a day but I've never smoked in the house, I smoke outside." That person would not be allowed to be a foster parent?

Stark: No, because the trouble is, Jon, they do smoke in the house.

Gaunt: How do you know that?

Stark: Because we have councillors on our council who are smokers who say we never smoke in the building, there's a policy we wouldn't dream. You go in their offices, there they are, puffing away illegally as they drop it on the floor.

Gaunt: So you are a Nazi then?

Stark: Erm, I find that ...

Gaunt: You are ... because ... No you are, you're a Nazi ...

Stark: No, no, no, no, no, no ...

Gaunt: Because what you're saying ... what you're saying ...

Stark: No, no, no, no. I'm not going to let you just say that, whatever you're going to say next, that is an offensive, insulting remark that is emotive and brings discussion down to the lowest key ...

Gaunt: Is that right? Is that right?

Stark: Which is why I was concerned about not appearing on your programme.

Gaunt: And that is why you have just shouted. Look at him shouting at me. Look at him shouting.

Stark: Because of your sort of offensive comments of that nature, which have probably [been] made to get me annoyed, which have made you successful. . .

Gaunt: Correct, you're just showing yourself up for the ignoramus you are because you are not even allowing me to finish . . . you're just shouting . . .

Stark: (shouting in background) You are rude. No, because you have used an insult that is probably actionable in law to be quite honest. . .

Gaunt: Well, I think your attitude is wrong.

Stark: Probably actionable. Probably actionable.

Gaunt: Take action then. Take action, because listen to me. . .

Stark: No doubt that will give you more publicity and make you more thrilled.

Gaunt: Take action if you wish . . .

Stark: Make you more thrilled . . .

Gaunt: Take action if you wish . . .

Stark: Make you more thrilled . . .

Gaunt: You are a health Nazi. You have no evidence . . .

Stark: Oh, you've put another word in front now, to carry out the legal part. Health Nazi, you'll probably get away with that one.

Gaunt: I, you didn't even allow me . . .

Stark: You've done that before . . .

Gaunt: You didn't allow me to finish my sentence.

Stark: Well, you've stopped me three times, so I don't see why I shouldn't stop you.

Gaunt: Do you want to carry on with the interview?

Stark: It's entirely up to you, Jon.

Gaunt: I would love to if you would just shut up for a minute.

Stark: You've been on at me to come on this programme, so I suppose you want to talk to me.

Gaunt: And you've waited 24 hours to come on. I'll go back to my point shall ...

Stark: Not at all, I do have a life and a job like yourself.

Gaunt: Really? I shall go back to my major question, shall I? When I said to you someone who smokes, right, who says they won't smoke in front of a child, you turned round and you said you don't believe them because you've got councillors who are liars, councillors who say they won't smoke in the building but do. Well, just because some of your councillors are liars doesn't mean the beautiful people who want to look after kids are, does it?

Stark: I don't follow that reasoning at all.

Gaunt: You've ... how do you not follow the reasoning?

Stark: Am I going to be able to reply or not?

Gaunt: Is every smoker a liar?

Stark: Am I going to be able to comment or not? Are you going to keep talking? Or would you like to interview yourself? You're obviously very good at interviewing yourself. I have said that the trouble is when people do smoke – and I have been on other programmes when people have smoked 60 a day, 20 or 30 a day – and I find at the end of the interview they say, well it's all right to smoke downstairs, isn't it? No, it isn't, passive smoking for children is very dangerous, there-fore we have to take that sort of policy.

Gaunt: How many children have you got in care in the Redbridge area?

Stark: About 60 at the moment.

Gaunt: Sixty.

Stark: About.

Gaunt: How many foster parents have you got?

Stark: We've got umm, umm, we've got about 80 or 90, but we also use private sometimes, about 18 smoke.

Gaunt: Have you ever been in care yourself?

Stark: About 18 smoke. No, have you?

Gaunt: Yes.

Stark: Oh. (Pause) Good.

Gaunt: What good that I was in care?

Stark: Well, no, that you've got a personal view, which will be valuable to the listeners to the programme.

Gaunt: Well, you should read my column in the *Sun* today, my friend, and I go back: you are a health Nazi because you're suggesting that every smoker . . .

Stark: I like the health bit.

Gaunt: Well, you're a Nazi then, if you want that, because you want to be actionable, then you get on with it. I'll go back to my point Mr . . . what's your name again? I've forgotten your name. Michael Stark.

Stark: Well, I can't remember yours either, it's very difficult, isn't it?

Gaunt: Michael St . . . no need to be rude. Michael Stark.

Stark: Well, you've been rude enough, so I don't see why I can't be rude back.

Gaunt: Tory cabinet member.

Stark: You give me that, [but] don't you like it back, Jon?

Gaunt: What I find odd, what I find odd is that you're the cabinet member for children's services and you're talking in an aggressive, bullying manner.

Stark: Well, that's what your programme's intending to do.

Gaunt: No ...

Stark: That's what you do, you wind people up and you use rude, emotive words ...

Gaunt: You just said, councillor, that you haven't heard of my name and you haven't heard of my programme, so how do you know what my programme does?

Anyway, we'll go back on to the main point. You haven't been through the care system yourself, you think smokers would lie and they would smoke in front of the children. You are putting a blanket ban on people who would smoke from fostering; you'd rather a child be wrapped up in bed on their own, would you, on a night in a children's home? Like I was, four or five to a room without a special to look after them when there is perfectly caring people out there that would like to take them on.

I'm not a smoker myself, by the way, but some people do smoke, some people do smoke and they make fantastic foster parents as well. Most of them are responsible, like most parents are nowadays, and wouldn't smoke in an enclosed environment with their child. What gives you the right to set yourself up as somebody who thinks that all smokers are liars, just because certain members of your councils are hypocrites and liars? Why do you therefore taint everybody with the same brush? What makes you so knowledgeable, councillor?

Stark: Can I have a go now?

Gaunt: Well, that's why I've just paused.

Stark: Oh good, I thought you were just making a speech.

Gaunt: Now you're being rude again. You're being rude again.

Stark: Well, yeah, you're being immensely rude. How calling someone a Nazi can be ...

Gaunt: Oh, we're going back to that.

Stark: Insulting.

Gaunt: Why don't we go back to answer the question of what I've just put to you?

Stark: Because I've tried to answer the question, if you just shut up for a moment, but it's very difficult to get you to, isn't it? Is it the Jon Jon programme? The instant, the point is that people do not live in the conditions that you were brought up in, which obviously has had an effect on you.

Gaunt: Oh, I see. Hold on a minute.

Stark: People are . . .

Gaunt: You're now going to insult me, are you, and say that somehow because I was in care and because of the experiences I've got, I am some kind of victim and I have some kind of psychological problem? I find that immensely offensive, not only to me but to everybody else who has been through the care system, you ignorant pig . . .

Stark: And foster parents look after them, and we make sure that they are looked after properly by foster parents and we have social workers that go into homes and make sure that they have a good environment to live in. On balance, we feel that the smoking environment, we know for very small children, who have very small airways . . .

Gaunt: Yes, I accept that. I accept that. I accept that.

Stark: Can, well, die if they find themselves [ill] as a result of smoking. Therefore on balance we feel . . .

Gaunt: Balance.

Stark: That a smoking environment is not acceptable for children on balance.

Gaunt: On balance?

Stark: Generally, with exceptions.

Gaunt: There is no exceptions in your world view.

Stark: There are exceptions; there will be exceptions.

Gaunt: Because what I've just said to you, my friend, is what about a smoker who says they won't smoke? Why are you suddenly saying, why are you coming over as some kind of health fascist and saying that everybody who smokes is a liar? I know foster parents who smoke, who would not smoke and I say the care of the child should come first. It is better that a child is with a foster parent than in the home system? I'm not denigrating all the people who work in the care system, because a lot of them do a very damn good job under extremely try...er, testing circumstances for very low pay. However, it is in the best interest for the children. There is 60,000 children approximately in this country who are in the care system. If they are put in a different environment, I am sure you would agree with me on that, why have you now put this ban in place to stop people who want to care for children? That is the point I'm making. It's not about a personal argument between you and me, although that's clearly what you want, it's about . . .

Stark: No, that's what you want Jon. That's what you employ.

Gaunt: It's about the child. No it isn't, my friend, because I'm talking on behalf of children.

Stark: Oh yes, you're talking to, on behalf of all the children.

Gaunt: Because I was, I was one. No, don't be an ignorant idiot, I was one of those children . . .

Stark: That will work. You lost the argument there. . .(laughs)

Gaunt: I was one of those children. I was one of those. I'm glad you think you can laugh at that plight of children. I was one of those children. I don't want you to have an argument with me about this. I want you to talk about the kids. Do you agree

with me it's better for a child to be fostered or adopted than
live through the residential care system? Do you...

Stark: We do not have people in residential care nowadays in the
way that you were brought up.

Gaunt: Where, where ...

Stark: Can I finish?

Gaunt: Yes you can, you can.

Stark: Thank you very much.

Gaunt: Go on, smug.

Stark: Doctor Barnados and institutions like that do not exist
nowadays ...

Gaunt: I wasn't in Barnados ...

Stark: (sighs) Oh dear, oh dear. Were you born talking? Doctor
Barnados ...

Gaunt: Do you have any residential care homes in your area?

Stark: Doctor Barnados was originally ... Well, that is in our
area actually. Doctor Barnados ...

Gaunt: Do you ...

Stark: Used to be a big residential care institution ...

Gaunt: Yes, I understand that.

Stark: With families of 10 and 12 children, that is all gone
now ...

Gaunt: I know.

Stark: They do and they specialise in great supportive work with
children with special needs and they are ...

Gaunt: Why are you talking about Barnados?

Stark: That is the area they specialise on.

Gaunt: Why?

Stark: Well, could you just let me finish?

Gaunt: Do you have residential children homes?

Stark: Would you like me to hang up and interview yourself?

Gaunt: Sorry about that, there is no point in continuing the interview.

The councillor hung up and frantic behind-the-scenes negotiations between producer Laurie Palacio and the council began in which it was agreed that Gaunt would apologise on air. Gaunt issued the apology to Stark later in the show, although it hardly seemed heartfelt. Once the show had finished, Gaunt left the building quickly as usual, stopping to tell Palacio that everything would be fine and that he shouldn't worry.

But everything would certainly not be fine. Once senior management, who had all been in a meeting during the broadcast, had heard a recording of the interview, an internal investigation was launched and Gaunt was suspended pending its outcome.

Unsurprisingly, Ofcom received more than 50 complaints after the interview and the watchdog found that Gaunt had breached its code for labelling Stark a 'Nazi' and an 'ignorant pig'. The regulator stated that the overall tone of the presenter's interviewing style was 'extremely aggressive' and those that complained described Gaunt's conduct during the interview as 'oppressive', 'intimidating' and 'like a playground bully'.

However, it wasn't the Ofcom findings that accounted for Gaunt's dismissal. What most disappointed talkSPORT management was that the presenter seemed unrepentant. He offered no apology to Moz Dee or Scott Taunton, who was appalled by Gaunt's flagrant disregard for the station when he taunted Stark to 'take action'. If the councillor had decided to go ahead with legal proceedings for being labelled a Nazi on air, it would have been talkSPORT that would have been facing hefty legal bills and possible damages.

The station's management felt they had little choice but to

dismiss one of their star presenters. Ten days after the interview, the still-suspended Gaunt was told his services would no longer be required by talkSPORT. Gaunt's sacking was the culmination of a fairly tumultuous year for the station, but it was not all bad news. On the one hand, two high-profile presenters had been dismissed but, on the other, two more had joined in the shape of Stan Collymore and Jeremy Kyle. Not only that, there would be more to come. Moz Dee's 'bigger, bolder and better' mantra was starting to bear fruit as the station entered its tenth year.

17

Rock 'n' Roll Radio

Untouchable? People have said that to me, but I would not be so pompous or arrogant. Everyone has their day and I have been doing it for ten years now, which is a long time. I'm over 50 so I have calmed down a bit.

ALAN BRAZIL

The ability to surprise and keep listeners on their toes has long been one of talkSPORT's greatest strengths. Moz Dee's decision to replace Jon Gaunt's rabble-rousing, mid-morning show with a new current affairs programme presented by Mike Parry and Andy Townsend was certainly a bolt from the blue.

As 2009 dawned, media speculation was rife about who would replace Gaunt but nobody foresaw Dee using the weekend breakfast show presenters. While Parry was certainly comfortable in the world of current affairs, with his newspaper background, this was a big challenge for Townsend, albeit one he embraced with great enthusiasm.

'It's new to me and I'm out of my comfort zone,' admitted Townsend. 'But I'm a dad, a taxpayer, a homeowner, so I have the same gripes as everyone else. I don't ever want to be perceived as a know-all and as someone whose opinion is right every time, but I do have an opinion I'm entitled to give.'

There was no reason why Townsend wouldn't have as much to contribute to a debate on the state of the economy as he would to a discussion on the previous night's football. In the same way, listeners who stayed with the station after the break-fast show would be equally affected by issues like immigration, policing and interest rates, so the transition worked.

Usually, the pair would adopt a more sporting theme to their first hour before easing gently into other areas of debate although, of course, if the sports story was big enough to be dominating the news – such as Cristiano Ronaldo leaving Manchester United to join Real Madrid – then Parry and Townsend would take that on for their entire show.

Having become used to working together over the weekend for more than three years, the pair now became even closer, as their show ran from Monday to Friday. Parry and Townsend would speak to each other at least two or three times a day to discuss ideas for the following morning and they would also chat over the weekend if a big enough news line emerged.

Their on-air relationship continued along the same lines as it had done at weekends. Just because they were talking current affairs didn't mean an element of humour couldn't be injected into proceedings. Parry was still his desk-thumping usual self, coming up with all manner of weird and wonderful ideas. One of his more recent brainwaves was that football goals should be made higher as the average height of goalkeepers has risen so much since the rules of the game were first drawn up.

He would also still treat – or possibly torment – his audience with renditions of some of his favourite tunes by singing live on air. On one occasion he performed the *Ghostbusters* theme tune in a duet with its original artist Ray Parker Jr. The listeners certainly approved of the pair's new show, if the rate of emails received in the talkSPORT inbox was anything to go by.

The calibre of guests they attracted also soared. On one poignant morning, Parry and Townsend invited the father and brother of murdered schoolboy Jimmy Mizen into the studios. The interview with the Mizens was some of the most powerful radio the station had ever transmitted.

The most notable guest to appear on the new mid-morning show was undoubtedly Gordon Brown, the prime minister, who paid a visit to talkSPORT Towers early in 2009. The station had tried for years to convince the PM to make an appearance, but, perhaps because of Downing Street snobbery about talkSPORT, nothing had come of their advances. But after a great deal of networking and conversation, current affairs man Sean Dilley and Dee went to meet Brown and his advisers at Number 10 and a deal was agreed to bring the prime minister to talkSPORT, where he would join Parry and Townsend in the studio for an hour one Monday morning.

Any location visited by a prime minister always has to be heavily screened by security and talkSPORT Towers was no exception, as police swept the building from top to bottom both the day before and on the morning of Brown's visit. With the station's offices not the tidiest of places, the build-up to the PM's appearance witnessed a huge internal clean-up, the likes of which had never been seen in the building. Even the notoriously unhygienic kitchen was spotless, as Townsend recalled: 'I've never seen the office as clean! The toilets were sparkling and there were at least three cups in the kitchen. It was unprecedented!'

If the office was smart then so were the staff, as everyone from presenters to producers to work placement juniors scrubbed up and donned their poshest outfits in Brown's honour. As the prime minister stood chatting to Moz Dee and the presenters in the boardroom, office manager Lauren Webster went to fetch him the water he had requested to drink. She returned and, not wanting to disturb the prime minister mid-conversation, she stood alongside him holding a cup of water in her outstretched arm. But the PM continued chatting to Dee and failed to notice Webster or the water. As the seconds ticked by, Webster started to feel like a spare part and was quite hurt at Brown's rudeness – not to mention the fact that her arm was beginning to ache. Eventually, Dee snatched the cup out of her hand and gave it to Brown as Webster scurried away. It was only later, while recounting the story to colleagues, that she realised she had been holding the cup towards Brown's blind eye – the PM had lost sight in one eye at the age of 16 – and he would have had absolutely no idea she had been standing alongside him for all that time.

Throughout the duration of Brown's talkSPORT appearance, the road outside the building was shut and virtually deserted apart from eight police motorbikes that were lined all the way up the street. And in the skies above talkSPORT Towers, a police helicopter circled. The PM's schedule was tight and strict timings governed his visit as he was whisked to the boardroom, where he had precisely 12 minutes to converse with Taunton, Dee, Parry and Townsend, before heading up to the studio.

Neither Townsend, who had rubbed shoulders with high-profile celebrities and politicians over the years due to his footballing exploits, nor Parry, who had interviewed every serving British prime minister since James Callaghan, were fazed by their studio guest. But the interview was far gentler than a Jeremy Paxman-style grilling on *Newsnight* and Brown even had time to discuss the fortunes of his football team, Raith Rovers.

But Parry and Townsend weren't trying to outwit Brown or catch him off-guard. This was a fantastic coup for talkSPORT that showed how the image and perception of the station had changed so dramatically. A prime minister visiting talkSPORT during its first few years would have been difficult to imagine. Now, the station was seen as a major broadcaster with millions of potential voters tuning in every day. Brown's advisers had realised that high-ranking politicians could not afford to ignore talkSPORT.

The message was obviously spreading as, on the morning after the budget, Alistair Darling appeared on the breakfast show, although he was not given anything light or fluffy to chew on by a furious Brazil. It was a phone interview rather than a studio appearance, but the fact that the chancellor was on talkSPORT the day after a major policy announcement spoke volumes.

Darling's budget had seen an increase in income tax placed on the country's highest earners and Brazil was livid, as it was a move that directly affected him. The Scot's opening gambit was: 'Alistair, I'm on my knees. You've kicked me in the shins!' Somewhat taken aback, Darling did his best to explain the rise in income tax, but Brazil was on full throttle and would not be silenced.

He proceeded to tell Darling that he had hit all the hardest-working British people, because all those who had attempted to better themselves through education and had then gone on to have successful careers were now having to pay more to the government. Brazil demanded to know why Darling hadn't targeted the spongers in society – in his mind, those who were living off the tax earned by those who worked hardest.

The chancellor was stunned and attempted to waffle his way

out of trouble. Brazil was also stunned, having no idea where his impassioned outburst had come from: 'A lot of times, I don't know who's on the show,' admitted Brazil. 'I had the right hump with the budget. I was really angry and then someone said "Right, you have got Alistair Darling coming on in five minutes" and I was like "Who?" "Alistair Darling." "Really?" Well, it was a surprise to me.

'I launched into him – "How dare you ..." That is not really my style and he was taken aback a bit and he didn't really know how to get out of it. He was waffling, he didn't expect it. I didn't expect it!'

The response from listeners was overwhelming. Many emailed the show in support of Brazil for having the guts to talk to the chancellor so honestly. However, some felt that the presenter, who earned way more than his average listener, was being slightly self-centred, as there were millions of Britons who were far more seriously affected by the global economic downturn.

It would have been hard for the station to trump having the prime minister and the chancellor broadcasting to the nation, but some would say they did just that with a startling coup that united Noel Gallagher and Russell Brand for a one-off show. With all due respect to the politicians, Gallagher and Brand were a damn sight sexier, funnier and more entertaining than either Brown or Darling.

While Gallagher, a talkSPORT fan, had made numerous appearances on the station to talk about his beloved Manchester City, the chances of attracting Brand seemed to be virtually zero, especially as he was tied in to broadcasting his own BBC Radio 2 show. But then Sachsgate broke. Brand, alongside Jonathan Ross, had left a series of lewd messages on former *Fawlty Towers* star Andrew Sachs' answer phone in which the comedian taunted the actor about how he'd had sex with his granddaughter. These calls had then been aired on Brand's show. It wasn't in particularly great taste and, once the newspapers had clamped their teeth on to the story, the public furore grew bigger.

Eventually, Brand resigned from his show and Dee immediately sent an email to the comedian's agent asking if his client would consider broadcasting a talkSPORT show. The programme director was pleasantly surprised to hear that Brand was interested, but was waiting for the dust to settle – at the same time as working on three films in the USA.

After a few months, regular discussions were taking place about Gallagher doing a show with Brand, but complications arose from the pair's extremely busy schedules. Brand was about to crack America and had a film crew following his every move for a documentary that iconic Hollywood director Oliver Stone was making about him. Added to that, Gallagher had released a new album with Oasis and the band were in the middle of a world tour.

But it seemed that the pair were extremely keen to do the show and a date in mid-April was found to record the programme before it aired the following evening. That would just about give management enough time to check if notorious ladies' man Brand had phoned any of his recent conquests' grandparents during the show. Fortunately, he managed to resist the temptation.

When the pair finally arrived at talkSPORT Towers, Dee was waiting to greet them and the sheer size of Brand's entourage was a throwback to the days of Abu Hamza and Mike Tyson. But they were guests. To that date, no talkSPORT *presenter* had ever turned up and brought a slice of Hollywood to the old sofas and squeaky studio floorboards.

The comedian was accompanied by an entire film crew – minus Oliver Stone – and his publicist, his publicist's assistant, his agent and his agent's assistant. Gallagher, travelling light, arrived with just his publicist. On top of that, there were numerous paparazzi waiting outside the building for the pair to arrive and most of them remained there in the pouring rain until the stars emerged hours later.

Most talkSPORT presenters tended not to think about their clothing too hard, given that they worked on radio. Unfashionable t-shirts and jeans would commonly be seen in the studios, but Brand and Gallagher brought a touch of style to the radio station that had rarely been seen. Brand wore a trendy cardigan over a designer vest top, with a beaded necklace completing the look, while Gallagher's lime green anorak was half-buttoned up to reveal a white t-shirt underneath. They looked like the major stars that they were.

There was something resembling a party atmosphere in the building that afternoon although, of course, normal programming was still on air as the new show was being pre-recorded in a different studio. The two-hour programme was themed loosely along the lines of football and entertainment, as Brand, a keen West Ham fan, and Gallagher exchanged banter about their teams and their celebrity lives. The huge Sachsgate-shaped elephant in the room was not left to be ignored. Instead, it was addressed in the opening seconds of the show:

Brand: You're listening to Russell Brand and Noel Gallagher on talkSPORT. I'm Russell Brand. Hello Noel.
Gallagher: Hello there.
Brand: Thanks for joining me in this foray back into radio, because last time obviously there were incidents.

Gallagher: There was one incident which wouldn't have happened on my watch.

Brand: It certainly wouldn't have done and I scarred not only myself but radio as a concept.

Further into the programme, Brand decided to call his old sparring partner Ross to catch up on old times:

Brand: Jonathan, it's Russell Brand.

Ross: Hello Russell. How are you?

Brand: I'm quite well. I'm doing this talkSPORT thing with Noel Gallagher. Do you want to be in it?

Ross: You're not back on the radio are you?

Brand: I'm on the radio, Jonathan, and I tell you what – it's easy being on radio. As long as you don't take any needless risks, it's good clean fun.

Ross: OK. Bung me on. When do you want to do it? Do you want to do it now?

Brand: Yeah. How about right this second? I'll call you back on a proper phone.

Ross: OK. Call me back in a minute.

Brand: Nice one Jonathan. Cheers mate. Later on, on the show, we will be talking to Jonathan Ross.

Gallagher: Well, this is two people who have obviously not learned their lesson.

When Ross came back on the show, he opened with the line: 'I can't help but think this probably isn't wise,' but he needn't have worried as the three stars stuck only to sporting topics throughout their conversation. A phone call was also made to the White House, where the pair left a message for Barack

Obama to see whether he really was a West Ham fan as had been reported. Former Hammers and City player Steve Lomas also appeared on the show to try to provide an answer as to which of the two presenters' favourite clubs was the better.

Gallagher even revealed that Wayne Rooney's wife Coleen had sent him a guitar, which she had requested him to sign for her husband's birthday. Instead, Gallagher returned the guitar after painting it blue and scrawling the lyrics to Man City anthem 'Blue Moon' all over it – he was hardly going to do a favour for one of City's most bitter rivals' star players.

The Brand and Gallagher show worked. The showbiz pair complemented one another well with the comedian's colourful, chatty style balanced by the musician's dry sense of humour. The programme received almost universal acclaim from critics and listeners and the station was hailed as brave for its courage in giving Brand another chance.

talkSPORT also made the broadcast available as a podcast and it was downloaded by more than one million people. The ambitious stunt to put Brand and Gallagher together had paid off spectacularly, with the station reaching a whole new audience. Although it was meant to have been a one-off broadcast, Brand was to return to the station the following year as a deal was signed which saw the comedian present twenty one-hour shows for the station which featured clips from his stand-up tour as well as backstage chat.

By the time Brand and Gallagher had appeared on the station, Stan Collymore was already an established talkSPORT broadcaster. Ahead of the start of the 2008-09 football season, programme director Moz Dee snapped up the signature of former Liverpool and Aston Villa star Stan Collymore. Having worked together at the BBC, Dee knew Collymore well and was able to offer him his own show every night of the week, as well as a co-commentary gig from a Premier League game on Saturday afternoons. The ex-striker signed on the dotted line and wasted little time in bringing his infectious enthusiasm for the beautiful game to the talkSPORT airwaves. He felt the station was made for him: 'I came in to the talkSPORT office and went straight into the kitchen,' said Collymore. 'I saw the state of the kitchen and thought "This is rock 'n' roll. I quite like this." I knew I'd be at home pretty much straight away!'

If Collymore hadn't been a footballer he would have undoubtedly spent every other week at Villa Park watching his beloved Aston Villa. As well as being a genuinely engaging and articulate broadcaster, Collymore was also a passionate football fan and listeners instantly warmed to him. He was a loud figure in press boxes on match days and when he hosted his phone-in shows after the matches, the ex-striker could often be seen standing or jumping up and down excitedly while making his points to fellow football fans who had called in to have their say.

Collymore hit it off with talkSPORT's commentator Nigel Pearson, who lives less than ten miles away from him in the Midlands. They never travelled to games together, however, because Collymore always stayed in the stadium after the match to present *Call Collymore*, the football fans' phone-in. The show aired on a Saturday evening immediately following the full-time whistles up and down the country. Often, Pearson would arrive at a ground in plenty of time to prepare for his commentary to find Collymore already in place in the press box, swatting up on his stats for the match. The former footballer was extremely thorough in everything he did for the station.

The new talkSPORT presenter's nightly football show saw him broadcast alongside Danny Kelly, an experienced radio man who soon felt the full force of the Collymore effect. One evening late in 2008, Arsenal were playing Spurs in what turned out to be an epic 4-4 draw, with Tottenham, Kelly's team, scoring two late goals. Earlier that week, Collymore had been his usual enthusiastic self, declaring how much he loved football live on air. With Spurs behind in the match, the former striker decided to give Kelly a morale-boosting pep talk during a commercial break: 'We went to a break and I said to Danny "Just open up a bit; Spurs could go for it", but he was a bit reticent and thought it wasn't very professional to do that,' said Collymore. 'Then, finally, when Aaron Lennon scored the last-minute equaliser he yelled "I love football!" They used that clip on trails all the time. That's what we're all about really.'

With a colourful background and private life – including a well-documented, stormy relationship with Ulrika Jonsson, whom he admitted to physically abusing – Collymore was not about to pretend he was some sort of saint now that he had his own radio show. Far from it, as the man exposed by the tabloid newspapers for being a keen exponent of the sexual fetish of 'dogging', he never flinched from references to his past. In fact, during his first *Call Collymore* football phone-in show after the opening game of the 2008-09 season between Arsenal and West Brom, one listener used the expression 'every dog has its day' in the course of making a point. Quick as a flash, Collymore interrupted and said: 'Oh no, we don't talk about dogs on this show!'

While Collymore's role at talkSPORT was to talk football, football then more football, on one poignant occasion he appeared on the mid-morning show where the topic was domestic abuse. The former footballer, who was covering for Andy Townsend all week on the show alongside Mike Parry, had been moved by newspaper pictures of pop star Rihanna's badly beaten face. In what was a supremely difficult moment for him, Collymore opened his heart to the nation and admitted how ashamed he felt of his past in relation to the way he treated Ulrika. He spoke of his depression that followed the shameful incident and became quite emotional. It was gripping, heart-wrenching radio that left listeners profoundly moved. Collymore began by introducing the topic:

> Collymore: I'm a little bit nervous, edgy, if I'm going to be per-fectly honest, but let's get through the topics and have a chat. In June 1998 in Paris, I did something to my then girlfriend that will live with me forever and rightly saw me as public enemy number one. Domestic violence was a part of my childhood as well as my adult life. It's corrosive, evil, and downright wrong. What are your thoughts? Are you a victim? Are you a perpetrator? One in four people I was just reading, a quite staggering statistic, male and female, are victims of domestic violence. This on the back of the Rihanna pictures in the paper. The pictures are quite horrific and brought back some very evocative and strong memories for me.

After outlining other topics that were up for discussion, Collymore continued:

> Collymore: You hear a lot of people talking about it, and the rights and the wrongs, and it's very corrosive, evil, undigni-fied. Of course, if you've suffered at the hands of it, frightening if you see it, and of course just plain wrong. This is born out of my own experiences.
>
> Firstly as a kid, my mum and dad were married for five or six years. My dad serially abused my mum, all of which I saw

at about four or five years of age. And my mum told me: 'Never, ever lay your hands on a lady.' She always says two things. She says: 'Go and enjoy your experiences in life, go and enjoy the world, go and travel and enjoy every day but never, ever lay your hands on a lady.'

Parry: I think you'll agree with me that a man doesn't need to be told that, does he? It's a rule of civilised behaviour, isn't it?

Collymore: It is a rule of civilised behaviour, but that was based, Mike, on what she had been through.

Parry: OK, right.

Collymore: Stitches, bruises, you name it.

Parry: Proper violence?

Collymore: And I didn't know as a kid what was going on and I saw it first-hand. Now I never, never thought that I would be in a position whereby I would hit anybody. I've got a short fuse. I'm aggressive, angry, sometimes even passionate... As a football player I liked to win, not at all costs, but I liked to win. So, when I ... in 1998 I'd been going out with Ulrika Jonsson, as everyone knows, and I've kind of become synonymous now as a wife-beater, if you want to call it that. I've never beat my wife, or serially beat anybody, but on that night in Paris we'd been out, had an argument, and I struck my girlfriend.

Parry: What frame of mind were you in at the time, Stan?

Collymore: Oh, angry, there's no doubt about it. And I think that the bigger issue of who ... the partner that you choose ... we want to get right into this about ... there's lots of different facets, and one of it is the partner you choose, the partner you spend your time with, the partner that brings out the best in you, that doesn't bring out anything in you.

And not excusing any behaviour but I would ... firstly, before we go into it, I would urge anybody that's in an abusive relationship whereby, even if you're constantly argu-ing, if there's no domestic abuse, if there's no violence, if there's no mind games being played, but if you're just in a relationship when you're constantly arguing and it's especially in the first six or twelve months of a relationship which set the tone for everything, get out of it please! Whatever you need to do, there are plenty of resources available for people to go and to talk and to get it off their chest. If you're angry, and if you're a person that potentially has a short fuse, poten-tially a person who could inflict harm on somebody else, please go and talk to somebody.

Parry: Even if somebody has never done it before, as you were a man that had never done it before. Are you saying that there are warning signs that that might develop into physi-cal violence and therefore you should walk away from them?

Collymore: Well, I think we all have relationships to a greater or lesser degree where we all argue with our loved ones. The relationship I'm in now I argue, we argue, like cats and dogs sometimes, for five or ten minutes here and there, but the feeling of the relationship is right and it's like anything if it feels right then it tends to be right.

That wasn't the case with Ulrika Jonsson and I, but again, that's no excuse for perpetrating physical violence, especially a strong, big, black male on a woman – or a little, blond male on a six foot tall woman. It's not acceptable. And after that in Paris, Mike, rightly so I became public enemy number one. I've no problem with that, because the time I gave myself after that over probably the next seven or eight years – I had major bouts of depression, self-loathing, like I say, evil. I felt I'd let my family down, well I *had* let my family down. My mum was disgusted, gutted, hurt, upset. I let my friends down; let myself down. And it was something that I wanted to understand about myself as to why. Something that I wanted to understand why anyone else would do it.

Parry: Have you found out?

Collymore: Yeah. That specific incident happened out of pure jealousy. It's as simple as that. Pure jealousy.

Parry: Attention from other men?

Collymore: Erm, on that evening, yeah.

Parry: But have you found out what inside your head made you do it?

Collymore: No, I haven't. You know, people saw red mist and use loads of crap – excuses, excuses. I'm sorry for using words like that, I'm a bit het up at the moment but it was excuses like red mist and ... that made me do it. I hear men and women, because you know one in four women will be a victim of domestic violence in their life.

At that point, the pair strayed from the subject slightly, but Collymore then added:

Collymore: I'm happy to talk about it, and if my experience can stop anybody today, male or female, hitting their partner, playing mind games with them, making them feel worthless, afraid, fearful, then the whole of this week, the whole of the experience that I have here at talkSPORT as a sports broadcaster, or joining you, will be worthwhile. It's not a cathartic experience for me, Mike ... Seeing the Rihanna pictures took me back to what Ulrika Jonsson's face was like.

Following a break for the news, Parry began by reading out an email that the show had received on the topic:

Parry: There's one here, Stan, that you've got to answer for me please. This is from Louise. She says: 'Violence against a woman or child is never excusable. A man who is being abused or who has abused should never marry or have children.'

Collymore: How do you do that? I'm in a wonderful relationship where I grow. I have a great relationship and there was somebody before that who I kind of met and talked to about domestic violence and helped me grow as well. So I'm not quite sure where you would draw the line.

Parry: The email you got just before the break said if you hit a woman, how do you know it will never happen again?

Collymore: Well, I don't, I suppose. You know, how do you know anything's not going to happen? I don't know.

Parry: Have you spoken to experts about how you can do your very best?

Collymore: Yes I ... just like the depression debate, there's a thing called Cognitive Behavioural Therapy, which is one of the main therapies that treats depression, which is based on various formulas that people have used over the years, which kind of give you tools to be able to go through depression and to be able to come out of the other side. And it's the same for issues ...

Parry: Were you depressed when this happened, by the way?

Collymore: No, I don't think I was, no. There are ... If you perpetrate any behaviour, whether it be, you know, going into car parks and looking for sex with people, whether it be looking for a rush, a thrill, by alcohol, drugs, violence, control or what have you, you deal with the same kind of pathways in the brain, you know. The whole point of why I'm trying to spark this debate is because I think that if you perpetrate physical violence on somebody, the first thing is to be

castigated, of course, and to have a really good look at yourself. Then you need to try and give yourself some tools that
are out there in the professional community.

Parry: To try and make sure it doesn't happen again.

Looking back on that emotional morning, Collymore was
pleased that he had been able to discuss such a personal issue on
air: 'When I did the show with Mike Parry, I wanted to make
sure that some of the topics were relevant to me in my life,' he
said. 'The most important thing was to say "Well, this happened – here's what I think of it, let's talk about it and get it out
in the open."'

'You just lay it bare, but people don't always hold your views.
People were more than welcome to come on and say "We
haven't forgiven you and we don't want you to broadcast" –
that's people's right. The biggest thing for me was to get it out
there and give people the chance to debate what is a very serious issue.'

Soon after Collymore joined talkSPORT, Jeremy Kyle also
began working for the station. Given his reputation for 'bear-
baiting' confessional TV chat shows, Kyle would not have been
the obvious choice to front a new Sunday lunchtime sports
show on national radio. But Moz Dee, looking to go a little bit
left field with the slot, saw something different in the television
presenter who was also a keen West Ham fan. Kyle's background
was in radio and he had actually started out in sales before landing his break at Midlands station BRMB. Dee was convinced he
was still very much a radio man at heart, so when he offered him
the chance to work at talkSPORT, Kyle gratefully accepted.

A sports fan and keen listener to the station, Kyle understood
exactly what talkSPORT was all about and the two-hour show

quickly became his favourite part of a hectic working week. The programme also gave Kyle the chance to show listeners who he really was, away from the weird world of in-your-face daytime television, lie detectors and DNA tests.

And the star signings didn't end there. In early 2009, ahead of a huge summer of Ashes cricket, former England star Darren Gough was the next sporting great to sign on talkSPORT's dotted line. Having worked under Dee at the BBC, Gough needed little convincing to make the leap across into commercial radio and he brought with him a huge personality, a sense of humour and an all-round sporting knowledge.

Gough was an extremely popular England cricketer, the Freddie Flintoff of the nineties, whose attitude and ability always to play with a smile on his face won him many fans. The Yorkshireman began by co-presenting the Friday drivetime show alongside Adrian Durham and then spent the summer reporting from the Ashes and hosting phone-ins after each day's cricket. But he was suddenly propelled into a far bigger role at the station with the dramatic news that Ian Wright was leaving the drivetime show.

After two and a half years, Wright was moving to work on the station's Saturday afternoon football show, still alongside Durham, in order to fit in with his new TV commitments. The former footballer was emotional about leaving drive, as he realised how far he had come since joining the station in 2007. He knew he would miss the daily office banter and the chance to be himself on air. What he certainly would not miss, however, was the abuse he received from Arsenal fans. They would often call their former hero on the show and accuse him of not being a true fan of the club because he dared to criticise the Gunners for not having won a trophy since 2005.

Although he was switching to a TV show, Wright believed that radio was now his natural medium and he was determined that he would return to talkSPORT on a daily basis before long. Since finishing the drivetime show, Wright has said: 'I will end up doing radio again and wherever Adrian Durham is, I'm coming to get him!'

Gough was drafted in to replace Wright and slotted in effortlessly as the ex-cricketer was a similar character to Wright. He was always open, honest and full of life and his new role as drive co-presenter gave him a platform where he could be himself, which he relished: 'You can get your opinions across a lot easier,' he said, comparing it to working for the BBC. 'It's a lot less scripted and I can be myself and my personality can come through.'

Like Wright before him, Gough lapped up the opportunity and quickly became part of the talkSPORT furniture. And like several other talkSPORT presenters, he soon found himself in a tricky position involving alcohol and broadcasting. It was the weekend of the final Ashes Test, after a nailbiting summer of cricket. Everything was on the line as both England and Australia could still claim the urn. talkSPORT's newest presenter had been right in the thick of the action, giving updates from the ground and even presenting a show from a pub next to The Oval on the second day. But on the potentially decisive third day, Gough could not be found anywhere near south London. His best friend was getting married and he was up in Doncaster for the wedding – as best man.

Like a true professional, however, Gough stayed glued to the cricket and provided talkSPORT with summaries throughout the day – well, at least until the ceremony started: 'Luckily, he didn't get married until half past three, so I was watching it on a TV right up until we went in church,' said Gough. 'And then obviously straight after [church] we had an hour and a half before we started all the other stuff, so I watched it again until the end of play. Then that was it, I joined in with the rest of the wedding all night.'

The former cricketer admitted he had enjoyed one or two drinks at the wedding over the course of the day, but was still able to provide his expert analysis without any problem: 'Well, I think I was all right, but sometimes when you think you're all right, you're not! But I gathered I talked a lot of sense.'

Gough was back in London the following day as England completed another memorable Ashes victory, which was covered comprehensively by talkSPORT.

The station was changing and growing rapidly. Major names from the world of sport and entertainment had been attracted by the on-air transparency talkSPORT offered them. With the new talent came a new level of professionalism but, sometimes, things still went wrong.

On one show, a joke made by presenter Andy Goldstein badly backfired. Alongside Jason Cundy, Goldstein fronted the weekend evening *Sports Bar* where humour and entertainment were the order of the day. Occasionally, Cundy would have other commitments with Sky Sports that prevented him from appearing on talkSPORT. On one such evening, Goldstein introduced the show by saying: 'Unfortunately, Jason Cundy can't be here this evening because he's dead!'

It was a daft, tongue-in-cheek comment that was quite in keeping with Goldstein's slightly offbeat sense of humour, but the fallout was quite spectacular.

Many listeners took Goldstein quite seriously and rumours about Cundy's death started spreading like wildfire. Cundy had actually battled back from testicular cancer in 1997, so it wasn't completely implausible for listeners to take Goldstein's unfortunate joke seriously. And they did just that – some people even laid wreaths outside Stamford Bridge, where Cundy used to play, despite the fact that the ex-footballer was alive and well in Isleworth, working for Sky.

Later that night after the show, Goldstein mentioned the joke in a phone call to his colleague, who didn't really take in what his co-presenter was saying. But, the following morning, Cundy received dozens of phone calls and texts checking if he was alive and well. His former Spurs team-mate Andy Sinton even called talkSPORT to check if he had passed away.

The rumour mill had gone into overdrive and it was only later that night, when Goldstein made a full and frank apology on air – with Cundy sitting alongside him proving that he was very much alive – that the affair drew to a close. The ex-footballer was completely unfazed by the drama: 'I wasn't the least bit bothered about it; it didn't upset me in any way, shape or form,' said Cundy. 'Some people were phoning up and saying "Thank god you have answered!" There was no real harm done in the end. It might have pissed a few people off, most notably my mum, who wasn't particularly impressed by the whole stunt.'

After a decade on air, talkSPORT had been through its fair share of scrapes – just like its presenters – but was now in the rudest of health, with ratings and revenue hitting new heights. Official audience figures from RAJAR announced early in 2009 gave talkSPORT its record reach, as more than 2.5 million people were now tuning in every week.

There was barely time to finish celebrating those results before talkSPORT had once again swept the honours at the Arqiva Commercial Radio Awards, winning station of the year

again, as well as picking up a top award for the sterling efforts
of its sales team. Those two awards, which were voted for by the
entire commercial radio industry, had never gone to the same
station in the same year. With 330 commercial broadcasters in
the UK, it was another fantastic achievement for talkSPORT.

And there were still big plans in place to ensure continued
growth in the future. Following on from the success of Germany
2006, Taunton signed a deal to ensure talkSPORT would be an
official FIFA broadcast partner for the 2010 World Cup in
South Africa. With the rest of the radio industry in turmoil,
talkSPORT continued to look healthy, even in the face of the
recession. Advertising revenue on the station was up as it continued to outperform the rest of the radio industry. After losing
so much money in the early days, talkSPORT was now making
around £6 million in operating profit every year.

There was no doubt that talkSPORT was in an extremely
robust position – even Alan Brazil was starting to take more
responsibility by listening to his body. Looking back on his first
decade at the station where he had played such a core role in a
massive success story, Brazil said: 'I don't tend to think too much
about tomorrow – my body will take me where it wants to. If I
am feeling tired, I might have a few early nights. If I don't feel
tired, I will have late nights. I do believe what my body tells me.
Bodies are brilliant things; it is remarkable how they can recover.
You put it under pressure and it responds. I rarely listen if my
boss tells me, but if my body tells me – Woah! Woah!' But this
was talkSPORT. And there were still times when Brazil listened
to neither his body nor his boss.

18

Colegate and Cheltenham Part II

When I catch up with him, he'll find out exactly what I think of him.

STAN COLLYMORE

There is only one talkSPORT.

What other radio station would defy the odds, the critics, the alcohol, the controversy, more alcohol, the rodents and a great deal more alcohol to make it to ten glorious years – and then celebrate the anniversary on the wrong date?

To insure against such an occurrence, a book was written to mark the occasion. The opening sentence of the opening paragraph of the book mentioned the date: 17 January 2000. Yet, on 19 January 2010, there was talkSPORT, shouting from the rooftops on 1089 and 1053 medium wave, letting the United Kingdom know it was celebrating its tenth birthday.

It was only two days late, which, by its own standards, was the equivalent of being punctual. Yet it summed up why it had hit such extraordinary levels of popularity with its listeners and been recognised by the broadcasting industry. That almost intentional unpredictability and institutionalised informality had served the station well. And just because it had reached double figures was no reason to suddenly adopt a more stuffy approach and alienate listeners. It was very much a case of business as usual, something to which breakfast presenter Alan Brazil was more than happy to adhere.

Despite his sincere and honest good intentions, Brazil was always susceptible to his demons. These otherworldly dark forces could be disguised in the shape of almost any human being. Essentially, these demons were pretty much anyone who offered him a drink. And, as the host of one of the nation's favourite breakfast shows, there was no shortage of invitations.

It was back at the scene of his greatest talkSPORT crisis where Brazil was to fall foul of the station's senior management once again. This Gloucestershire town has proven to be Brazil's nirvana, but also his undoing. This was the place on which hundreds of thousands of revellers and horse racing enthusiasts converge for four days every year – almost all of whom wanted to buy the former Scotland international a pint, and almost all of whom did. Cheltenham. Steeped in tradition and attracting the world's greatest horses, it also possesses an unfathomable quantity of Guinness.

Brazil arrived in his south-west Mecca in 2010 with a relatively clean talkSPORT licence. Naturally, he was liable to miss the odd show now and again due to the occasional heavy night – in October 2009, he'd gone to Paris to see Sea The Stars, one of his favourite horses, win the Prix de l'Arc de Triomphe and failed to return for the following morning's breakfast show – but his days of regular candle-burning at both ends were long gone. At the age of 50, the lifestyle had caught up with him and he reluctantly acknowledged that. But that didn't mean he couldn't still enjoy a one-off blowout. Especially when he was doing an outside broadcast from his favourite sporting event of the calendar. And especially when station bosses, in their infinite wisdom, had deemed that the *Alan Brazil Sports Breakfast* would be broadcast live from a bar every morning of the festival.

The Front Rooms was a bar and live music venue that had hosted plenty of boozy evenings for locals looking to party late into the night. Yet nothing would have quite prepared the bar's manager for talkSPORT's finest celebrating the Cheltenham festival. And so, at 6am on Tuesday 16 March 2010, Brazil, with his co-presenter Ronnie Irani alongside him for company, took to the air to begin a four-day stint that he would never quite see through.

The Scot had been suffering from persistent throat problems in the preceding weeks, that had led him to miss a number of shows. The illness had caused his voice to sound even more gravelly than usual to the point where he could barely make himself heard or understood – and this was without a drop inside him. Naturally, a throat ailment like that would not have been improved by the dehydrating effects of alcohol and, despite his improved behaviour, Brazil was hardly a tea-totaller. An irritable dry throat combined with the excitement of broadcasting live from a Cheltenham bar was an accident waiting to happen.

The presenter had a ball for the first couple of days of the festival. He was joined for the live broadcasts by bookmakers, associates and fans, and he revelled in the atmosphere and relished being in the spotlight. But two full days and nights at Cheltenham had taken their toll by the time he came on air on the Thursday. Lacking sleep and still full of the jollities of the previous night, he struggled his way through the show and station management were far from amused, ordering Front Rooms staff not to serve their star man. That particular missive was taken seriously and, when Brazil returned for Friday morning's final festival show, events took a spectacular turn for the worse.

If the wheels had started to come off on Thursday's show, they had long since gone solo and rolled down the road by the time it came to the following morning's broadcast. With his throat dry and the night before seemingly merged with the new day, Brazil used a commercial break to request a pint of the black stuff from the bar. At 7.45am. With the orders from London fresh in the bar staff's ears, he was politely turned down with a full explanation that they had been instructed not to serve him by his bosses. The barman may as well have draped a red bedsheet across an already seething bull.

Brazil hit back the only way he knew how – if he wasn't allowed to drink on air, he'd simply drink off it and he informed producers that he wouldn't be returning to the mic after the interval. There wasn't much protest from talkSPORT's on-site team, who were well aware such a situation had been on the cards, and Irani took over the main anchoring role while a succession of pre-booked studio guests were asked to stay for slightly longer. In fact, former Cheltenham Town manager-turned-pundit Martin Allen arrived early for his slot and was quickly ushered into Brazil's chair, where he remained for the next hour and 40 minutes, keeping Irani company until the show ended. All that time, Brazil was perched on a stool at the bar, happily supping pints with friends and punters while watching proceedings.

The disciplinary action was swift, with the Scot immediately suspended pending a full inquiry into the events that had caused him to refuse to go on air. There were echoes of Cheltenham 2004, with an uneasy silence emanating from the station and speculation that the presenter had finally pushed his luck once too often. And the rumour mill went into overdrive when Brazil didn't present the following Monday's programme. However, the gossip proved to be unfounded as the man who had been with the station since its launch was quickly absolved of all blame by the inquiry and returned to the breakfast show hotseat with his trademark 'Maaaarning!' in double quick time. Brazil's poorly throat had proved to be a blessing in disguise.

As for The Front Rooms, sadly there was to be no happy ending. Four days of Alan Brazil clearly took its toll on the Cheltenham entertainment venue, as it was forced to shut within weeks of the talkSPORT visit. Whether the Scot had actually drunk it dry or there were other financial forces at play will remain one of life's great unsolved mysteries.

What was no mystery was the rude health in which the station found itself in terms of its listening figures. Like almost every other business, the effects of the global economic downturn and the subsequent UK recession eventually caught up with talkSPORT, but this didn't have any impact on ratings. And that was chiefly because the mix of sport, banter and news was appealing to listeners from a diverse range of backgrounds. And, occasionally, the station continued to make the headlines in its own right, thanks to some astonishing exclusives.

One Wednesday afternoon in October 2009, Adrian Durham and Darren Gough were engaged in a lively football debate on their drivetime show. Durham takes up the story: 'We'd been talking about goal-line technology and I was giving my usual reasons why I don't want it, when Bruce Forsyth called in to tell me that I was an idiot because we needed it! I just remember seeing his name on the system and I was thinking that he knows Goughy from *Strictly Come Dancing*. I thought that was why he was phoning. But then I thought, "Let's get him on air so we can talk about Anton Du Beke" as there was a big storm at the time because he'd called a fellow contestant a Paki.'

Du Beke had been guilty of making the racially offensive remark when describing the appearance of his celebrity dance partner Laila Rouass on the BBC hit show. The slur had provoked a media storm, with hundreds of viewers complaining to regulatory body Ofcom. And, in the middle of this furore, the show's presenter had called in to talkSPORT.

'We got him on air and went through the motions of having the debate,' continues Durham. 'As I recall, he went on about how he should do the show instead of me because I didn't know what I was talking about. So I said: "You come in and do this and I'll do *Strictly* with Tess [Daly] ..."'

'Once we'd done that, I asked him about Du Beke and he went for it. It was one of those golden moments on talkSPORT when you have somebody that huge, a legend, a gold standard entertainer, one of the greatest this country has ever seen – and I was about to get a news line out of the man as well!'

Durham managed to extract more than a news line, as his exchange with the television presenter made the front pages of many of the following day's newspapers after Forsyth defended his colleague who'd been accused of racism. The conversation went as follows:

Durham: While you're on, Bruce, can I ask you a question?
Forsyth: Yes.
Durham: Your colleague Anton Du Beke has been hitting the headlines for the wrong reasons. He's apologised and she's accepted, so should that be the end of it?
Forsyth: Of course it should, for goodness sake ... We used to

have a sense of humour about this. You go back 25, 30, 40 years and there has always been a bit of humour about the whole thing. At one time the Americans used to call us 'Limeys', which doesn't sound very nice, but we used to laugh about it. Everybody has a nickname. Anton is such a sweet guy, it's such a terrible shame.

Durham: You know Anton Du Beke, and a lot of people reading these stories won't know him at all. What can you tell us about him?

Forsyth: OK, he can be a bit mouthy and can say quick things off-the-cuff, like I do. If someone says something to me then I'm straight back. Quick reflex of the tongue is what we've got. But when you're like that you can slip up every now and again. You can say something that you don't mean. But I'm sure there was nothing vindictive about what he said and it [Du Beke's apology] should be accepted and the page should be closed on it. It's a damn shame and I feel for him and Laila – she's a lovely girl.

The phone call continued with more discussion about that particular series of the BBC show, but Forsyth's defence of Du Beke's comment didn't go down particularly well with BBC viewers, as the Corporation received hundreds more complaints following his impromptu interview. Forsyth even had to issue a statement through the BBC, clarifying his position and withdrawing his call to have 'a sense of humour' about the affair.

The statement read: 'What Anton said to Laila was wrong and he has apologised unreservedly for this. Nor do I in any way excuse or condone the use of such language. To be absolutely clear, the use of racially offensive language is never either funny or acceptable. However, there is a major difference between this and racist comments which are malicious in intent, and while I accept that we live in a world of extraordinary political correctness, we should keep things in perspective.'

Despite putting Forsyth in an awkward position, Durham reflected that the incident had highlighted to him how fortunate he was to be in a position to have someone of Forsyth's stature calling in: 'What a great job, I thought to myself that night. I grew up on a council estate watching *The Generation Game* with Bruce Forsyth and suddenly I was talking to him. You realise the football managers and players listen – but you don't think such a household name is listening to you. Yet because I'm on the radio in his home or in his car, he was speaking to me like he knows me. It was an honour and a privilege to speak to him. The next day, I had a day off and I was sitting in a coffee shop in Hertfordshire, reading newspapers that were full of [stories about] Bruce Forsyth speaking on talkSPORT. Somebody told me that if you added up the newspaper space [the story took], there was the equivalent of about half a million pounds of advertising space. I felt very proud I had made news worth that money.'

And Forsyth wasn't the only heavyweight of Saturday night prime-time television to make an appearance on talkSPORT at that time, as *The X Factor*'s Cheryl Cole made an appearance on Andy Goldstein and Jason Cundy's *Sports Bar*. The exclusive was secured through the former Chelsea footballer's wife Lizzie, who was attending a party where several WAGs were present and phoned her husband to confirm that Cole was happy to appear on the show. Or so it seemed. In fact, this was merely the preamble to what must rank as arguably the greatest of talkSPORT's many cock-ups.

This was through no fault of either Goldstein or Cundy, who

remained blissfully unaware that his wife was about to play an extraordinary prank on live radio. When Lizzie called Cundy to tell him that she had Cheryl Cole with her at the birthday party of another radio presenter, Emma B, the former Chelsea player would have had no reason to suspect foul play. But, as legendary prankster Jeremy Beadle himself might have put it, 'what Jason *didn't* know' was that his wife was not stood alongside *The X Factor* star, but was in fact stood next to impressionist Francine Lewis, who just so happened to have a formidable Cheryl Cole voice as part of her repertoire.

The unsuspecting Cundy rose to the bait and, live to the nation, welcomed Cole to the show and began by asking her about then-husband Ashley's performance earlier that day for Chelsea before moving on to *The X Factor* – and Simon Cowell's haircut. Cole/Lewis said on air: 'I've told him that he needs to change his hairstyle. I've told him time and time again, he just doesn't listen to anyone. He think he's gorgeous; you know what he's like.'

Sounding delighted with these revelations they'd managed to prise out of Cole, the presenters continued by probing her about the alleged rivalry that had been building between her and fellow talent-show judge Dannii Minogue. 'Despite what people say in the press, we all get on really well,' Cole/Lewis told the talkSPORT listeners. 'Dannii is great. Everyone is just fantastic. I love Louis [Walsh] to bits.'

The interview then moved on to England manager Fabio Capello's plans to ban WAGs from the following summer's World Cup in South Africa, but the impressionist bizarrely decided not to say anything too controversial on this subject, perhaps becoming as convinced by her own performance as the talkSPORT presenters: 'I've just been too busy, to be honest. I haven't even thought about it. I don't really get involved with the other WAGs, I just do my own thing.'

Lewis spoke as Cole for fully five minutes and at no point did she drop her guard, meaning that once it was over, there was delight all round at talkSPORT Towers. The station sent out a press release alerting all the national newspapers about its scoop and stories began to appear in various media outlets and blogs, with quotes attributed to Cheryl Cole about Simon Cowell's hair.

Meanwhile, several talkSPORT shows played a recording of the interview on their programmes over the following 24 hours. Cundy was so thrilled that he even went as far as buying his wife flowers and an expensive bracelet to thank her for setting up the interview. By that stage, Mrs Cundy could not bring herself to tell her husband the truth – the hoax had now gone too far. It was only when talkSPORT was contacted by Lewis's agent, who called to request a recording of the interview so she could show-case her client's talent, that anybody came even close to the whiff of a rat. Although, even then, talkSPORT didn't provide Lewis's agent with the tape, as the station was still convinced that the real Cheryl Cole had appeared on the *Sports Bar*. Finally, Cundy was asked to explain what had happened and it was only then that his wife came clean and revealed she had duped her husband, the radio station and all its listeners.

She released an apologetic statement to the *Mail on Sunday*, which ran with the full story a few weeks later: 'This was a light-hearted joke that went wrong. I'm very sorry for any embarrassment caused to my husband, talkSPORT or Cheryl Cole.' The radio station itself took the only possible stance it could in the circumstances and had the good sense to laugh at itself. A talkSPORT spokesman was quoted by the *Mail on*

Sunday saying: 'As a WAG herself, Lizzie is a regular in the pages of *Hello!* Magazine, so when she called the station to say she was with Cheryl Cole we had no reason to doubt her. We can see the funny side and we hope the real Cheryl does too. No one's job is on the line; Jason will be on this week as usual. But I think we'll be keeping the chat to football.'

Based on the theory that all publicity is good publicity, talkSPORT's 'Colegate' probably didn't do the station much harm, merely reinforcing its image as the place on the dial where anything can happen at any given moment – and usually does. And the following summer the station made all the front pages of the nationals for the right reasons when it pulled off a genuine scoop; this time without the help of Miss Lewis.

On 10 July 2010, wanted gunman Raoul Moat shot himself after a six-hour stand-off with armed police in Northumberland. Moat was on the run after shooting and seriously injuring Samantha Stobbart, his ex-girlfriend, killing her new partner Chris Brown and shooting police officer David Rathband, who was permanently blinded as a result. The manhunt lasted for a week and Moat became the subject of a media frenzy. In the immediate aftermath of Moat's death, several pages on the social media giant Facebook were set up in tribute to him, including one which was called 'RIP Raoul Moat, you Legend'. This page attracted 35,000 members and provoked David Cameron, the prime minister, to condemn it in the House of Commons, saying: 'I cannot understand any wave, however small, of public sympathy for this man.'

The outrage at this site quickly became the focal point of the story, with Cameron urging Facebook to shut it down, as well as all other similar pages. But the social media giants stood firm, saying: 'Facebook is a place where people can express their views and discuss things in an open way, as they can and do in many other places. And as such we sometimes find people discussing topics others may find distasteful, however, that is not a reason in itself to stop a debate from happening. We believe that enabling people to have these different opinions and debate about a topic can help bring together lots of different views for a healthy discussion.'

The prime minister was powerless in his attempts to shut the site down and lodged an official complaint with Facebook. But talkSPORT didn't bother complaining. Instead, the radio station incredibly managed to do what Cameron couldn't and the page was removed. The amazing coup was pulled off by the late night presenter Ian Collins and his production team, who successfully tracked down the page's creator, Siobhan O'Dowd, and persuaded her to appear on talkSPORT. O'Dowd had actually texted into the late night show when her controversial site was being discussed and, although she'd changed her mobile number by the time producers had convinced her to appear on the show, she texted in again.

In a powerful and astonishing piece of live broadcasting, O'Dowd was interviewed on the telephone by Collins, who became embroiled in a passionate exchange with the woman, who was seemingly oblivious to the fact her webpage was offending 99.9 per cent of the country. They spoke for eight minutes, during which O'Dowd defended herself and the page by arguing: 'To be honest, I didn't think this would be the kind of reaction I would get. Everyone is entitled to their own opinion. Even Facebook said that and that's why they wouldn't shut it down.'

When Collins challenged her that she was effectively canonising a killer, she countered with: 'I don't agree with the shootings – that were harsh, like.' At that point, Collins, who had remained quite calm in the early part of the interview, spoke from the heart: 'You're very casual about the fact that a woman has had her stomach blown out, one man is dead and another is blinded,' he said. 'A legend has to have done something to be called a legend ... Why do you think he's worthy of hero status?'

'He hid from police for a week – that were funny,' responded O'Dowd. 'He were right underneath their nose ... and they still couldn't find him ... I think he's a legend for keeping them on their toes for a week.'

It didn't make for easy listening, but it was undeniably compelling. The following day, almost certainly as a result of the interview, which was then splashed over many of the morning's papers, O'Dowd removed the page from Facebook. The show's producers spent much of the day fielding calls from journalists, both in the UK and abroad, who were desperate for O'Dowd's contact details, but their requests were turned down. talkSPORT had its story and it was keeping it. Almost inevitably, the press tracked O'Dowd down to her Burnley home and she continued to feature in the papers in the following days.

But possibly the biggest scoop the station had ever landed fell into its lap in early 2011, when Sky Sports presenter Richard Keys opted to deliver a live *mea culpa* with talkSPORT following his off-air comments about female assistant referee Sian Massey. A sensational media storm had blown up after a tape of Keys and pundit Andy Gray was made public, in which the pair suggested a woman was not fit to officiate at the Premier League match between Wolves and Liverpool. Further tapes of the two surfaced in the following days, and the former footballer was sacked. Keys was still at Sky when he chose to appear on Paul

Hawksbee and Andy Jacobs' afternoon show to bare his soul to the nation and beg for forgiveness.

The interview with the face of football on Sky Sports made for riveting listening for the millions who tuned in. Keys could not apologise enough. 'I'm not proud of what happened at the weekend,' he told H&J. Given the immense pressure he was under, he occasionally sounded confused and by then must have already been deliberating whether to resign. That morning, he had been locked in talks with programme director Moz Dee, with whom he had been acquainted for many years – he had called Dee at 6am, keen for a chance to go on air, and had arrived at the studios later that morning.

The station kept quiet about Keys' presence in talkSPORT Towers all morning, but the buzz from within the building would have been palpable even on the South Bank. Keys went on air at 1.30pm and, 30 minutes beforehand, talkSPORT began to trail their coup using all available social media and broadcasting tools. Very soon, dozens of press, TV cameramen and satellite trucks had surrounded the Hatfields building. Thinking on his feet, chief executive Scott Taunton toured the floors and found his burliest employee – magazine art editor John Mahood, who had once been a Glasgow doorman – and seconded him to bouncing duties on the front door. For several hours, Mahood stood defiant against a hungry media pack, keen to find out when they could feast on Keys.

But their wait was to be in vain. Keys had a vehicle waiting for him in the talkSPORT car park behind the building and made good his escape via the basement and a side exit. Within hours of leaving, Keys had handed in his resignation and talkSPORT was all over every newspaper, website and media outlet imaginable and had gained an army of new listeners.

Incredibly, the story didn't end there, as within three weeks Keys was back in the talkSPORT studios presenting his own new show, alongside his former Sky Sports sparring partner Andy Gray. In what was described as a 'sensational coup' by Dee, the pair had been persuaded to make an immediate return to broadcasting and, once again, the station was making headlines. Admittedly, not all the press was positive, but a helping of controversy had never done the station any harm previously and from a publicity point of view, talkSPORT had never had it so good.

The paparazzi returned to Hatfields on 14 February 2011, as Keys and Gray arrived for their first show. The impact of employing heavyweight names as regular presenters was immediately felt, as guests in their opening shows included Harry Redknapp, Paul Ince and Roy Hodgson.

Redknapp had also been part of the station's impressive roster of World Cup pundits in South Africa the previous summer, a tournament that saw talkSPORT hit new heights of popularity. Sadly, the same could not have been said about the England team. As an official FIFA licensed broadcaster once again, the station had provided live commentary of all 64 games of the tournament, with record audience numbers tuning in. The talkSPORT crew did an outstanding professional job at the finals, but of course there were plenty of amusing moments behind the scenes that also made it back from Africa – not one of them featuring Alan Brazil. He stayed in London.

The fun began before a ball had been kicked or a boarding pass had been issued, as the station threw a World Cup preview bash in Marylebone. This was not *just* about the free drinks, as it also formed the basis for an outside broadcast during which talkSPORT's star summer signings whet the listeners' appetites for the festival of football that lay ahead. Tottenham manager Redknapp was the major addition to the station's squad for the tournament, and he joined Stan Collymore and others in central London.

All the station's presenters were in attendance, including Andy Jacobs, who became the least likely talkSPORT broadcaster of all time to disgrace himself. If bookmakers would have taken odds on which of the station's anchors would get themselves thrown out of the World Cup preview outside broadcast, it's likely that Jacobs would have attracted considerably lengthy odds and little interest from punters. Certainly when compared to other notorious party animals.

Yet, it was the softly spoken afternoon show presenter who caused a ruckus after a spat with one of the venue's bouncers. Taking an important phone call during the show, Jacobs had sought somewhere quiet to speak on his mobile phone and had innocently wandered off into the kitchens of the Marylebone bar. Unfortunately, the kitchen staff weren't entirely happy with a member of the public marching up and down shouting into a mobile phone while they were trying to prepare food and asked Jacobs to leave, a request he didn't take to particularly well. After much shouting and gesticulating – both into his phone and towards kitchen staff – Jacobs was frog-marched off the premises by bouncers. The sight of the 5ft 5in, silver-haired 57-year-old being escorted out of the building was highly amusing to several of his colleagues, although he was eventually allowed back in – but only when Ian Wright intervened.

The former drivetime host was making an appearance at the event himself, and when he arrived on the scene to find Jacobs outside remonstrating with the doormen, he did his best to calm the situation. A few minutes of sweet-talking and autograph signing later, Wright had successfully managed to negotiate Jacobs back in to the building. There was more drama to come once the station's World Cup team had made it out to South Africa, where a luxury Johannesburg lodge awaited them. The station had leased the five-star premises, with facilities including a fully stocked bar, kitchen staff to wait upon them hand and foot and a studio in the basement, for the duration of the tournament, to ensure star presenters such as Collymore were well looked after.

And the former Liverpool and Aston Villa forward made himself at home very quickly. One evening, some of the crew were gathered around the huge plasma TV screen in the lodge's living room when Collymore suggested watching a DVD through his laptop. He spent an age unwiring the television's complicated cable connections and hooking the system up to his computer but, sadly, his engineering prowess was not quite the same as his goalscoring capability. When the TV was switched back on, there was no picture to be seen and, after a further interminable period of rewiring to return the TV to its original connection, a blank screen still awaited the team. Collymore had broken the television and the lodge owners had to be called out to rescue the situation.

That wasn't the only occasion an emergency visit from the station's temporary landlords was required, following another night of dramatic tension. In the run-up to the tournament, the UK press had bombarded the front and back pages with scare stories of the dangers that the crime-troubled country possessed for fans attending the World Cup. By and large, these stories were vastly exaggerated, although there were some incidents at the start of the tournament, with journalists being robbed and some members of the England squad were victims of theft at their Royal Bafokeng retreat. With this fresh in the mind of talkSPORT presenter Adrian Durham, he was awoken one night by the sound of somebody attempting to get into his bedroom.

'I was in a room on my own next door to Ian Danter's,' he explained. 'It was 2 or 3am and I remember hearing this elephant charging down the corridor towards our rooms. All the stories we'd heard of journos getting robbed flashed through my head and I thought this was our time – I was genuinely scared.

'I had locked my door and I heard it being rattled quite hard. Then I could hear Danter's door being shaken and whoever it was still couldn't get in. So I texted Danter under my bed clothes, as I didn't want any light to emerge from underneath the door and attract attention to myself. I wrote to him "Did you know somebody is trying to get in your room?"'

'He joked: "It must be Parry after a heavy night!"'

'I replied, still petrified: "How do you know it's not some axe murderer?"'

'Danter texted back and said: "Because I think he would have got in . . ." at which point I laughed out loud and the game was up.'

Whoever the 'elephant' was, he eventually found his way back into a room and everyone else could get back to sleep.

The station's World Cup squad saw the funny side of that initially disturbing incident and they were laughing again soon after, when they heard of a fantastic wind-up at the expense of John Anderson, their England correspondent, who was staying in a media apartment block away from the lodge. Following a seemingly innocent conversation with *Daily Mirror* reporter John Cross, Anderson had revealed he was meant to be sharing a flat with someone called Tony from Eurosport. Never having heard of the fellow before, Cross immediately told Anderson: 'You don't mean "Terrible Tony", do you?' at which point the talkSPORT man's face turned pale.

Cross, and several other hacks, snappers and anyone else he could wheel in on the act, then spent days convincing Anderson that 'Terrible Tony' was so-called due to his less than exemplary behaviour at previous tournaments. 'Terrible Tony' tales included time served in prison, an arrest at the 2006 World Cup, a ban from Euro 2008 for assaulting a journalist in the press 'mixed zone' and, as if that wasn't enough, this nightmare of a man also regularly stole from colleagues due to his alcoholism. Anderson had heard enough by this stage and requested a new apartment, only for the genuinely not-so-terrible Tony to finally turn up in South Africa. The talkSPORT man soon realised the unassuming gentleman before him meant he'd been the victim of an elaborate hoax.

Another prank victim was talkSPORT's fearless roving reporter Ian 'Moose' Abrahams. The sports newsreader had infuriated colleagues by repeatedly leaving the ISDN and studio equipment in the basement switched on, meaning somebody else always had to switch it off. One evening, Abrahams was out at a local bar, when 'Villa' Matt Smith noticed the equipment had been left on again. Durham decided this was too good an opportunity to miss and texted Moose to ask if he'd left the studio on. The reporter replied back apologetically admitting he had, so Durham responded by saying 'There's been a fire. I think you'd better get back.'

In record time that would have flattered Usain Bolt, the larger-than-life Moose stormed back to the lodge, raced down to the basement while his colleagues chuckled to themselves upstairs. After a few seconds, they heard him calling up the stairs: 'There's not been a fire has there?' as their laughs became increasingly louder.

But Moose was also helping enhance the station's coverage of the tournament with his no-fear approach to securing exclusive stories. Following the World Cup semi-final, talkSPORT's most intrepid reporter hid himself in the victorious Dutch team hotel's lobby, keeping a low profile by repeatedly ordering coffees from the bar. He sat there for an hour and, presumably more intensely focused after so much caffeine, approached Netherlands left-back Giovanni van Bronckhorst for a photograph. The footballer obliged but refused to do an interview, as the team had been instructed not to. Shortly after, Dirk Kuyt entered the lobby, and this time Moose's persistence paid off as the Liverpool man led him around a corner where they'd be out of sight to record the interview. Both men were looking over their shoulders as they spoke but Abrahams had his story, trumping rival stations.

And talkSPORT's strong performance in South Africa had clearly riled its closest competitor, with BBC Radio 5 Live's Alan Green seeming to resort to various digs during his World Cup commentaries. On more than one occasion, he warned BBC listeners to 'beware of cheap imitations', which many took to be a reference to talkSPORT, and which certainly wound up Collymore. According to the *Daily Mail*, the talkSPORT man was furious with his former colleague and was apparently looking for Green before the World Cup quarter-final between Argentina and Germany. Collymore was quoted in the paper as saying: 'There are a number of us who are very upset about what Green's been saying about the station. It's disrespectful to a team who have been working extremely hard during the tournament. When I catch up with him, he'll find out exactly what I think about him.'

Collymore was to have his own back towards the end of the year, when he was reporting live from Old Trafford at the Manchester United v Arsenal top-of-the-table Premier League encounter. His excitable and enthusiastic broadcasting style meant that his voice could not only be heard on 1089 and 1053, but also on the BBC's 909 frequency above Green and co's commentary, much to the anger and irritation of the 5 Live team. It was a moral victory for the commerical station, who had had the Beeb on the run back in South Africa thanks to their superb coverage which went beyond the usual commentary and phone-ins. On several occasions, talkSPORT sent its presenters and reporters out to see South Africa and learn about the country's history and this resulted in absorbing and emotional radio.

Durham and Mick Quinn visited Soweto one morning, where they were shown around Nelson Mandela's house and given a full insight into apartheid South Africa. The trip had a profound effect on the pair, particularly Quinn, and their subsequent broadcast – where clips were played from their educational visit – was especially poignant. 'I have a politics degree and, despite being well aware of everything that happened there, it hit me hugely,' recounted Durham. 'Quinny only found out the full extent of apartheid on that trip to Soweto and it changed him, it blew him away. It was heart-warming to see that change. I think we all grew as people, living together in Johannesburg and getting a little snippet of that life as it was beforehand. It was a privilege to be there at that World Cup.'

Unfortunately, as is so often the case, the tournament was one to forget for England, as the perennial underachievers managed a timid second-round exit at the hands of Germany – although there was cause for some humour, as a result of an incident in that game when Frank Lampard took a shot that crossed the line but was not given as a goal. That would have drawn England level at 2-2, and the frustration experienced by millions of England fans was summed up by presenter Mark Saggers, who was anchoring the station's live commentary of the knockout tie.

Although he wasn't broadcasting live at the time, Saggers' comments were being recorded and his subsequent rant at 'the goal that never was' was replayed frequently on talkSPORT over the following days (minus the swearing) to cheer up a disgruntled nation of football fans: 'Yes! Yes! It's a goal! It's a goal! It's a goal! It's a goal! It's a goal! It's a goal! It's a goal! It's a goal! It's a... It's a goal! Booooooo! Booooooo! It's a goal! It's a goal! Ohhh! [sees replay on TV monitor] Miles over the line! You cheating bastards! Oh fucking hell! It's this far over! Oh, come on! You bastards!'

The former BBC man would never have known his comments would be broadcast to the nation, but this was talkSPORT and he took it in good spirits. For all its new-found air of professionalism, the station was still more than capable of stunts like that, although usually its funniest moments were entirely unintentional. In many ways, nothing had changed at talkSPORT Towers since the early days.

Take, for example, the 2009 Hall of Fame event that talkSPORT organised. The idea was hatched to create a star-studded annual extravaganza at which several sporting greats would be honoured by being inducted into the talkSPORT Hall of Fame. Voting took place throughout the year, with two stars from each of a number of sports being awarded the honour of a place in the station's eternal roster of greatness.

The original guest invite list that was drawn up for the event read like a who's who of the biggest names from the world of sport and the trendiest names from the entertainment world. All the stars were on that list from Joe Calzaghe to Calum Best, Konnie Huq to Liz McClarnon and Lee Sharpe to Eric Morecambe.

That's Eric Morecambe. Of Morecambe and Wise fame. Who has been dead since 1984.

Still, mistakes are always made and the station probably wasn't expecting to hear back from Mr Morecambe once the error had been discovered. The problem was that talkSPORT didn't hear back from anyone, and that was due to another cock-up as the RSVP email address on the beautifully embossed invitations contained a typo. Instead of an address which ended @utvgb – indicating the station's owners UTV Media Great Britain – the email printed ended with @utvbg. Or, in other words, UTV Media Breat Gritain.

The ceremony itself was also not without its problems, mainly because the radio station that prided itself on being the voice of millions of football fans across the country managed to induct Pelé into the Hall of Fame. On the surface, that would seem to be an entirely justifiable course of action. Internationally acknowledged as one of the finest – if not *the* finest – players ever to set foot on to a football pitch, the Brazilian icon won three World Cups and is a worldwide ambassador for the game. The problem was that the list of inductees, handsomely printed on more embossed card on each table, claimed that Abedi Pelé – the relatively obscure former Marseille striker who never played at a World Cup – was set for the most unlikely of honours. Only talkSPORT could induct the wrong Pelé into its Hall of Fame.

And the station's penchant for embarrassment and hilarity were themes that continued to be espoused by star presenter Mike Parry, a man who regularly took to the airwaves in all manner of absurd costumes and disguises. And Porky repeated his particularly nasty habit of singing duets with any musicians who were booked to appear in the talkSPORT studios. The man Brazil continued to refer to as the 'short-armed ginger tube' butchered 'Bat out of Hell' live in the studio with Meat Loaf and also managed to utterly destroy 'These are a Few of My Favourite Things' with West End performer Connie Fisher. Not that these, or the many other truly appalling duets in which he starred, deterred him from further exhibitionism.

On one evening, Parry was at White Hart Lane watching his Everton team take on Tottenham in a Carling Cup tie and became involved in a bizarre incident, which was captured on a mobile phone camera by a Spurs fan and then seen by hundreds of thousands on the internet. Perhaps slightly worse for wear, Porky took leave of his corporate box seat and began provoking home fans by lifting his shirt and exposing his midriff. Soon after, he pretended to climb down towards the opposition fans below him, but was soon stopped in his tracks by a steward who gave him a ticking off. As if that humiliation were not enough, home fans began chanting 'We want Parry out' and 'You're getting sacked in the morning!' Porky dodged the bullet by making light of the affair and allowing himself to be ribbed for the whole of the following morning's show by Andy Townsend.

Amazingly, the night immediately following that ignominious incident, the station remained in the spotlight, but this time for all the right reasons, by claiming the prestigious title of Media Brand of the Year at the highly respected 2009 Media Week Awards. It was a magnificent recognition of the power of the radio station and proved just how far it had come from its troubled early days. But, this was talkSPORT, and the station couldn't just win such a prestigious title without something going wrong. Sadly, the gong itself never made it back to the talkSPORT trophy cabinet, as the man who was entrusted with its safe keeping for the night, communications director James Mallinson, managed to leave it in the back of a taxi.

Another taxi, or more accurately the lack of another taxi, caused the station further trouble soon after, when boxer Kevin Mitchell had been scheduled to appear on the evening *Kick Off* show with Danny Kelly. A car had been booked to pick up the fighter from his east London home on talkSPORT's usual mini-cab account and, when producers called the firm to check everything was set up, they were assured all was as it should have been. Kelly continued to trail that Mitchell was due in the studio later in the show, while producers kept an eye on the clock. The boxer was nowhere to be seen with minutes left until he was due on air, so producers called him to be informed that the taxi had never shown up. The cab firm could offer no explanation, meaning they were in a remarkably similar position to Kelly, who had to inform the listening millions that Mitchell would not be appearing in the studio after all.

Another 'administrative error' – as an excuse-weary corporate statement might put it – led to the bizarre situation of one talkSPORT show being broadcast in pitch black darkness. Following every live Premier League commentary on a Saturday afternoon, the station would hand the mic over to Collymore and the listeners, who would debate the day's talking points from whichever stadium the former footballer had co-commentated on that day's match. Usually, the same member of the talkSPORT production team would make the necessary logistical arrangements to ensure that the club concerned knew to keep the stadium open and its floodlights on until after the programme was scheduled to finish at 7pm.

One Saturday evening at Goodison Park, Collymore and his

producer were the last men left in the stadium, as the nation's liveliest football debate entered its final hour. Sat in the same seats they'd occupied in the press box throughout the day and with the cold winter night having long since fallen on Merseyside, it was only 45 minutes until they could seek comfort indoors. Suddenly, they were plunged into total darkness as the Everton floodlights seemed to give up the ghost. For the remainder of the show, the pair couldn't see each other or their equipment as they continued to broadcast. News emerged later that there had been no floodlight failure at Goodison. The explanation was far more simple: the talkSPORT employee who normally arranged the extended stadium opening was away that week.

And the station suffered a prolonged period of absences later in 2010, after a bug struck talkSPORT Towers which took no prisoners – presenters included. Even while they were on air.

Fresh from his headline-making exploits after getting the Raoul Moat-fan Facebook site shut down, *Late Night Show* presenter Ian Collins turned up for his show one evening, murmuring something about a dodgy curry. In fact, he'd been out with colleagues to mark one of the producers' last night on the show. Despite reaching the ripe old age of 43, Collins had never sampled the delights of Indian cuisine before and began to talk himself into trouble about the possible ramifications of consuming his first south Asian dish. As the show came closer to airing, he ramped up his sickness talk but still took his seat in the studio as usual at 10pm.

But just seven minutes into the programme he frantically signalled to producers in the control room, who went to a commercial break as they watched Collins dart from his seat, sprint out of the studio and throw himself into the nearest toilet from where he didn't emerge for a good 15 minutes. A severe – possibly psychosomatic – stomach disorder curtailed Collins, who spent the rest of the night vomiting while his show was meant to be on air. Instead, anyone tuning into 1089 at that time would have heard a recording of Collins' interview with O'Dowd repeated on a loop, while an emergency presenter was sought. The previous show's anchor, Danny Kelly, had already left, while the ever-reliable Ian Danter was uncharacteristically unavailable. Eventually overnight man Adrian Goldberg arrived at talkSPORT Towers to prepare for his show, but was sent straight into the studio where he performed admirably with no preparation.

It quickly became apparent that Collins had not eaten a dodgy curry – not unless everyone in the building had been dining at the same tandoori. A full-scale gastroenteric illness had taken over talkSPORT and, within a week, the following email was sent to all staff:

> Hello everyone,
> We appear to have run out of toilet paper!
> More is on it's [sic] way, due later today. Please use it sparingly until then.
> BUT PLEASE, PRETTY PLEASE, don't put the paper towels down the toilet! They will clog it up, and that's worse.
> Sorry about this.
> *Peter Ockelford*
> *Senior Station Engineer*

Fortunately, toilet paper stocks were replenished and staff were soon fully recovered, much like the radio station which had seen off the worst the global economy had to offer and come out fighting in spectacular fashion.

Ahead of what was to prove to be a tremendous World Cup for the station, talkSPORT announced it had signed a deal with the Premier League to snatch two further packages of live broadcasting rights away from arch rival BBC Radio 5 Live for three seasons from the 2010-11 campaign. The station would now cover two live games every weekend, the Saturday match at 5.30pm and the Sunday lunchtime fixture.

This was a major coup for talkSPORT, which left the BBC fuming and chief executive Scott Taunton was more than happy to put the (football) boot in: 'This is a great day for talkSPORT and commercial radio in the UK. To have won the rights to broadcast live and exclusive Barclays Premier League football on both a Saturday and a Sunday, when no other national radio broadcaster – including the BBC – has commentary, puts the station at the very heart of Premier League football in the UK.'

On top of that, a deal was signed for talkSPORT to own exclusive broadcasting rights to the 2011 Rugby World Cup in New Zealand, while the station also managed to scoop its first Sony gold award. Elsewhere, the schedules were shaken up as overnight man Mike Graham teamed up with his namesake and former New York journalist buddy Parry to present the weekday morning show together.

The station also managed to scoop its first Sony gold award for the magnificent 'Dear Stan' trailer. Created by Peter Gee's team, the promo was a pastiche on Eminem's hit single 'Stan', to advertise Collymore's phone-in programme. It contained such gems as: 'I know you probably hear this every day, but I'm your biggest fan; I even liked you when you played for Real Oviedo, man!'

With all the station's great success, there were still difficult decisions that had to be taken. Andy Townsend had decided to concentrate on his television duties after the World Cup in South Africa, while the arrival of Keys and Gray had followed the exit of one of talkSPORT's founding fathers. When Mike Parry resigned, the announcement of his departure was buried under the news of the Sky Sports pair's arrival.

The former programme director, and co-presenter of arguably the station's best ever show alongside Brazil, had resigned the week before the capture of Keys and Gray had been announced, according to an interview he gave to the Portsmouth newspaper *The News*: 'It was over a contractual dispute which has been dragging on since last summer after the World Cup. I've had lots of job offers, which I'm considering. I'd be mad to quit a job like that and not have something else in the pipeline, wouldn't I? Andy [Gray] gets my blessing. He's one of my footballing heroes and I'm delighted he's going to be doing the job that I can no longer do.'

There was outrage at the news from Porky's loyal legion of fans, although he was back on the airwaves within days, fronting arch-rivals BBC Radio 5 Live's 606 football phone-in show.

By taking controversial decisions such as letting Parry leave, the *enfant terrible* of British broadcasting had grown up, but only on its own terms and in its own distinct way. There was still no other UK outlet that came close to matching talkSPORT's unique tone.

With three million listeners, the future was looking bright and the potential arrival of even more star presenters was on the cards. The station had come a long way from having an engineer underneath the studio desk desperately trying to fix a technical problem just minutes before it was due to launch.

Did it really matter if the station celebrated its tenth anniversary on the right day? Of course not. There was only one thing more impressive, and more talkSPORT, than celebrating a milestone like that on the right day – doing it on the wrong day. Nobody else would have dared.

However, the studio floorboards did still squeak sometimes. The odd rodent could still be spotted in the production floor kitchen from time to time. A rogue fire alarm could even still take the station off air briefly every now and then. Occasionally, it was still the same old story with talkSPORT.

But what a story it was.